Soldiers in Revolt

Army Mutinies in Africa

HURST & COMPANY, LONDON

First published in the United Kingdom in 2017 by
C. Hurst & Co. (Publishers) Ltd.,
41 Great Russell Street, London, WC1B 3PL
© Maggie Dwyer, 2017
All rights reserved.
Printed in the United Kingdom

The right of Maggie Dwyer to be identified as the author of this publication is asserted by her in accordance with the Copyright, Designs and Patents Act, 1988.

A Cataloguing-in-Publication data record for this book is available from the British Library.

ISBN: 9781849048293

This book is printed using paper from registered sustainable and managed sources

www.hurstpublishers.com

CONTENTS

Acknowledgements ix
Abbreviations xi

1. The Popular Allure and Academic Neglect of Mutinies 1
   Beyond indiscipline 4
   Mutinies in Africa 8
   Book overview 12

2. Out of the Shadows of Coups 15
   Identifying mutiny 16
   Researching the mutineers' perspective 20
   Documenting mutinies in West and Central Africa 24

3. The Typical Mutiny: Patterns in Participants, Tactics and Outcomes 29
   The uncomfortable place of rank-and-file soldiers in Africa 30
   Private problems 33
   'The problems are between the generals and us' 37
   Mutineers' playbook 41
   Mutineers' public relations campaigns 44
   Violence as an ace or a bluff 46
   The predictably unpredictable nature of mutinies 49
   Determining success in a mutiny 52
   Conclusion 54

4. Public Discourse, Protests and Revolts 57
   Global trends lead to ground-level complaints 58
   Dual mobilisation 63

CONTENTS

Borrowed scripts	67
Freedom to mutiny	73
Conclusion	78

5. The Price of Hardship: Deployments and Peacekeeping — 79
   - *Risks, entitlements and respect* — 81
   - *Familiar complaints, new importance* — 84
   - *Pay problems* — 86
   - *The problem with transparency* — 88
   - *Revealing the greener grass* — 92
   - *Cohesion and division* — 95
   - *Conclusion* — 97

6. A Coup Hidden in a Mutiny: Case Study of Sierra Leone — 101
   - *The shifting role of the military* — 102
   - *The Tigers are tested* — 105
   - *From objections to actions* — 109
   - *Operation Mutiny becomes Operation Coup* — 112
   - *'A change that changed little'* — 115
   - *A new military with new problems* — 118
   - *Conclusion* — 123

7. Mutinies with Unintended Consequences: Case Study of The Gambia — 125
   - *The reluctant creation of the Gambian armed forces* — 126
   - *The divisive effects of the Confederal Army* — 128
   - *Dissatisfaction among the peacekeepers* — 130
   - *Mutinies lead to a contentious caretaker* — 134
   - *The unresolved problems grow* — 136
   - *The third and final strike* — 139
   - *Potential problems below the surface* — 143
   - *Conclusion* — 145

8. An Escalating Cycle of Mutinies: Case Study of Burkina Faso — 149
   - *A temporary civilian–military union* — 150
   - *A tested tactic* — 153
   - *Familiar dissatisfaction reignited* — 154
   - *The military enters the scene* — 156

CONTENTS

Mutiny finale	159
Depth of the grievances	161
The exceptionally uninterested sectors	164
New changes replicate old patterns	167
Memory of the mutinies continues	169
Conclusion	173
9. An Altered View of Mutinies	175
Future of mutinies in West and Central Africa	176
A revised view of mutinies	178
Notes	185
Bibliography	217
Index	231

ACKNOWLEDGEMENTS

I am deeply grateful to the many soldiers in Burkina Faso, The Gambia, Sierra Leone and elsewhere throughout West Africa who generously and patiently shared their stories with me. Many went out of their way to welcome me to their bases and homes, as well as include me in their social networks. This work was only possible through their trust, and I hope this book accurately portrays their experiences. Because of the sensitive nature of mutinies, the vast majority of the interviewees and others who assisted in the research are not named; however, particular thanks go to Mana, Issa and Luke.

While the book focuses primarily on soldiers, informants outside of the military were critical in furthering my understanding of armed forces in Africa. I also owe these civil servants, journalists, politicians, activists, union leaders, academics and students my sincerest thanks.

It is a privilege to have had the opportunity to be a part of the Centre of African Studies at the University of Edinburgh throughout the research and writing of this book. I benefited greatly from the support and encouragement of my colleagues at the centre and am particularly appreciative of the advice and guidance of Paul Nugent and Sara Rich Dorman.

The book has been revised following input at various conferences, workshops and seminars. Discussions at events hosted by the African Studies Centre Leiden, the Nordic Africa Institute and Peace Research Institute Oslo were particularly helpful in developing my ideas about African militaries. Special thanks goes to 'Funmi Olonisakin for her feedback and to Patrick McGowan for sharing his extended coup dataset. I am also appreciative of the insightful comments of the anonymous peer reviewers and the support of Hurst.

I am thankful for the financial support of the Harry Frank Guggenheim Foundation and the Gerda Henkel Stiftung Foundation, which allowed for several field research trips.

ACKNOWLEDGEMENTS

Finally, I am endlessly grateful to my husband Gerhard for his unwavering encouragement, support and good humour.

Sections and earlier versions of some of the chapters have been published as journal articles. Parts of Chapter 3 were published in *Africa Spectrum*, parts of Chapter 4 in *Conflict Security and Development*, parts of Chapter 5 in *African Affairs*, parts of Chapter 6 in *Politique Africaine*, and parts of Chapter 8 were published in *Third World Quarterly*.

ABBREVIATIONS

AFISMA	African-led International Support Mission to Mali
AFPRC	Armed Forces Provisional Ruling Council (The Gambia)
AMISOM	African Union Mission in Somalia
APC	All People's Congress (Sierra Leone)
AU	African Union
CGT-B	Confédération Générale du Travail du Burkina
CNR	Conseil National de la Révolution (Burkina Faso)
CO	Commanding officer
EO	Executive Outcomes
ECOMIL	Economic Community of West African States Mission in Liberia
ECOMOG	Economic Community of West African States Monitoring Group
ECOWAS	Economic Community of West African States
GNA	Gambian National Army
GNG	Gambian National Gendarmerie
GRSP	Gambia Revolutionary Socialist Party
GSG	Gurkha Security Guards
ISU	Internal Security Unit (Sierra Leone)
MBDHP	Mouvement Burkinabé des Droits de l'Homme et des Peuples
MINURCA	Mission des Nations Unies en République Centrafricaine
MINUSMA	Mission Multidimensionnelle Intégrée des Nations Unies pour la Stabilisation au Mali
MOJA	Movement for Justice in Africa
NATAG	Nigerian Army Training Assistance Group
NCO	Non-commissioned officer

ABBREVIATIONS

NPFL	National Patriotic Front of Liberia
NPRC	National Provisional Ruling Council (Sierra Leone)
ONUC	Opération des Nations Unies au Congo
PANAFU	Pan African Union
PPP	People's Progressive Party (The Gambia)
PSO	Peace Support Operation
RSP	Régiment de la Sécurité Présidentielle (Burkina Faso)
RUF	Revolutionary United Front
RWAFF	Royal West African Frontier Force
SAP	Structural Adjustment Programme
SSD	Special Security Division (Sierra Leone)
TSG	Tactical Support Group (The Gambia)
UN	United Nations
UNMIL	United National Mission in Liberia
UNOMIL	United Nations Observer Mission in Liberia

1

THE POPULAR ALLURE
AND ACADEMIC NEGLECT OF MUTINIES

Our knowledge of military mutinies is a contradictory mix of allure and neglect. Mutiny has been seen described as 'one of the most terrifying, yet fascinating, forms of rebellion since it erupts within the very military institutions that are supposed to ensure a society's order and security'.[1] The act is universally illegal, often carrying a potential sentence of capital punishment, making it a highly risky decision for soldiers.[2] The high-stakes actions of mutineers have grabbed media headlines and inspired numerous fictional novels and classic Hollywood films such as *The Caine Mutiny* (1954) and *Mutiny on the Bounty* (1962). Despite this fascination, mutinies have received limited academic attention, particularly in an African context.

Mutinies are by no means a recent phenomenon, and therefore the lack of attention cannot be attributed to novelty. It is an act that 'is as old as soldiering', with recorded cases of mutiny dating back to antiquity.[3] Yet one needs only to look back over the last couple of years in West Africa to see that mutiny is not an outdated tactic for militaries in the region.

Hence the general neglect of studies on African mutinies does not equate to a lack of mutinies on the continent. Colonial powers were challenged by mutinies within the Gold Coast Artillery Corps in 1858 and 1863, the Royal Niger Constabulary in 1898, the Sierra Leone Frontier Force in 1900 and the West African Regiment in 1901.[4] The pattern of mutinies in Africa continued through the Second World War and into the end of the colonial period.[5] In

1944, for example, soldiers in the Belgian Congo plotted an unsuccessful mutiny against low pay and poor health conditions and later carried through with an uprising opposing mandatory smallpox vaccinations.[6] In the same year, Senegalese soldiers mutinied in Dakar to demand back-wages and improved living conditions.[7] This mutiny, and subsequent massacre of many of the mutineers, is depicted in the film *Camp de Thiaroye* (1988), directed by Ousmane Sembène. The Somali Camel Corps, which was particularly known for its rebellious behaviour, mutinied in 1937 and 1944.[8] In the latter mutiny, the troops specifically demanded pay and status on a par with Asian troops within the British Empire.[9] In assessing a number of these mutinies, John Iliffe notes that 'African colonial troops used mutiny both as collective bargaining and to defend their honour.'[10] As will be demonstrated below, more recent mutinies in Africa have had similar aims.

African soldiers found mutinies as appealing in post-independence times as they did during the colonial era. Congolese soldiers wasted little time in initiating their first postcolonial mutiny just days after the country gained independence in 1960.[11] A similar pattern occurred in East Africa when soldiers in Kenya, Tanzania and Uganda also orchestrated mutinies in 1964, soon after gaining independence. The revolts caused such panic among the new African political leadership that British military assistance was requested to help quell the revolt. In response, the United Kingdom deployed thousands of troops to its former East African colonies. Although the mutinies were put down quickly, the countries faced long-term challenges in reconstituting the armies in the aftermath.[12] A decade later, a series of mutinies spread over several months preceded the 1974 Ethiopian Revolution.[13] These mutinies at points of political transition have received the most academic attention. However, beyond these examples, there are only a limited number of studies of mutinies in recent decades in Africa, perhaps giving the impression that mutinies have lost steam since the 1960s and 1970s.

The next chapter will demonstrate that the number of mutinies has not decreased since the early independence years; nor is there an end in sight to the tactic. Indeed, mutinies continue to have major consequences for African states. Mutinies in Burkina Faso in 2011, for example, contributed to the largest government changes in President Blaise Compaoré's twenty-seven-year reign, and a mutiny in Mali in 2012 preceded a coup that interrupted over two decades of democratic transitions of power. Nigeria's ongoing fight to counter Boko Haram has been the trigger of mutinies as well as being hampered by them. The seriousness of mutinies for the Nigerian military is reflected in the sixty-six death sentences handed out to mutineers in 2014.[14]

POPULAR ALLURE AND ACADEMIC NEGLECT

As mutinies continue to have significant consequences for African states, there is a need to further understand their origins, dynamics and common characteristics. This book is the first to look at mutinies across time in Africa. It views mutinies as a recurring phenomenon in West and Central Africa, rather than the more common approach of viewing them as singular, exceptional events. In so doing, it also provides a new look at ways in which primarily rank-and-file soldiers express their discontent within a military structure. This view from the lower ranks is key to comprehending how militaries function, and particularly understanding the internal struggles that can threaten their ability to function effectively.[15] My findings suggest that there are common situations and problems within military organisations that heighten the chance of mutinies throughout the region. Understanding common triggers to mutinies is the first step in developing ways to reduce them, a goal that governments, military leaders and even rank-and-file soldiers would likely support.

In order to provide a more comprehensive understanding of a core element of the sovereign nation state, the study of mutinies inevitably requires a broader focus than internal military matters alone. The occurrence of mutinies is linked to both national politics and international relations. Mutineers often formulate and reinterpret their grievances against the backdrop of popular political themes and international trends such as peacekeeping. Their complaints, even when specific to a military context, regularly draw on wider issues of regional underdevelopment.

Although centred on military grievances, this examination of mutinies also looks at junior soldiers as a part of wider society. The history of military engagement in African politics means that armies in many African states are not distant organisations fighting foreign opponents. They are an integral part of state affairs, and the actions of the military have very real effects on many people's daily lives. Similarly, the military can be seen as a microcosm of the tensions that play out in wider society. Ethnic, regional and class divisions in the civilian realm are also present in the military. Issues that exacerbate these divisions within the civilian population can quickly spread to the military. This intertwined relationship between civilians and military personnel helps explain why mutinies in Africa are often not restricted to internal military matters. Thus the study of mutinies need not be limited to military historians but should be of interest to anyone seeking to gain a deeper understanding of the complex dynamics of African states.

Beyond indiscipline

Broadly speaking, mutinies constitute collective revolts by soldiers that are not focused on taking control of the state. Rather than being mere acts of indiscipline, mutineers' actions are a means to convey soldiers' grievances. It is the rationality of these actions that this book explores. The book addresses two overarching themes. The first is that mutineers are usually driven by a combination of material demands and a perceived injustice. As such, mutinies typically represent much larger issues than the initial demands suggest and regularly have larger effects than the immediate impact. Secondly, soldiers use mutinies to communicate with the senior leadership. Through the mutiny, mutineers attempt to open a dialogue with their hierarchy and vocalise their expectations. Together, these themes challenge the standard way in which mutinies are often viewed, either as pay disputes or as acts of indiscipline. Instead, mutinies can more accurately be viewed as soldiers communicating deeper perceptions of tensions and injustices within a military environment.

These themes have similarities with observations found in studies of mutinies in regions outside of Africa in both past centuries and more recent times. The overlap between findings on modern African mutinies and research on (mostly) Western mutinies from a historic perspective suggests that there are some universal traits to mutinies. While this current section will focus on the commonalities, the following section will also show that there are significant differences, particularly in when and how soldiers in West and Central Africa mutiny.

Despite the widely different contexts in which mutinies have occurred over time, they share the common trait of challenging authority and this makes them universally feared by military commanders. In the words of the military historian Richard Watt, 'a mutiny is like a horrible, malignant disease and the chances that the patient will die an agonizing death are so great, that the subject cannot be mentioned aloud'.[16] Rather than declare the dreaded word, military leaders use a variety of other terms such as an 'incident', 'strike', 'protest', 'disaffection' or a 'temporary breakdown in discipline'.[17]

Militaries are founded on a hierarchical system of discipline.[18] Within any military hierarchy, there are two distinct sectors: enlisted soldiers and officers.[19] Enlisted ranks are always subordinate to the officer corps and are required to show obedience to their superiors. When soldiers mutiny, they challenge their superiors and directly contradict the foundation of a military structure. As Elihu Rose explains, a mutiny 'is more than a breach of regulations; it is a negation of the military essence'.[20] He argues that mutinies are 'the antithesis of discipline', and, as such, they are detested by militaries universally. However, this book challenges the idea of mutiny as the 'antithesis of discipline' and shows that there is often a level of discipline within mutinies. Moreover, mutinies should not be seen as an attack on the hierarchy but as an objection to particular individuals or forms of behaviour within that hierarchy. This is consistent with research on other mutinies in Africa and beyond.[21] For example, in his analysis of the 1964 Tanganyika mutinies, Nestor Luanda found that the mutineers were seeking 'to recreate (rather than destroy) hierarchy'.[22]

Military authorities and non-specialists generally view mutinies as being primarily sparked by mundane material issues such as pay, living conditions and food. The grievances of mutineers are regularly seen as 'basic and immediate'.[23] Although material grievances may be easy to understand, scholarship on mutinies from a worldwide perspective has at times criticised both military commanders and the more classic academic studies of mutinies for an overemphasis on the material grievances, which paints a deceptively simple explanation of mutiny. Focusing too heavily on such complaints is unhelpful in assessing how or when soldiers decide to mutiny. Christopher Ankersen questions at what point 'things get bad enough' for soldiers to decide to mutiny.[24] This is a particularly relevant question for West and Central African militaries because there are ample opportunities for grievances to emerge among rank-and-file soldiers in most states in the region. Owing to the generally poor economic conditions in much of the region, at any given time soldiers could find fault with their uniforms, equipment, housing, food or salaries. Still, rank-and-file soldiers in Africa are not in constant revolt, nor are mutinies limited to times of extreme hardship, which suggests that there are other aspects beyond material conditions that contribute to mutinies.

One reason why the material school of thought has long been dominant is that mutinies are usually associated with the junior ranks of military hierarchies. This sector of the military has historically been less educated, made up of people from lower socioeconomic classes, and has often been treated as unsophisticated, both by academics and military organisations. Therefore, when rank-and-file soldiers mutiny it is also viewed as an unsophisticated, instantaneous reaction rather than a planned and logical protest.[25] This attitude is reflected in the way the 'the ranks have remained invisible, in theory as well as in research' in Africa.[26] There has been little academic attention on the corporate claims and material conditions of ordinary soldiers, perhaps suggesting that their actions are not as worthy of the analysis that has been given to the officer corps.[27] The tendency to downplay or simplify actions by rank-

and-file soldiers may help explain the lack of attention to mutinies within the literature on African militaries.

Another cause for the predominant focus on material issues may be 'institutional vanity'.[28] Rose explains that mutinies are 'antithetical to an ethos whose fundamental tenets are duty, loyalty, honour, and patriotism, and the unit that participates in a mutiny brings discredit upon itself, its officers, and its service'.[29] It is more convenient for military leadership to claim that mutineers are primarily driven by material interests than to address issues that may bring dishonour to the organisation, particularly the officer corps, and thus undermine its key tenets.

Whatever the reasons for this prevailing focus on the material aspects of mutinies, there is now a consensus among many who have recently written about mutinies that we must look beyond 'the mundane material grievances that have become cliché' in order to discover the less tangible motivations.[30] These more existential issues often relate to the desire of soldiers to feel that they are valued or not taken for granted.[31] This book demonstrates that African mutineers are usually motivated by what they believe is unfair treatment and the irresponsible behaviour of their superiors within a military context.[32] Excerpts of discussions with former mutineers will help delve deeper into perceptions of justice within a military context, which are often not clearly portrayed in media reporting of the events.

Along the same lines of Ankersen's question about what makes material conditions 'bad enough', one could also question when perceptions of injustice become 'unacceptable enough' to trigger a mutiny. This is a complex question, with no single answer. By observing trends within the occurrence of mutinies, we can identify shifts in shared beliefs about what soldiers find acceptable as well as what they believe they are entitled to. The following chapters will demonstrate two situations in which the views of acceptable treatment by superiors among soldiers appear to shift at the same time that material grievances also increase, creating the perfect conditions for mutiny. This occurred in West and Central Africa alongside the mass protests of the 1990s. Chapter 4 will argue that the democratisation movement inspired an altered sense of expectations within the military, which drew from many of the demands made by civilians at the time. Just as civilians were increasingly focused on issues of accountability among politicians, so too were soldiers towards their superiors. This occurred at a time when economic constraints also led to increased economic hardships for the soldiers. The overlap between civilian and military demands is not limited to the 1990s, and Chapter 8 will show a similar trend in recent mutinies in Burkina Faso. Chapter 5 will demonstrate another pattern of altered expectations alongside increased hardships, but this time as a result of deployment experiences. In the case of deployments, the sense of injustice appears to be linked to veteran status and perceptions of a broken contract.

This book's analysis of mutinies shows that material grievances and perceptions of injustice are closely intertwined. For example, complaints by rank-and-file soldiers over payment delays are often linked to accusations of corruption within the officer corps. Understanding that material grievances are often working in conjunction with feelings of injustice helps explain why mutineers' actions often appear risky out of proportion to their material demands. Chapter 7 will detail a mutiny in The Gambia, for instance, in which the soldiers demanded fifteen days' pay. The risk taken for a relatively small amount of money may seem illogical in a material sense, but it becomes more understandable when viewed as an attempt to alter the behaviour of the hierarchy into a manner that soldiers find acceptable and could potentially have longer-term benefits. These soldiers not only demanded their pay but also insisted that the officers who were responsible for the delay be held accountable.

When mutinies are seen as more complex than a simple request for material demands, it becomes easier to see why they often have much larger consequences than the immediate mutiny. Addressing material complaints is a fairly straightforward task; however, the deeper divisions of mistrust, suspicion and disrespect that often accompany the mutiny are much harder to fix and can create long-lasting divides within a military. The idea that even seemingly small mutinies can have great effects is a theme shared with other scholars studying mutinies. For example, Geoffrey Parker's work on mutinies in the Spanish army between 1572 and 1607 showed that even though the soldiers lacked political motivations, their actions had political significance.[33] Although looking at a very different case from Parker, Ali Mazrui and Donald Rothchild make a similar observation about the East African mutinies in 1964: 'Army mutinies, even when concerned with pay, have an importance that extends beyond the mutinies themselves. They have repercussions which always exceed the intentions of the mutineers.'[34] Similarly, Rose, looking at mutinies from a broad perspective, states that 'The military may regard mutiny as a purely internal matter but its effect can easily spill over the institutional boundaries and affect society at large.'[35]

The image of mutinies as exposing deeper discontent is closely linked to the other key theme of this book—communication. When mutinies are viewed as demands for material items or as acts of indiscipline, the mutiny is 'normally summarily addressed by the authorities with little introspection concerning the genesis of the event'.[36] Instead, it is more valuable to view mutinies as a form of communication in which mutineers are taking a great risk to convey a message to their hierarchy. Military hierarchies intentionally stifle communication and direct it in a one-way manner down the chain of command, thus giving rank-and-file soldiers few means to communicate their grievances to higher authority, especially if their grievances involve their immediate seniors. Mutinies are used by (mostly) junior soldiers as a way to open a dialogue with senior leadership in an environment in which the voices of the lowest in the structure are often unheard.

This book's analysis of common tactics among African mutineers will show that a key goal of their actions is to draw attention and communicate a message. Interpreting mutiny as a form of communication through collective action is not the dominant way of thinking about mutinies, especially among military personnel. In the official investigation into one of the only notable mutinies in the British Royal Navy during the Second World War, for example, the authors seem to have been surprised that 'no particular precautions were taken to keep this meeting [about common grievances] secret' and that 'the men in fact wanted it to be discovered'.[37] The examination of numerous African mutinies in this research also shows that it is common for soldiers to openly discuss complaints and the idea of mutiny. This is understandable if mutiny is viewed as a mode of communication in which the function is to convey a message, not keep it secret. There is also an element of bluff in the pre-warnings mutineers often provide. Soldiers seem to hope that even the hint of a mutiny will be enough to bring attention and resolution to their grievances (and later examples will show that it often works).

This book looks at mutinies as a form of communication as well as how soldiers communicate during a revolt. Mutineers use the media as a mode of communication, an aspect that is changing quickly with new forms of media and one that has not been addressed in other research on mutinies. Examining the messages conveyed both by the mutineers themselves and through the act of mutinying allows for a unique glimpse into the tensions within the military, which are often hidden internally by strict hierarchy and externally by military cultures of exclusivity.

Mutinies in Africa

Mutiny is not an act specific to African militaries. However, certain aspects of African mutinies veer from patterns seen in studies of mutinies elsewhere.

One difference is that much of the analysis of Western mutinies is specific to combat scenarios. As Timothy Parsons explains, 'most cases of collective indiscipline in Western national armies occurred when danger of active combat broke down institutional prohibitions on insubordination and mutiny'.[38] This focus on combat mutinies within the existing scholarship could give the impression that mutinies are largely confined to times of war. However, my data on African mutinies does not support this claim. The vast majority of the cases examined in this book did not occur in a combat setting. Yet there is a relationship between deployments and mutinies in Africa, as will be further detailed in Chapter 5.

Mutinies are an important topic in West and Central Africa regardless of whether the country is at war, at peace or somewhere in-between. Some of the logic underlying mutinies in combat settings can be applied to mutinies in non-combat settings. However, the argument that mutinies result largely from battlefield conditions (such as fear, mental fatigue, sleep deprivation) is not as convincing when seeking to explain the mutinies examined in this study. Lawrence James links the prevalence of mutinies in world wars to the frequent use of conscripts who often had low morale owing to their perception that they had been 'dragooned into service'.[39] This explanation does not hold weight in a modern African context, as most countries in the region do not have a shortage of military recruits and do not rely on conscription.

The focus on mutinies in times of war also portrays the revolts as spontaneous actions directly linked to immediate life-threatening combat scenarios. For example, Geoffrey Parker's and Guy Pedroncini's studies of Western historical mutinies conclude that there were 'few premeditated or purposeful acts of indiscipline. Instead most mutineers acted out of despair, fatigue, or momentary anger.'[40] In contrast, my analysis of African mutinies shows they were often premeditated, with soldiers regularly warning the leadership ahead of time. Chapter 3 will demonstrate that the tactics used by mutineers indicate that they were not spur-of-the-moment decisions, but rather planned actions with specific goals. This point will be further developed in Chapter 5, which shows that while some mutinies are linked to peacekeeping missions, the mutineers often revolt when they return home, not while on the deployment. Thus the soldiers have ample time to consider the action and its consequences.

In addition to battlefield mutinies, there is also a heavy focus on naval revolts in the scholarship on Western mutinies.[41] Naval mutinies are a particularly dramatic type of rebellion since the confined space and sea location puts added pressure on commanders. The dataset presented in the next chapter does include mutinies among navy personnel, but none at sea. The prevalence of studies of mutinies on board ships and combat mutinies presents an image of mutinies as generally contained within a military environment, usually not affecting civilians. However, this is another significant difference with modern African mutinies, as the latter regularly occur in populated city centres and many have resulted in high civilian casualties. While mutinies have traditionally been seen as an internal military matter, this book suggests that studying mutinies can further our understanding of the way internal military divisions can affect civilian populations. Additionally, Chapter 4 will show that mutinies do not only affect civilian society, civilian society can also influence soldiers' decision to mutiny.

Civilian populations play a larger role in African mutinies than in mutinies in a non-African context owing to the internal function of many armies on the continent. African militaries 'were historically created not with a view to responding effectively to external threats but with the explicit goal of subjugating local communities'.[42] This pattern extended beyond the end of colonialism, with many independent African leaders using their armies for regime protection against opposition, rather than the defence of territorial boundaries. This often coincided with coups, and most African countries have had periods in which the military has controlled the state.

While militaries were touted as modernisers in early independence years, today there are few who would champion military control of the political sphere in Africa. A retrospective look at military leaders in political office shows a very poor record of economic performance and a tendency towards authoritarianism.[43] Yet it is important to acknowledge that military leaders have often espoused populist ideas and garnered civilian support and have at times been seen as vanguards of change. It would therefore be inaccurate to assume that militaries are always viewed warily by civilians. The civilian–military relationship in Africa is one that fluctuates and varies by country and time. The case studies in this book will highlight the complex and diverse roles civilians play in influencing the decision to mutiny as well as the impact that revolts can have on those outside of the armed forces.

A final difference in African mutinies is less in how they are carried out and more in the way they are perceived. Studies of Western mutinies often approach the topic as a puzzle in seeking to explain why soldiers would act with such disregard for their training and professional code of conduct. Yet there is not a similar sense of surprise when African soldiers revolt. This is likely because mutinies fit with a dominant narrative of African militaries as unprofessional. Writing in the late 1970s, Samuel Decalo explained that 'many African armies bear little resemblance to a modern complex organization model and are instead a coterie of distinct armed camps owing primary clientelist allegiance to a handful of mutually competitive officers of different ranks seething with a variety of corporate, ethnic, and personal grievances'.[44] Robin Luckham provocatively describes attempts at democratisation under military rule in the 1990s as 'taming the monsters'. More recent critiques similarly argue that 'African militaries tend to lack skills, technical expertise, and combat-readiness, and often put their interests, and those of their patrons ahead of those of the state.'[45]

While there are large differences between African militaries and across time, these observations still have some merit. There is no denying that some African soldiers have abused their power, both through political channels and through intimidation and maltreatment of the civilian population during routine tasks. There are ample examples of abuses on a large scale. For example, there is evidence of widespread theft among West African troops during peace operations in Liberia and strong allegations of mass murders carried out by the Nigerian military during its missions against Boko Haram.[46] Some abuses have coincided with mutinies, as Chapter 3 and the case study of Burkina Faso will detail.

Yet the emphasis on what African militaries lack often neglects the strong sense of pride that many African soldiers have for their job. This sense of professional identity is easier to observe in field research than through the academic literature or via media reports. While conducting research throughout West Africa, I was invited to dozens of soldiers' homes or into their rooms in the barracks. It was very common to see walls lined with framed military certificates marking promotions or training sessions. On many other occasions, soldiers showed me photo albums of passing out ceremonies, parades and other military events. It was clear in these cases that the individuals took pride in their identity as soldiers and in their professional achievements. Similarly, a lack of uniforms was a common theme in interviews with mutineers as well as in their public statements. In 2016, numerous soldiers in Sierra Leone complained that it had been several years since they had been issued with new uniforms. Many had bought second-hand T-shirts in patterns that loosely resembled camouflage, and others asked if I had the ability to source uniforms from the UK. These concerns are not merely about clothing but represent a desire to look professional. The sense of pride around military service often increases around deployments, as further explained in Chapter

5, and international training opportunities that have grown after a lull following the end of the Cold War.

Despite persistent criticisms about many African armed forces, it is important to understand the pride many soldiers feel for their membership in the military because it often helps drive mutinies. Soldiers typically see themselves as professionals and expect the hierarchy to treat them as such. This is no different from soldiers in many other parts of the world. Much like Western mutinies from hundreds of years earlier, African mutineers also 'emphasize the righteousness of their cause' and believe their service entitles them to wages and other privileges.[47]

Book overview

This book begins with a focus on the broad patterns of mutinies in Africa and becomes narrower as it progresses. Chapter 2 will examine the occurrence of mutinies in Africa through the presentation of original empirical data. It will further assess the concept of mutiny and compare it with coups. Chapter 3 focuses on the common grievances stated by mutineers and patterns in how they physically carry out a mutiny. The chapter examines the position of the rank and file in comparison with the officer corps, in which there is a particularly severe divide in wealth and prestige due to the role of militaries in postcolonial Africa. An assessment of acts within the revolts will show that mutineers in West and Central Africa use a fairly limited number of tactics, thus making it possible to anticipate mutineers' courses of action. However, the predictability of a mutiny's outcome is limited, partially due to the tendency of mutinies to spread, altering the number and specific participants as well as the goals. The chapter demonstrates how the common tactics used by mutineers serve common strategic goals.

Chapters 4 and 5 address patterns in the occurrence of mutinies in West and Central Africa. Chapter 4 focuses on the political and economic conditions in Africa in the 1990s that may have made the region particularly mutiny-prone during this period. Conversely, it also assesses why mutiny was not a popular tactic in the preceding decades. This chapter argues that soldiers' decision to mutiny is often linked to particular political systems. Chapter 5 addresses a more nuanced trend of when soldiers mutiny, which is less apparent in a chronological charting of mutinies but becomes clear with an examination of the qualitative aspects of the mutiny dataset. This chapter shows that mutinies often follow deployments and particularly deployments on multinational missions. It will explain how deployments alter the conditions in which soldiers find grievances as well as their view of their entitlements. The analysis brings to light the potential heightened risk that deployed units have to mutiny and shows the common grievances that soldiers find among these deployments.

The next three chapters consist of the case studies presented in a chronological order. Chapter 6 looks at Sierra Leone, Chapter 7 examines The Gambia and Chapter 8 focuses on Burkina Faso. The case studies will provide a detailed analysis of the mutinies as well as situating the events within the political and military context of the state at the time they occurred. Additionally, a summary of relevant and related events that followed after a mutiny will serve to show the potential long-term impacts of the incident. The case studies will refer back to the other chapters in order to show places in which the cases support the earlier identified patterns as well as where they contradict.

The book concludes with Chapter 9, which summarises the key findings and provides an assessment of the future of mutinies in this region.

2

OUT OF THE SHADOWS OF COUPS

Although it is a punishable offence in any military, there is no consensus over what precisely constitutes a mutiny. It is often an emotive term, which can be used or substituted strategically, both by soldiers and authorities. This chapter starts by explaining why 'confusion over the meaning of mutiny is the norm'.[1] It will highlight some of the key differences in how academics and military authorities understand mutiny. It will also address how mutiny is defined in this book.

In an African context, the discussion of mutinies is often intertwined with coups. When soldiers in Africa take to the streets, there is usually an assumption that the position of the head of state is directly under threat. The notion at times has led to swift crackdowns and punishments for soldiers who participate. This fear that armed forces gathering en masse will lead to political upheaval is steeped in a history of political interference by militaries across the continent. While there have been various scholarly commentaries on the relationship between coups and mutinies, particularly in the early independence years, there have not been any studies that directly examine the link. New empirical data on mutinies presented in this chapter, as well as the interviews and case studies presented in later chapters, show that one should not assume a linear progression from mutiny to coup. Examining mutinies as a unique phenomenon adds more depth to our understanding of the continuum of indiscipline and a more nuanced understanding of the various ways African militaries make demands and challenge authority.

There is a sense of taboo around the issue of mutinies, which challenges efforts to collect empirical research on the topic. Yet, as will be discussed below, mutinies are not normally secret events. They often occur in public spaces and are reported in the media. Additionally, they are actions that have been significant events in the lives of the soldiers who took part. One former mutineer described a revolt he had been involved in as the 'biggest thing' in his professional career. Many of these soldiers were willing to share their experiences in great detail. This chapter will detail the research design and discuss the various sources of data for this book, including both media reporting and in-depth interviews with mutineers.

Identifying mutiny

Scholars who write about mutinies share a common frustration when defining the term. The debate over the definition of mutiny centres on the term's ambiguity. One might assume that mutiny would be easy to identify given that militaries are structured around numerous military codes and laws. However, military codes are often the least precise when defining what a mutiny actually is. In these codes, mutiny is 'the accepted legal term for almost every refusal to obey orders',[2] and therefore vastly different actions can fall into the category of a mutiny.

For studies in the social sciences, most scholars have searched for a meaning that is more specific. Additionally, comparative studies benefit from a cross-national meaning that extends beyond specific national laws. This book identifies a mutiny as an act of collective insubordination in which military personnel revolt against lawfully constituted authority in order to express grievances and make explicit demands. Mutineers' actions may attempt to influence political authorities in order to have their demands met, but their goal is not to seize political office. This definition is closely related to the one presented by Rose, based on the term's first use in sixteenth-century France.[3] While there are variations in definitions between authors writing about mutiny, 'collective insubordination' is the cornerstone of most descriptions.[4]

There are several important aspects to the definition used in this study. One is the word 'collective', which shows that a mutiny must involve a group of soldiers. A single individual who refuses orders is guilty of misconduct or insubordination, but a group that acts together can be charged with mutiny. This is explicitly stated in most military codes. The British military code, for example, which is the basis of many of the military regulations in Anglophone

Africa, states that a mutiny involves indiscipline 'in concert with at least one other person subject to service law'.[5]

This definition indicates that mutinies involve individuals who are currently part of the state's official security structure revolting against their legitimate authority figures who are also part of the structure.[6] This is important because it helps distinguish a mutiny from a rebel movement, in which armed individuals may be making demands, but are doing so from the outside. The fact that mutineers are still employed by the military, and generally want to keep that status, is an important trait that guides their tactics. It is precisely because soldiers are in a contract with the state that they often feel entitled to the claims they make.

Mutiny is often associated with junior ranks, and there are some scholars who include the rank of the soldiers as part of the criteria of a mutiny.[7] My definition does not narrow mutiny to one sector of the military. As will be discussed further below, most of the participants in West and Central African mutinies are rank-and-file soldiers, but there are cases in which officers have also taken part. Additionally, there are some scholars that include tactics as a way to identify a mutiny. For example, Jimmy Kandeh argues that 'mutinies are by definition violent acts of defiance'.[8] This book does not use direct acts of violence as criteria of mutiny. However, the next chapter will demonstrate that mutineers' membership in an organisation centred on amed action makes a threat of violence key to a mutiny.

The last part of the definition is related to the objective. It clarifies that mutinies are generally seen as expressions of collective grievances, not attempts to overthrow governments. Thus it also draws an explicit line between coups and mutinies. This is necessary for the purposes of categorisation, but the events in practice can often change dynamics and motives, challenging the ability to place them into neat categories.

With over eighty successful coups since independence and as many unsuccessful attempts, it is not surprising that African citizens and officials alike are suspicious when soldiers take to the streets to air their grievances.[9] Media reports are unhelpful in differentiating the two events, often claiming that mutinies are coup attempts even when there is little evidence of any desire for political control. Academics have also contributed to the idea that mutinies and coups are closely linked. For example, Ruth First classified mutinies as the initial stage of a coup cycle and Luckham explains that mutinies have been the first phase in the military's incursions into politics in Africa.[10] These scholars link mutinies and coups but still discuss them as separate entities, suggesting there is a difference between the two events.

The idea that there is a relationship between mutinies and coups in Africa has merit and will be discussed later in this section. However, the implicit assumption that mutinies in Africa regularly lead to coups is not supported by the evidence. My research found that most mutinies never escalated to a coup attempt. While coup leaders and mutineers may have similar grievances, such as a lack of promotion opportunities, the manner in which they attempt to address these grievances is different.

The tendency to group mutinies with coups in an African context is likely linked to the rich literature on coups. There are numerous coup datasets, hypotheses and forecasts, and these have been continually updated and tested since the 1960s. However, this also means that we have much more data on the few cases of mutinies that preceded the removal of a head of state. For example, the mutinies in Ethiopia in 1974 that came before the popular revolution and the mutinies in Côte d'Ivoire immediately before a coup in 1999 are well known cases of mutiny. In contrast, mutinies that have not contributed to political changes have largely been ignored. The incidents have very real implications for those involved but are often only visible in archived newspapers or military records. Thus the data on a select number of mutinies may have skewed our perception of the typical trajectory of these revolts.

The most basic distinction between mutinies and coups is found in the definitions of the two events. Coups are defined as 'events in which existing regimes are suddenly and illegally displaced by the action of relatively small groups in which members of the military, police, or security forces of the state play a key role, either on their own or in conjunction with a number of civil servants or politicians'.[11]

While there are some variations in definitions of mutinies, as explained above, they never stipulate that mutinies require the removal of a regime. As Jonathan Powell and Clayton Thyne point out, it is the goal of overthrowing the chief executive that serves as the primary dividing line between coups and the 'less extreme mechanism of pressuring leadership', such as mutinies.[12]

The differences go beyond the definition to include variations in participants, tactics and goals. Although both coups and mutinies involve the military, they typically originate from different sectors of the military. Generally, coups originate from the officer ranks. By contrast, mutinies in Africa are almost the complete opposite in that they typically originate from the rank and file. There is some flexibility in this pattern, as senior enlisted soldiers and junior officers at times participate in both coups and mutinies. However, it is safe to say that junior enlisted soldiers would be unlikely to orchestrate a coup, just as senior officers rarely start a mutiny.

In addition to the particular actors, the number of participants also varies between the two events. A coup typically includes very few individuals, at least in the planning phases.[13] Coups are intended to be exclusive and secretive.[14] In a coup, 'the conspiratorial strike is the secret to its success, not the mobilization of popular masses'.[15] Mutinies are exactly the reverse. Mutineers want to include many participants and are generally seen to gain strength with increased numbers. Mutinies risk failure if they do not have a sufficient number of participants; coups risk failure with too many participants.

Since a coup can be conducted with very few individuals, the act itself does not require much support beyond those involved. A mutiny generally draws a larger number of participants and therefore the grievance must have some level of popular appeal among peers. A small group of individuals can be the sole beneficiaries of a coup, and thus coup-plotters are often accused of being driven by idiosyncratic motives related to greed and power.[16] A mutiny must appeal to the larger mass, and its goals typically benefit a wider group. This is not to suggest that mutinies cannot involve greed as well. However, a mutiny is likely to be initiated over a communal grievance.

As previously mentioned, there are different goals when soldiers conduct a coup compared with when they conduct a mutiny. The former want direct political control, while the latter want a specific grievance addressed. Coups can be seen as an 'all or nothing' scenario in which the actors strive to take complete political control. Mutineers want their grievances addressed and their conditions improved but are usually more flexible in how this is done. As will be explained in the next chapter, the tactics used by mutineers are designed to extract concessions or negotiations and are thus different from the zero-sum mentality of the military personnel that attempt coups. The flexibility of mutinies often equates to a longer execution phase than coups. Coups, particularly those carried out by senior and mid-level officers, are regularly conducted in a matter of hours.[17] Conversely, mutinies are often prolonged affairs, lasting days, weeks or even months. The demands of mutineers often shift over time, and the size of the group can change as other units join or the group splinters. Their tactics also shift, usually escalating the level of violence and threats.

Lastly, soldiers see mutinies and coups as very distinct actions. Later examples will show that mutineers are often adamant that they are not the same as coup-plotters. Even soldiers who had never been involved in either were quick to explain in interviews that these actions were not synonymous. Military tribunals often treat coups and mutinies differently, usually handing down harsher penalties for coups, which are associated with treason. However, death penalties for mutineers in Nigeria in 2014 serve as a reminder that mutiny is also considered a very serious offence by military authorities.[18]

While differentiating coups from mutinies, my research also shows that the two events can be interrelated.[19] As Parsons explains, there is a 'broad continuum of indiscipline in the military ... One form can lead to another, or each type of indiscipline can remain a separate and discrete incident.'[20] Mutinies can escalate to a coup when soldiers' demands are not met or when a zealous member decides to take control. Alternatively, a series of mutinies can lead to a 'creeping coup', as in Ethiopia in 1974.[21] This grey area between coups and mutinies has often led scholars to combine the terms, such as Luckham's description of events in Sierra Leone in 1968 as 'the coup-mutiny' or Boubacar N'Diaye's identification of events in Guinea in 1996 as a 'mutiny/coup'.[22] The case study of Sierra Leone in Chapter 6 will further demonstrate the blurred lines between the two events.

Researching the mutineers' perspective

This study takes two distinct but complementary approaches to examining mutinies. One is a dataset that documents the occurrence of mutinies in West and Central Africa from 1960 to 2014. The data were compiled through a systematic search of media reporting, supplemented with academic texts, biographies, leaked and declassified intelligence reports and interviews. These data will be further examined in the following section.

The other approach involves case studies of mutinies in Sierra Leone, The Gambia and Burkina Faso. For this part of the study, research trips were carried out in 2011, 2012 and 2016, spanning a total of ten months. The research involved over 200 informants, of which roughly fifty were former mutineers. The remainder were other soldiers and officers familiar with the mutinies and civilians who also had in-depth knowledge of the events, as detailed below.

The internal workings of militaries are often shrouded in secrecy and exclusivity, making researching military misbehaviour a difficult task. Most military records are not open to the public, and military hierarchies often require numerous levels of authorisation. Long periods of time were spent on or near military bases to build the requisite trust and rapport needed to discuss these sensitive issues. This allowed for countless conversations with soldiers and their families about military life. These discussions provided deeper insight into how soldiers viewed their conditions as well as their role within their units, communities and the state.

There is no single entry point to access mutineers for research. Most contacts for this book were made through other soldiers that I developed networks with over time and who helped identify and introduce me to others from their previous units. Military personnel in Africa, like in other parts of the world, are frequently transferred to different locations throughout their careers. Therefore, units that once mutinied together have usually been dispersed to different bases over time. In some cases, individuals have left the military, either by order or voluntarily. As a result, much time was spent locating individuals and travelling between interview locations. For example, the Sierra Leone interviews were conducted at ten different military bases spread throughout the country. In the case of The Gambia, the repressive Jammeh regime led many who had been in the military to leave the country after their service. Some of the interviews with former mutineers were conducted outside of The Gambia with former soldiers now living in the UK, the United States and Senegal.

Pre-existing contacts with the foreign diplomatic community assisted with introductions within the military in Burkina Faso. Yet these international channels were limited to building contacts with officers and provided no access to the junior ranks. In Burkina Faso, I had the most success identifying rank-and-file soldiers and eventually former mutineers through contacts with local university students. Many students are of the same age group as junior ranks and knew soldiers from their hometowns, neighbourhoods or circle of friends. These links demonstrated the close relationships that many soldiers maintain with civilian youth. These relationships are easy to overlook as the literature tends to draw distinct lines between civilians and military. Their importance with regard to mutinies will be expanded on in each of the case studies.

While I met the vast majority of interviewees through social networks, I also approached military headquarters to introduce my research and request assistance. In a few instances, top officials were interested in discussing the topic, but more often they wanted nothing to do with the project. In some cases, this led to more complications. After showing up at the military headquarters in Banjul in The Gambia, I was later approached by plain-clothed officers and escorted back to the headquarters for questioning by the intelligence service. This served as a reminder that mutiny is considered a sensitive and threatening topic, particularly by those at the top of the hierarchy.

As part of the research trip in 2012, I travelled by road, using public transport between Sierra Leone and Burkina Faso. Long distance road travel in the region led to countless interactions with soldiers outside of the formal interviews. Soldiers were present at border crossings and manned checkpoints throughout the route, particularly in Guinea. On some parts of the route, for instance in Burkina Faso, armed soldiers stood at the front of the bus to deter criminals following a pattern of bus robberies. At a heated dispute at a minibus station in Guinea, soldiers in uniform were called over to mediate and decide which party was in the right. These examples, and many others from the trip, highlight the internal role of many African militaries. They demonstrate the everyday interactions that many civilians have with military personnel, even those living far from military bases.

Through this long road journey, I spent several weeks each in Guinea and Mali. By chance, the trip coincided with a mutiny and coup in Mali in 2012. This made military revolts a natural point of conversation for many in the region, including state security forces which had an increased presence on the streets and at checkpoints. Travel by minibus and shared taxis does not follow a schedule, and it is common to spend half a day waiting for a vehicle to have enough passengers to move on, leaving ample time for casual discussions. Thus the more formal interviews from the case study countries were supplemented with dozens of unplanned conversations with soldiers and others from Guinea and Mali.

While most of the former mutineers were rank-and-file soldiers, interviews were also conducted with officers. Some of these officers were directly involved in countering or negotiating with the mutineers. In the case of Sierra Leone, the officers were involved in the revolt. Unsurprisingly, the perceptions of the officer corps were often different from those of the rank-and-file soldiers. This reflects varying positions within the military hierarchy and related differences such as background, class and lifestyles. I reflect on these differences throughout the case studies.

My list of interviewees also extended beyond military personnel, representing the complex interactions between mutineers and civilians. These sources of information included politicians, journalists, human rights activists, trade union leaders, university students and members of the international diplomatic community. The case study of Burkina Faso involved the most non-military interviewees, as the mutinies occurred alongside civilian protests and civilians were victims of violent acts by the mutineers. The military and non-military sources together help portray a more holistic picture of African mutinies.

The case studies of Sierra Leone, The Gambia and Burkina Faso reveal different 'types' of mutinies, which occurred under different styles of political leadership. The mutinies in The Gambia in 1991 and 1992 are what I term 'contained mutinies', whereas the mutinies in Burkina Faso in 2011 are an example of violent mass mutinies. The case of Sierra Leone in 1992 represents the overlap between mutinies and coups and will show how plans for one may lead to the other. At the time of the examined mutinies, Sierra Leone was under military leadership, The Gambia was led by a civilian who had been in office for twenty-four years, and Burkina Faso was controlled by a long-standing military-turned-civilian leader. The case studies also show varying outcomes, often beyond the goals of the mutineers.

Despite many of the clear differences between the case studies, when looked at in detail there are also similarities, particularly in the causes of the mutiny and the tactics used by the mutineers. These three case studies show that, even when mutinies occur in very different settings with varied participants, there are common trends within the conduct of the event. The case studies will put the mutinies into historic and political context, which is key to a full understanding of how and why mutinies take place. The case studies will also allow for post-mutiny analysis, demonstrating that the revolts often have long-lasting effects on a military and a state.

In addition to providing a more detailed look at mutinies, the case studies offer a different and important perspective—that of the mutineers. In many mutiny studies, the voice of the mutineers is noticeably absent. This is understandable as mutiny studies are often focused on historic cases and rely on archival data, which tends to favour the government perspective. Similarly, in media reporting of mutinies, government representatives are typically the main source of information. When mutineers express their grievances, it is usually through a spokesperson. Neither of these outlets allows for the perspective of individuals. Through interviews with former mutineers, the motivations and justification of individuals participating in mutinies will be given due attention. While mutiny is an action that requires some group cohesion, conversations with former mutineers show that there is often variation in motives and beliefs among the individuals involved.

The two-part research design allows for the identification of broader patterns of mutinies across time while not neglecting the ground-level perspective. Each approach has strengths as well as limitations. The dataset identifies broad patterns but is less valuable when looking at the context of the mutiny, whereas the case studies are rich in context but are difficult to make generalisations from. However, combining the two approaches allows mutinies to be viewed as incidents that follow general patterns but are also subject to nuance.

SOLDIERS IN REVOLT

Documenting mutinies in West and Central Africa

One of the main challenges in studying mutinies is the lack of longitudinal data on their occurrence. This book attempts to tackle that hurdle with an original dataset of mutinies in West and Central Africa between 1960 and 2014. West and Central Africa was chosen as the region of focus for its high-level of military indiscipline and dissatisfaction,[23] as demonstrated by the Military Intervention Scores in Pat McGowan and Thomas H. Johnson's research, which rated West Africa as having the highest rate of intervention in the continent.[24]

To track incidents of mutiny, I carried out a systematic review of *Africa South of the Sahara*, *Africa Confidential*, *Africa Research Bulletin* and *West Africa* to identify cases of mutinies from independence to 2014. These sources were chosen as my primary starting point because of their consistent and high-quality reporting on the region. I also used the Armed Conflict Location and Event Data (ACLED) Project dataset, which documents acts of political violence and protests in Africa from 1997 onwards. Additional information about the mutinies came from academic writing, memoirs, news outlets, declassified intelligence reports and interviews conducted during field research. Lastly, Patrick McGowan generously shared his extended dataset of coup-related events across the continent from 1957 to 2003, which allowed for more in-depth comparisons between coups and mutinies.

In order for an event to be included in the study, it must involve the following traits: (1) a group of soldiers who remain within the state's military structure; and (2) use of mass insubordination to express stated grievances and goals separate from the desire for political power to higher political and military authorities. These two criteria are closely linked to the definition of mutiny presented earlier. A key trait of all the mutinies in my dataset is that soldiers expressed grievances to the government or military hierarchy with hopes that the government would respond in their favour. In other words, the first action was not to take control of the state.

This categorisation ultimately relies on establishing a motive. In most cases, this was determined by mutineers' public statements or related media reporting, which regularly lists the soldiers' demands. In some cases, tactics used during the mutiny also helped clarify the goals of the soldiers. However, there is a grey area between forms of indiscipline, as noted in the previous section. The case study of Sierra Leone addresses this topic specifically, as I chose to look at an incident that was labelled as both a coup and mutiny by various sources.

Using this methodology, I arrived at a list of seventy one mutinies in West and Central Africa between 1960 and 2014 (see Table 1). This is a conservative figure for a number of reasons. First, both governments and militaries have an incentive not to publicise a mutiny. Mutinies often challenge the legitimacy of individual officers or the military command structure. There is a common belief within the military that a mutiny is always the fault of the officer in charge of the particular unit.[25] This gives officers a motive to avoid announcing that a mutiny has occurred, particularly when mutineers are calling attention to misdeeds by their officers, as with accusations of corruption. Mutinies also pose a threat to public order, and there are often fears that they could spread to other units, giving government officials an incentive not to announce mutinies. Therefore, some mutinies are likely to have occurred that were never reported as such in the press.

Unreported mutinies are especially likely when the government controls the media, as is the case in many African states at various points since independence. The sources used are largely Anglophone and tend to focus on the former British colonies. With the increase in internet reporting and social media, it has become easier to identify mutinies, particularly when conducted in a public location. Additionally, mutineers since the 1990s have increasingly used the media as a 'weapon'. This issue will be discussed further in the following chapter.

The dataset of mutinies does not include every incident of mutiny within West and Central Africa. Rather, it can only account for those that are publicly documented, which is likely an underestimate of the real number of occurrences. This is the opposite problem to that faced by researchers attempting to document coup attempts or plots. There is often speculation that governments will announce false coup attempts or coup plots to justify the arrest of opposition figures or those deemed a threat to the political leadership. While there may be some political manipulation of mutiny reporting, the public nature of mutinies and their mass participation make them easier to verify than plots. Datasets of coup attempts and plots are hindered by false reporting, whereas the mutiny dataset used in this book is challenged by a lack of reporting, particularly in earlier decades.

One other complication in creating a list of mutinies is determining how to count the mutinies. As will be demonstrated in the following chapter, mutinies often spread between units and geographic areas, and it is common to see multiple units mutinying in different locations within the same country. It would be possible to count this as either one mutiny or multiple mutinies. In this scenario, I counted multiple units mutinying at the same time as a single incident, largely because reporting usually does not identify all of the various participating units. However, when there was a clear end to a mutiny or pause for negotiations followed by another revolt (usually from a new unit), this was recorded as a separate mutiny.[26]

Developing a dataset of mutinies is much more than an exercise in counting incidences, as qualitative material was also collected for each of the mutinies. This allows for analysis beyond when mutinies have occurred. Details about participants, demands, tactics and outcomes were also examined. The following chapters will take a deeper look at trends within mutinies by drawing on the qualitative material gathered in the dataset as well as through interviews.

Table 1: Mutinies in West and Central Africa from 1960 to 2014

Country	Year	Country	Year
Democratic Republic of Congo	1960	Republic of Congo	1997
Ghana	1961	Burkina Faso	1997
Democratic Republic of Congo	1961	Niger	1998
Togo	1963	Côte d'Ivoire	1999
Liberia	1963	Niger	1999
Niger	1963	Burkina Faso	1999
Republic of Congo	1966	Côte d'Ivoire	2000
Democratic Republic of Congo	1966	Côte d'Ivoire	2000
Nigeria	1966	Nigeria	2000
Democratic Republic of Congo	1967	Benin	2000
Nigeria	1970	Central African Republic	2001
Benin	1972	Côte d'Ivoire	2002
Sierra Leone	1982	Niger	2002
Burkina Faso	1983	Burkina Faso	2003
Côte d'Ivoire	1990	Côte d'Ivoire	2003
Côte d'Ivoire	1990	Guinea Bissau	2004
Chad	1991	Burkina Faso	2006
The Gambia	1991	Burkina Faso	2007
Democratic Republic of Congo	1991	Guinea	2007
Democratic Republic of Congo	1991	Guinea	2007
Benin	1992	Guinea	2008
Republic of Congo	1992	Côte d'Ivoire	2008
The Gambia	1992	Nigeria	2008
Niger	1992	Guinea	2009
Central African Republic	1993	Guinea	2010
Central African Republic	1993	Burkina Faso	2011
Democratic Republic of Congo	1993	Burkina Faso	2011

Côte d'Ivoire	1993	Burkina Faso	2011
Niger	1993	Guinea Bissau	2011
Central African Republic	1996	Mali	2012
Central African Republic	1996	Chad	2013
Central African Republic	1996	São Tomé and Príncipe	2014
Republic of Congo	1996	Nigeria	2014
Guinea	1996	Nigeria	2014
Republic of Congo	1997	Chad	2014
		Côte d'Ivoire	2014

The list above indicates that mutinies have not taken place at an even pace across time. African states experienced a series of mutinies in the early independence years but very few occurred in the 1970s and 1980s. However, mutinies gained traction in the 1990s and have remained a popular tactic among soldiers ever since. The relatively consistent use of mutiny in West and Central Africa since the 1990s makes a case for the timeliness of research on these types of revolts. The increasing number of mutinies among African soldiers is in contrast to rates of coups. Successful coups peaked in the 1960s with nineteen cases in West and Central Africa before declining over time, with nine in the 1990s and four between 2000 and 2009.[27] The following chapters will further examine mutineers' tactics, goals and success rates to shed light on why soldiers continue to see mutiny as a potentially beneficial action. Chapter 4 in particular will propose reasons why soldiers have been prone to mutiny during certain decades more than others.

In comparing the above mutiny list with datasets of coups and coup attempts by Powell and Thyne for the same countries in the same years, there are five incidents that appear in both lists.[28] In several of these cases, protests by soldiers over corporate grievances escalated to an eventual overthrow of the state. This pattern occurred in Togo in 1963 and Côte d'Ivoire in 1999, for example. In the other cases, researchers labelled the incidences as failed coup attempts, whereas other data suggest the soldiers' primary motive was to express grievances to their superiors, not to take control of the state. This variation in interpreting motives occurs on the ground as well, with political and military leaders often assuming that a mutiny is a coup attempt or, much less often, calling a coup attempt a mutiny. As the following chapter will discuss in greater detail, large groups of soldiers can have different individual goals within a single group, and thus in some cases it is possible to classify an incident as both a failed coup attempt and a mutiny.

The comparison of the datasets also shows that the vast majority of incidents listed in Table 1 have not been examined in coup studies. While it is important to acknowledge the cases where mutinies have escalated into attempts to take political control, it is the large number of cases in which this did not occur that I am most interested in. It is these mutinies that have often been overlooked in research on African militaries.

3

THE TYPICAL MUTINY

PATTERNS IN PARTICIPANTS, TACTICS AND OUTCOMES

There is a debate in the existing scholarship over whether mutinies follow a standard pattern. The American military historian Fletcher Platt claims that 'there is no such thing as a typical mutiny'.[1] Rose, on the other hand, argues that this 'only partially true, since mutinies, like men, have attributes that permit at least some generalizations'.[2] My research supports the idea that generalisations can be made about mutinies; however, the patterns I describe in this chapter often contradict generalisations made by other researchers examining Western mutinies from previous centuries.

It should not come as a surprise that there is typical behaviour within mutinies, given that they are conducted by groups of individuals with shared training experiences and a lifestyle that emphasises conformity. While mutinies show an obvious break from the discipline instilled in a military environment, mutineers often use military manoeuvres and strategy to their advantage during a mutiny. What is perhaps surprising, though, is that we know very little about what a typical mutiny looks like in West and Central Africa. This chapter aims to fill this gap by looking at common traits in the demands made by mutineers as well as the way mutinies are carried out. Attempting to document what is typical in the actions of mutineers has practical value in attempting predictive analysis. However, perhaps more importantly, it also helps identify recurring dissatisfaction within the ranks in the region.

This chapter begins by briefly discussing the role of the military in African states in order to show the historic roots of many of the mutineers' grievances, particularly those in which they object to the advantages given to the officer corps. The findings show that most mutineers' grievances involve conditions of service, in particular aspects of pay or other material benefits such as housing. However, underlying these grievances are perceptions of injustice in their own conditions compared with those of the senior ranks. Although rank-and-file mutineers do not make claims that they deserve equivalent pay or benefits to senior officers, there is a common feeling that the level of differentiation is extreme. This analysis builds on the works of scholars such as Robin Luckham, Michael Lofchie and Jimmy Kandeh who have emphasised the significance of class differences within African military structures.[3] While these authors place emphasis on the position of junior officers, my analysis will expand on the discussion by showing the way in which class differences are often interpreted by the rank-and-file soldiers.

Following the discussion of common mutineer grievances, the focus of the chapter then shifts to the act of mutiny. Soldiers use a limited number of tactics when conducting a mutiny, indicating that mutineers are not reinventing strategies with each revolt. Furthermore, these common tactics serve to draw attention to the cause of the mutineers and open a dialogue with the senior leadership. Examples in this and later chapters demonstrate that often mutineers are not acting simply on impulse but rather have a particular strategy in their actions. Still, even mutinies with plans are limited in their predictability becaue of shifts in participants and goals as well as the various ways in which a government can respond. Lastly, this chapter will discuss the success rates of mutinies. Mutinies in Africa can often be considered a short-term success for the mutineers but are limited in creating long-term changes.

The uncomfortable place of rank-and-file soldiers in Africa

One consistent feature of mutinies that applies to both African and non-African settings is that they tend to be made up of personnel from the junior enlisted ranks of their service. Occasionally, non-commissioned officers (NCOs) take part and more rarely junior officers, but for the most part mutinies involve the lowest level of the military hierarchy. Before delving into the specifics of mutineers' grievances and how they generally conduct mutinies, it is worthwhile to briefly situate the military, and particularly the rank-and-file soldiers, within African states. As will be elaborated on in the next section, mutineers' grievances, even those of a material nature, regularly involve accusations against their superiors. These complaints are often grounded in a history in which the divisions between the ranks have increased as militaries in the region have become involved in politics.

The role of the military has changed in many African states since independence, but generally the military has been one of the most powerful organisations in any given state. This is not simply based on its manpower or access to weapons but is due to the military's history of participating in, influencing and often dominating politics. When militaries throughout the region began launching coups in the 1960s, they marketed themselves as selfless saviours who would 'modernise' the state.[4] For many, their presence in politics was welcomed, as the military was viewed as the only 'group with the necessary skills to uplift newly independent nations', due to their position and training during the colonial era.[5] However, coups soon became endemic, with few countries spared and many coup organisers becoming victims of coups themselves. The military's performance in the political realm did not live up to its promises, and in many cases military regimes were particularly repressive. By the 1980s, the image of African militaries as saviours was long out of fashion and the focus turned to ways to 'demilitarise' or 're-civilianise' politics. However, it was difficult to relegate the military back to the barracks once they became involved in politics.

One of the main ways political leaders (both civilians and leaders from a military background) tried to insure themselves against a coup was to make certain the military, especially the officer corps, was satisfied. Decalo explains that there has been a 'very visible trade-off of material benefits, both to the military as a corporate body and to officers as individuals, in exchange for political fealty':[6]

the armed forces [have] become yet another important constituency that has to be 'taken care of' through spoils of office.

Corporate trade-offs may include the provision of often unnecessarily sophisticated equipment and firepower that enhances the prestige of the military, and an ever increasingly large army that, *inter alia*, raises the status of its leaders, as well as the number of officers needed, all with prestige and remunerative repercussions, etcetera. Individual perks include not only rank and pay promotions, duty-free cars and other luxury imports, but also appointments overseas as military attaches, as well as places on refresher training-courses in prized foreign staff-colleges.[7]

In addition to these immediate benefits for senior officers were often more long-term opportunities, including positions within the government and access to land or other entrepreneurial prospects. As a result, in 'most African states, civil or military, army officers play a major economic role in the commercial sector'.[8] These economic advantages are often highly profitable for a select number of individuals. Herbert Howe, for example, shows that expensive and generally unnecessary weapons systems are often desired not just for issues of prestige, as described by Decalo, but also for the commissions they can earn senior officers.[9] Additionally, the officer corps in many states has come to enjoy a high degree of impunity due to their political connections.

As a result of the military's history in Africa, its role in politics and the privileges awarded by governments (including foreign governments), senior military officers are often considered elites within society. However, these 'spoils enticements ... have mostly benefitted senior officers' while creating a sharp division between the ranks in the military.[10] Although the military is often referred to as a homogenous organisation with particular privilege, in reality there are vast differences within the organisation as a whole.

The prestige awarded to the military as an organisation often has limited tangible benefit for rank-and-file soldiers. While soldiers may be in an enviable position compared with some civilians because they have a (supposedly) regular salary, the pay for rank-and-file soldiers is typically low, and in some states it is often the case that rank-and-file soldiers will receive their salary erratically, as various examples throughout this book will demonstrate. It is also common for enlisted ranks to supplement their salaries through other means, both legal and illegal. Housing for the lowest ranks is often limited, and junior soldiers regularly live off base. The advantage of joining the military is likely not the initial pay but the ability to advance up the ranks. However, a lack of promotion opportunities is a persistent complaint among junior soldiers. There is of course a challenge in making generalisations across many states, as not all rank-and-file soldiers live in poor conditions and not all of the senior officers have become wealthy from their position. However, the persistent claims of the gap between the lifestyles of the senior officers and those below them indicate that it is a common trend in the region.

Rank-and-file soldiers in Africa are in an uncomfortable position because they are the least influential members in what is often considered the most powerful and elite organisation in the country. The military institution may project an image of prestige, but this has limited value in the daily life of many junior soldiers. Still, the limited economic opportunities in most states in the region, especially for individuals without higher education, create an incentive for soldiers to maintain their position in the military. As this book demonstrates, instead of relinquishing their position out of dissatisfaction, they often attempt to work within the system to have their conditions improved.

In terms of their socio-economic status, rank-and-file soldiers usually have more in common with lower classes of the civilian society than with senior officers. While there is often overlap between junior soldiers and the civilian sector, there is also an intentional divide. This divide goes beyond the standard division in most militaries where soldiers separate themselves from civilians through uniforms, grooming standards and so on. The divide between rank-and-file soldiers and civilians in West and Central Africa also has to do with the history of using militaries for internal policing. Soldiers were often tasked—and in many cases still are—with regime protection and shielding political leaders from internal opposition. In this role, the military was often in direct contact with the civilian sector but in an antagonistic way, particularly when ordered to curb civilian protests. Ethnic military recruitment in some states has further exacerbated tensions between the military and civilian populations when the military is seen as being aligned with a particular ethnic group or region.

In many ways, the rank-and-file soldiers are caught between the lower classes of the civilian population and their military superiors. When rank-and-file soldiers mutiny, they often appear to have been influenced by the actions of the civilian population as well as their military superiors. For example, demands for improvements in their work conditions often sound very similar to demands made during strikes by trade unions or student organisations. However, mutineers also use intimidation and threats of violence and instability. Much as coup leaders present an image of policing the civilian politicians, mutineers often present themselves as policing the officer corps.

Private problems

One of the most basic but significant questions regarding mutineers is 'what do they want?' For the military leadership, this is a very practical concern because it relates to how a mutiny can be resolved. As will be further detailed later, when leaders discover what the demands of mutinies are, they often decide to acquiesce or negotiate. Assessing common demands from mutineers is also valuable beyond those directly involved in engaging the mutineers, as it gives an insight into the perceptions of the lower ranks. Their demands highlight their expectations as well as where they find fault.

From qualitative data from the seventy one cases of mutiny described in the last chapter and interviews with mutineers, it is clear that the vast majority of mutineers' grievances revolve around their daily life or terms of service. In West and Central Africa, mutinies are generally used as a means for junior soldiers to negotiate with their superiors over their conditions of service.

Most grievances expressed by mutineers fit into categories related to monetary/material issues, leadership or military processes. However, soldiers do not limit themselves to one category, and it is common to see all types of complaints in a single mutiny. These common grievances are elaborated on below, but it is also important to note that the groupings are not concrete, as there is a lot of overlap between the categories. Each type of grievance is usually accompanied by a fairly direct demand: monetary/material concessions, leadership changes or revisions to military processes. However, the following section will explain how an underlying perception of injustice surrounding these complaints makes the demands less straightforward than they often appear.

The most frequent grievance in West and Central Africa involves pay or other material issues. In roughly 75 per cent of the mutinies examined in this book, soldiers made direct demands for payment or other material concessions. Payment grievances typically consist of accusations of delays in receiving pay or claims that the pay is inadequate. These two complaints are not mutually exclusive, with some mutineers claiming that their inadequate salaries are late. A more specific payment criticism involves special payments for deployments. These particular demands will be addressed in more detail in Chapter 5. Closely linked to salary complaints are grievances over material issues such as housing, food, equipment and uniforms. These material issues are closely tied to, and often inclusive of, salaries. In some states, for example, it is common for monthly salaries to include both money and food, such as a supply of rice. Similarly, if soldiers reside on base and if the base provides meals, a portion of their salary goes to cover those expenses. Mutinying soldiers often claim that the food, housing or uniforms provided by the military are insufficient or of less value than the money deducted from their salaries. A common demand includes larger monetary payments with which soldiers can then buy their own food or pay for their own housing.

The second most common grievance involves specific complaints about the leadership. These demands are closely linked to the material complaints, as the officers are usually accused of having a role in missing pay or lack of other material items. The spokesperson for mutineers in Guinea in 2008 demonstrated this type of grievance by stating that the generals 'do not care about the needs of the soldiers' and accusing them of 'hiding' the soldiers' back-pay.[11]

In some cases, the soldiers appear to have had negative interactions with the particular officers they accuse. For example, in 1997, mutineers in the

THE TYPICAL MUTINY

Republic of Congo demanded the removal of the commander of a particular training centre, who is likely to have been an individual with whom the soldiers had contact.[12] However, often mutineers seem unsure of whom to blame and call for dismissals at the most senior levels. This occurred in Guinea in 2008 when soldiers asked that the defence minister be dismissed and in The Gambia in 1991 when soldiers called for the most senior officer in the military to be relieved of service.[13] In these two cases, it is unlikely that junior soldiers had personal interactions with these senior persons and thus their calls are more symbolic of a distrust of the hierarchy in general. In both cases, the demands of the mutineers were met and these senior officials lost their positions. However, in many instances these changes are largely symbolic, as was the case when a Gambian colonel was removed from his position following calls from mutineers in 1991 and 'punished' with an ambassadorial position in Europe.[14]

The third common type of grievance has to do with procedures within the military system. In these cases, the soldiers complain about decisions or specific processes that they deem to be unjust or not advantageous. Examples include objections to decisions to downsize the military or transfer units to different bases. It is also common for grievances to include the promotion process or more general accusations of favouritism within the military. These types of grievances also overlap with material concerns and leadership complaints. For example, concerns over promotion procedures are closely linked to claims that military leaders manipulate the process.

An overview of the common grievances shows that mutineers are typically self-interested and fairly pragmatic. Mutineers rarely push for changes beyond their own conditions of service, nor do they make radical requests for changes to the military structure. When asking for promotions, it is almost always within a reasonable scale. Rank-and-file soldiers may ask to be promoted up one rank but not to be promoted to an officer rank. Similarly, mutineers may demand better housing but do not expect their housing to be on a par with officers or even NCOs. Through their demands, mutineers show a general respect for, or at least acceptance of the military hierarchy.

Another example of the pragmatic side of mutineers is their heavy emphasis on numbers and facts. This was apparent in my interviews with former mutineers. They would often go to great lengths to explain their salaries in precise numbers (including how often they were paid) as well as listing other various costs such as rice, a pound of meat, transport to visit family, uniforms and boots. This is apparent in media announcements by mutineers as well. For example, in 1996, soldiers in the Central African Republic announced: 'We pay for our uniforms which cost CFA 25,000; a pair of boots costs CFA 25,000, and we get 29,041—and we have families and children.'[15] The same group later explained on the radio how they had 'continued to receive the salary of a second class private, CFA 29,041 for 15 to 16 years'.[16] Similarly, soldiers in Guinea in 2008 explained their pay grievances in relation to the cost of rice in order to show that a bag of rice costs roughly half their monthly pay.[17] In these cases, there seemed to be a strong desire to demonstrate how their salaries could not cover the basic costs of living, and the soldiers were making the point that their actions were driven by necessity. By providing the exact details of their salaries and expenses, soldiers also distinguished themselves from the officers whom they often accuse of economic irresponsibility. However, characterising themselves as sensible negotiators is likely to be a strategy in itself, and there are plenty of examples of behaviour within mutinies, such as looting, which could not be justified by claims of necessity.

Qualitative data from the mutinies presented in the previous chapter also allow for an examination of whether there is a certain 'type' of unit in which these grievances appear most often or a type of unit that is more prone to mutiny. The simple answer is that there is no significant difference in the units that have mutinied in the region. The vast majority of units with documented cases of mutiny were in armies. However, this corresponds to the dominance of armies in terms of personnel within military structures in the region. Air forces and navies tend to be small by comparison, if states in West and Central Africa have them at all. Yet mutinies are not limited to armies, and nearly every type of military unit can be accounted for in the dataset: army, navy, air force, gendarmerie, parachutists, commandos, presidential guards, foreign-trained units and units with foreign advisors. The only feature that seems to appear more frequently among units that mutiny is a shared deployment experience. The propensity of mutiny following deployments will be the subject of Chapter 5.

There are differences in mutiny rates for rural and urban-based units. Most of the mutinies examined in this book took place in a capital city. This is to be expected considering that soldiers are typically bringing their complaints to the government or military headquarters, both of which are usually located in the capital. Furthermore, most capitals host a sizeable number of military personnel and units. The urban-centric nature of militaries in the region reflects the internal function of many African armies. Some attempts to reform and restructure militaries, such as those carried out in post-war Sierra Leone, have placed emphasis on redistributing soldiers and bases away from the capital. Still, most major urban centres in West and Central Africa are also home to large military bases.

Yet mutinies are not restricted to capital cities or urban centres. Roughly 20 per cent of the mutinies occurred in rural regions, away from major cities. In some cases, the grievances that triggered the mutinies occurred at rural bases, but soldiers took their complaints to the leadership in the capital. Thus the physical location of a mutiny does not always coincide with where the grievances developed. Similarly, Chapter 5 will explore mutinies in which complaints began while abroad on deployments but the act of revolt took place in the soldiers' home country. It is also possible that urban mutinies attract more attention in the press, as media outlets also have a higher presence in urban centres. Therefore, incidents of mutiny in rural areas may be more likely to go unreported.

The lack of a concrete pattern in the types of units that most often mutiny further suggests that many of the grievances expressed by mutineers are widespread. They extend throughout military organisations and are not linked to one particular aspect of the structure. For instance, in the research on mutinies from a non-African perspective and coups in an African context, there has been speculation that internal military tensions and revolts often centre on divisions created by the development of elite units within the military.[18] However, there is no indication that elite units, or the envy they attract from 'regular' units, significantly contribute to more mutinies in West and Central Africa. While it may be difficult to predict mutinies based on the type of unit or where they are based, the following two chapters will identify particular contexts in which soldiers often decide that their conditions of service are unacceptable.

'The problems are between the generals and us'[19]

Mutineers' demands for payment, improved housing or removal of an officer are often linked to perceptions of injustice. This sense of injustice regularly develops around large discrepancies in the privileges and economic advantages between the ranks. All hierarchies have divisions between the rank-and-file soldiers and their senior officers, but the divisions in West and Central Africa are often particularly severe given the unique role of the military in the region. In interviews, former mutineers regularly discussed their own conditions in comparison with what they saw as the excessive lifestyles of officers. For example, a rank-and-file soldier involved in the 1992 revolt in Sierra Leone described the cause of the incident in the following way: 'We are at the warfront, we are not being paid on time, we are not well catered for, we need better medical facilities. And authorities are sitting in Freetown, driving luxurious cars.'[20] In conversations with Sierra Leonean soldiers in 2011 about their present conditions, their complaints sound similar to those of decades earlier. One soldier commented on the lifestyle of officers in the following way: 'if you have 10,000 [USD] and you are driving a car that costs 60,000–70,000, where did you get the money? They are building homes, mansions in Freetown. And we are grumbling, soldiers are grumbling.'[21] The soldier's answer to his own question was that he believed the money came from peacekeeping pay, a topic that will be further examined in Chapter 5. Here we see that it is not necessarily the inequality that soldiers object to, as any hierarchy has inequality, but rather what they view as excessive, which they represent using words like 'luxurious' and 'mansions'.

This perception of the senior officers' lavish lifestyle is a direct contradiction of traditional military ethos, which emphasises austerity. While austerity is rarely a term used to describe senior officers in Africa, there still appears to be a disdain for officers whom the rank-and-file soldiers deem to be living too extravagantly. The actions of soldiers in Burkina Faso in 2011 represent this belief. Mutineers vandalised and set fire to the homes of several senior officers, including the army chief of staff.[22] Similar targeted attacks occurred on the residences of senior officers in Guinea in 2008.[23]

It is difficult to quantify the salary differentiation between the ranks as official pay scales in Africa are usually unavailable, and it is likely that rank-and-file soldiers are not aware of the particular salaries of their senior officers. No rank-and-file interviewee in my research ever gave a specific figure for an officer's salary and in fact salary was rarely mentioned. This is consistent with public statements by mutineers as well. Instead, complaints centre on the idea that officers were making money through other means as a result of their position. Mutineers are not alone in their observations. International analysis and investigations into procurement procedures have highlighted that weak oversight measures often lead to the self-enrichment of 'military oligarchies'.[24] Reports from the Strategic Studies Institute put it more bluntly by stating that Nigerian 'senior officers all become immensely rich through theft, while junior officers and enlisted men live in poverty', with the researchers even going as far as to call for a 'wholesale replacement of the officer corps'.[25]

The perceived injustice becomes especially apparent when soldiers believe that their efforts are responsible for officers' success. A Burkinabé rank-and-

THE TYPICAL MUTINY

file soldier expressed this opinion by stating that 'if he is a high officer, say a colonel, he gets to that position through the help of those below him. He is taken care of by his juniors, but then he has no respect for them ... There is much selfishness with the officers.'[26]

This issue of class differentiation and perceptions of corruption among officers by the ranks as detailed above is also a key argument in Kandeh's work on the junior ranks that conduct coups:

> Ordinary soldiers observe and take exception to the sudden embourgeoisment [sic] of their officers, which many have come to rightly believe occurs at their expense. Resentment based upon perceptions that officers are 'stiffing' the ranks, 'chopping them small,' and siphoning their supplies has often been the center of the grievance narratives of subaltern mutineers and insurgents.[27]

However, the feelings of resentment among the rank and file go beyond the material advantages and include other privileges. For example, Burkinabé military interviewees consistently complained of a system in which senior officers were able to bring their sons into the military, regardless of whether or not they had the necessary qualifications. The perceived impunity of the officer corps was also a key concern of mutineers in Burkina Faso in 2011. Rank-and-file soldiers felt that they were singled out for punishment because of their rank, while officers went uncharged for similar or worse offences.[28]

Many of the accusations made by mutineers are not of criminal offences but rather frustrations that their leadership does not abide by the required military procedures. These perceived double standards among the ranks lower troop morale and undercut the ethos of discipline, which is key to military functionality. In an interview with a Burkinabé soldier, I asked what had caused the 2011 mutinies. He responded that 'the main main main cause is no respect for authority, no discipline, even the superiors do not respect military rules'.[29] This individual expresses the idea that discipline must start at the top of the hierarchy and seems to suggest that, if superiors do not respect rules, nor will their subordinates.

When soldiers discussed their general complaints about the officer corps, they usually made a point to explain that there were exceptions, individuals who did not fit the pattern. There was one particular officer in Sierra Leone, for instance, who was described in a heroic manner by numerous interviewees. During one interview with a soldier, I remarked 'Every time I talk to soldiers they bring up Lt Bangura, why is he so popular?'[30] The soldier's response was that 'He demonstrated by example.' The interviewee then elaborated on this with statements such as 'He is the only person who wakes up at 6.00 in the morning, 8.00 in the morning everybody is supposed to be in the office ... He participated in the cleaning every last Saturday of the month.'[31] Thus the respect for Lt Bangura was a result of his willingness to follow the same regulations and expectations that were applied to the rank-and-file soldiers.

Leadership is a central focus in most research on mutinies. There is a dominant theme among mutiny scholars and military personnel that mutinies are the fault of individual officers. Rose explains that the 'view of command responsibility is a *leitmotif* throughout military history, as prevalent today [as it was] almost 200 years ago.'[32] Joel Hamby's work, entitled 'A Leadership Model for Mutiny in Combat', specifically addresses how individual leaders can avoid causing mutinies or how they can handle mutinies if they occur. He leaves the reader with no doubt of his opinions for the causes and solutions of mutinies: 'There is no magical silver bullet that will prevent mutiny; only leaders who lead effectively can forestall the phenomenon.'[33]

The examples from West and Central Africa, as presented above, vary from the dominant view, which blames mutinies on individual leaders. In the cases examined in this book, soldiers tend to express grievances about the leadership as a whole rather than attributing blame to a single individual. The African examples demonstrate that there are divisions between the rank-and-file soldiers and their officers that go beyond the expected hierarchical divisions that develop from differences in education, training or experience. The soldiers raise objections about a system in which the gaps between rank-and-file and senior officers are often enormous in terms of economic advantages. Added to these economic differences are other concerns, such as unequal treatment under the law.

By viewing the gap between the ranks as a more systemic problem with historical roots, it becomes clearer why mutinies have become a recurring regional problem, not just single exceptional incidents. Hamby argues that 'the passions involved [in mutinies] burn out quickly', which is consistent with his broader claim that mutinies result from weak leaders and can be resolved with changes to leadership.[34] However, my research suggests that passions rarely die easily, and in fact we very often see mutinies reignite in the same countries. This is largely because the authorities may address the surface complaints (salary, food, housing) while failing to acknowledge the underlying issues, a topic that will be further addressed later in the chapter and will be highlighted again through the case studies.

THE TYPICAL MUTINY

Mutineers' playbook

Discussions of the common tactics used by mutineers are oddly absent from nearly all writings on mutinies. The opposite can be said for coup analysis, in which there has been detailed and extensive work on tactics.[35] This is a major blindspot in the mutiny literature because it means that it is very difficult to know what to expect once a mutiny begins. The analysis of tactics is valuable beyond its practicality and is also useful in determining broader goals.

The image in most people's minds of an African mutiny is likely one of soldiers gathered in streets firing weapons into the air. This is a fairly accurate starting point for a mutiny. Discharging firearms and mass gatherings in a strategic location (military headquarters, State House, parliament building, etc.) are among the most common tactics mutineers use. The firing of weapons is closely linked to another common action, breaking into the armoury. In most parts of West and Central Africa, junior soldiers do not readily have access to firearms, and therefore the first step for many mutineers is to seize weapons and ammunition from the armoury. Brandishing weapons or firing weapons can serve as both a symbol of power and a threat to those not involved in the mutiny.

While the media portrayal of mutineers as gun-wielding soldiers creating a chaotic atmosphere for their own benefit is partially true, it is also an incomplete picture. Mutineers are often strategic and creative in their tactics, gaining inspiration from their own military training as well as from successful actions used by other armed groups and civilian organisations.

Hostage-taking is a common course of action among mutineers. At least fifteen of the mutinies in the table in the previous chapter involved the taking of hostages. This tactic is not specific to a particular time period. It was used in the Republic of Congo in 1966 when mutineers captured the head of the army and gendarmerie.[36] Similarly, this also occurred in the Central African Republic mutinies in 1996 when mutineers took the army chief of staff, the energy minister and the National Assembly speaker hostage.[37] The tactic appears to have been particularly popular among Nigerien soldiers, with hostage-taking episodes occurring during revolts in 1992, 1993, 1998, 1999 and 2002. Their abductees included the head of the parliament, ministers, military commanders and local authorities.

Hostage-taking is a recognised tactic among non-state armed groups in Africa, one that has been used by militants in the Niger Delta, al-Qaida in the Islamic Maghreb, and Somali pirates. However, it is not a strategy that would commonly be used in a military context. In hostage-taking by both armed groups and mutineers, the value of the hostage resides in the ability to pressure an exchange. Armed groups are usually attempting to exchange hostages for the release of prisoners or money, for example, while mutineers exchange hostages for meetings with senior leadership or promises that their demands will be met. One important difference between hostage-taking by mutineers and other armed groups is that the former are often abducting individuals from their own organisation and state, whereas non-state armed groups regularly target international personnel. Furthermore, mutineers seldom attempt to hide their identity or location. Lastly, mutineers are usually not overtly threatening the lives of their hostages. In the cases of hostages taken by mutineers examined here, there were no incidents in which the hostages were killed. Mutineers want to make procedural changes in the military or desire material gains; they do not want to be excluded and removed from the system. Therefore, they must use caution when dealing with hostages, as an injured or dead hostage would not help their cause.

It is more common for mutineers to take civilian political representatives hostage than to abduct military officers. In some ways, this may seem counterintuitive. One could assume that rank-and-file soldiers would take hostage those that they blame for their problems, which tends to be military officers. However, rank-and-file soldiers abducting officers and expecting the military hierarchy to respond keeps the act as an internal military matter, and generally speaking the mutineers are suspicious of the military hierarchy. By involving political representatives, mutineers work around their chain of command and bring their complaints into the political realm. They also attract wider attention to the perceived wrongdoings of their seniors.

Mutineers often take over strategic locations as a way to assert their power and threaten authority. The tactical value of these locations ranges from relatively minimal to highly important. For example, mutineers in Nigeria in 2008 blocked traffic for several hours on a major road in order to draw attention to claims that they had not been paid their allowances.[38] While the mutiny did bring attention to their complaints and likely inconvenienced many local people, it did not threaten the nation's stability. Other mutineers have captured more valuable targets. For instance, air force mutineers took over the control tower and terminals at the Abidjan Airport in 1990.[39] Similar incidents of mutineers holding airports have occurred in the Democratic Republic of Congo (1966, 1991) and Niger (1992).[40] Mutineers in the Republic of Congo in 1997 held both the rail station and the power station, disrupting rail services and leaving local towns without electricity for several days.[41]

Controlling public or strategically important locations is similar to hostage-taking in that it brings the grievances of the mutineers into a more public forum. Unlike hostage-taking, controlling locations affects not just key political or military personnel but the general civilian population as well. Targeting transit infrastructure, especially airports, also has international implications when air traffic is diverted. The longer mutineers hold strategically important locations, the more fragile a government appears, which could affect international trade and investments. Furthermore, when the actions of mutineers affect civilians there is the threat that civilians will react, further destabilising the situation. There is the possibility that civilians will criticise the way the government handles the situation or perhaps even side with the mutineers. Both scenarios have occurred in Burkina Faso, the former in 2011 and the latter in 1983.

In addition to its strategic value, the decision to capture transport infrastructure can also be seen as mutineers working in a domain with which they are familiar. While militaries worldwide are often thought to have an external focus, in West and Central Africa the military regularly take on an internal function, similar to policing. The protection of key infrastructure is often part of their responsibility, and it is particularly common for the military to be active in transport infrastructure as with military-manned road checkpoints or military personnel serving as airport security.

Public gatherings, firing weapons into the air, taking hostages and holding key infrastructure all serve the purpose of drawing attention to the mutineers' cause. These tactics are not meant to be discreet; mutineers want people to know their mission. This is an important difference between coups and mutinies. Whereas coups are meant to be a definitive action, mutinies are a step in a process of negotiations. The tactics aim to gain attention and open a dialogue with the leadership in an environment in which the hierarchy does not easily allow individuals to express their opinions. Channelling concerns up the chain of command, which is the required procedure within a military hierarchy, often involves navigating a range of obstacles. One is that the direct chain of command is often the problem, particularly when soldiers accuse their superiors of having a hand in their missing salaries. Secondly, the demands of mutineers are often larger than could be addressed by their immediate superiors, Most militaries do have some form of official grievance procedure, in which soldiers could register their concerns. Yet every soldier that I asked about this option immediately dismissed it. They suggested that it either would not work or would cause more problems for the individual who submitted the complaint.

There is often ambiguity in whether mutineers aim to gain an audience of senior military leadership or senior political leadership. Part of the explanation for this could be that there is often a lack of clarity in the role and relationship between senior political and military leadership in the region. Moreover, as junior members of the hierarchy, mutineers may be unaware of how decisions, especially regarding funding, are made. In general, mutineers seem to prefer dealing with the political leadership, a trend that represents their general distrust of their senior military officers. This preference can be seen in the way they often physically approach State House or demand meetings with the president.

Mutineers' public relations campaigns

The desire for mutineers to grab the attention of government officials, and often a wider audience, makes the media a natural tool for mutineers. Media allow mutineers to circumvent their chain of command and address their concerns to political authorities, and the media have become increasingly accessible in recent years. The above-mentioned mutineer tactics have been used fairly consistently since the 1960s. However, the use of media by mutineers is a relatively new tactic, having gained in popularity in the 1990s. This trend coincides with and has been enabled by increased media freedoms from the 1990s onwards.

By engaging directly with the media, mutineers can create their own public relations image. As the examples below will show, soldiers often try to counter the image portrayed by government sources, which is almost always negative. For example, descriptors of mutineers by government sources include 'ruthless', 'uncontrolled individuals', 'diehards', 'criminals' and 'dangerous'. Mutineers use the media to provide an alternative narrative, and often one in which they are the victims of an unjust system rather than aggressors.

Radio has been the preferred media outlet for African mutineers, which mirrors radio's popularity within the region. There are several ways mutineers use the radio waves. The less common manner is to use radio announcements to speak among their group. For example, mutineers in the Central African Republic in 1993 first explained over the radio that they were revolting because they had not been paid for eight months and then called on other soldiers to return to the barracks and take up arms in case of attack by other

THE TYPICAL MUTINY

troops.[42] In this instance, mutineers saw a radio broadcast as the quickest way to get a message across to both the government and their fellow soldiers. However, most mutineers do not use the public radio to send instructions to each other, but rather to justify their actions and lay out demands, sometimes in very specific detail. In 1996, for example, mutineers in the Central African Republic made the following announcement: 'First, we demand the payment of overdue salaries for 1992, 1993, and 1994. Second, the unfreezing of salaries. Third, the restoration and improvement of the Central African armed forces ... Fourth, we demand that no legal proceedings should take place after the mutiny since we will stop today.'[43]

In a separate message, the same group stated: 'Our living conditions are mediocre; we are treated badly and we are exposed to disease. This is why we have left the barracks. We made these demands from our barracks, but all to no avail. We have been forced to take to the streets.'[44]

The announcements serve to personalise the mutineers. The mutineers aim to portray themselves not as soldiers who are committing a military crime but rather as individuals who simply cannot provide for themselves or their families with their current salaries. They also claim that they have mutinied as a last resort and thus suggest that the blame is on their leadership for not responding to earlier complaints.

While the above examples are of media used during an actual mutiny, in 2012 Nigerian soldiers contacted the media in order to threaten the government with a potential mutiny. Nigerian soldiers, serving as part of the United Nations/African Union mission in Darfur, told the Radio France International Hausa Service that they would mutiny if they were not paid their allowances and airlifted back to Nigeria. In a related petition sent to the government, the soldiers stated: 'Nobody seems to listen to us or the plight of our families back home. Even though it is against the ethics of the military to go to the press, we are pushed to the wall because nobody listens to our cries apart from the media.'[45]

In this case, the soldiers stress the desire to be listened to by their superiors and their willingness to take extreme measures to get attention for their concerns. Much like the example from the Central African Republic above, these soldiers also acknowledge that their actions go against a military code of conduct but claim that it was a measure of last resort.

The rapid increase in internet use and particularly social media allows the mutineers' messages to reach much farther than radio announcements. Whereas the Nigerian soldiers' threat was announced on the radio, the story was also posted online and picked up by bloggers and reposted via Twitter, thus reaching an incalculable number of people throughout the world. In another example from Nigeria, in 2013 a letter from an anonymous organisation calling itself the 'Group for the Salvation of the Nigerian Army and the Motherland (GROSNAMM)' was widely circulated on blogs, internet message boards and Facebook, followed by hundreds of reader comments. The report detailed the career paths of dozens of senior officers and accused the Nigerian military of nepotism and ethnic favouritism in recruitment and promotions (among other things). It cautioned of growing tensions in the military and warned of a pending mutiny.[46] Considering that mutinies often involve junior rank-and-file soldiers, many of whom will likely be of a more technology-savvy generation than their older peers, it is reasonable to assume that new technologies and social media will increasingly be used in future mutinies.

All of the commonly used tactics such as discharging firearms, mass gatherings, taking control of strategic locations, holding hostages and making media announcements are designed to grab attention, open a dialogue and pressure negotiations. These tactics would be extreme if conducted by civilians, yet in a military perspective they can be considered measured. There are certainly cases in which mutineers turn to violence and destruction, but as this section has demonstrated, most tactics at least in the initial stages of a mutiny are calculated decisions. This analysis of tactics stands in opposition to many other writings on mutinies, which describe the act as 'spontaneous'. Although there are certainly incidents within mutinies that are unplanned, mutinies in West and Central Africa are usually not reckless reactions. Taking control of an airport, breaking into an armoury, capturing hostages and making media announcements all require a degree of planning and coordination in the execution phase. However, even if we view mutinies as largely planned actions, rather than impulsive decisions, they still have a high degree of unpredictability, which will be the focus of the next two sections.

Violence as an ace or a bluff

An important part of mutineers' strategy is the ability to create and control instability. Unlike those in industrial or agricultural employment, soldiers do not have any tangible goods to demonstrate or measure their worth. Instead, the value of the military rests in its ability to manage violence.[47] Within this context, it is perhaps not surprising that violence is a key tool for mutineers.

The *threat* of violence is an integral part of a mutiny; however, the *use* of violence is not. Of the seventy one mutinies examined in this book, less than

THE TYPICAL MUTINY

half involved direct acts of violence. This is consistent with other studies using non-African data, which have also shown that mutinies tend to be non-violent.[48] Mutineers use their position in the military to threaten to create a situation of instability or escalate the instability they have already created. Their main bargaining chip is their ability to control the situation and return to the desired state of 'normalcy'. Yet this is often an overly ambitious claim, especially when the group lacks cohesion. Anger, aggression and indiscipline can dominate over strategy, and individuals often act on their own accord. Involving large numbers of participants is often both the strength and the downfall of mutinies. A large group quickly gathers the desired attention but is also difficult to control.

When mutinies become violent, the number of casualties can be very high. In the mutinies in the Central African Republic in 1996, estimates of fatalities ranged from 200 to 500.[49] In mutinies in the Democratic Republic of Congo in 1967, there were around eighty killed and 100 wounded, while revolts in the same country in 1991 resulted in 100 fatalities.[50] The Côte d'Ivoire mutinies in 2002 led to 270 deaths, and mutinies in Guinea in 1996 resulted in fifty deaths and 300 wounded.[51] Significantly, many, if not most, of these casualties are civilians. Therefore, although mutinies are usually seen as internal military matters, in West and Central Africa they have had severe consequences for civilian populations. Understanding mutinies, and in particular the ways to avoid or resolve them, is important not just from a political stability standpoint but also from a humanitarian perspective.

The variation in levels of violence within mutinies leads to the question of whether there are different types of mutinies. Other mutiny scholars have stated that attempts to create a mutiny typology have proven more difficult than anticipated, and my findings mirror this.[52] The fluid nature of mutinies makes it challenging to categorise them in the way that coups are at times described as a 'palace coup' or a 'coup from below'. Mutinies often start out in one fashion and change drastically as time goes on. It is more valuable to view mutinies along a continuum.

On one end of this spectrum are mutinies that involve a generally cohesive unit with demands that are often specific to their particular group. I refer to these as self-contained mutinies. In many cases, these units have recently deployed together and share common grievances about their deployment experience. Since these units have a history together, they often appear to respect a hierarchy within the group, and mutineers in this scenario seem less likely to use violence. Mutinies in The Gambia in 1991 and 1992, as described in Chapter 7, fall into this category. Another example of a self-contained style of mutiny occurred in the Republic of Congo in 1997. In this case, sailors locked themselves in their base in an attempt to demand better pay and living conditions and the removal of their base commander.[53]

On the opposite end of the continuum is a more chaotic style of mutiny, which I refer to as violent mass mutinies. These mutinies often appear to be self-destructive in nature. Although the mutinies may start with a single unit, their complaints are regularly broad in scope, which gives their campaign mass appeal. As more soldiers and units throughout the country join in, they add their own personalised goals and complaints. These soldiers are unified in anger and frustration, not necessarily intimately shared experiences or specific demands.

Rose notes that the individual motivations of mutineers begin to vary as a mutiny spreads. He explains that, during a mass mutiny, 'the full gamut of the human condition is revealed. Some troops join because of intimidation, some because of opportunism. Some are true believers; some are only swimmers with the tide. Some would face the severest penalties for their principles; some would denounce their fellows at the first opportunity.'[54]

With these wide variations in the group's motivation and goals, it then becomes especially difficult to organise cohesive demands or negotiations. When mutineers in these situations use violence, it seems to quickly spread and often also involves property destruction, looting and rape. As a result, this type of mutiny has the highest probability of negatively affecting the civilian population. The mutinies in Burkina Faso in 2011 can be considered violent mass mutinies, as can the mutinies in the Democratic Republic of Congo in 1961, the Central African Republic in 1996 and Guinea in 1996.

In some ways, a mutiny is like a high-risk game of poker. As a revolt progresses, the mutineers are raising the stakes, often with hostages or strategic locations, and always with the threat of violence, hoping for the government to fold. When the mutineers resort to violence, they have put all their chips on the table and force the government to respond. However, the chaotic environment created by a violent mass mutiny makes negotiations difficult and the government often responds with force. Therefore, the use of violence is often counterproductive to the mutineers' goals.

The use of violence can also isolate the mutineers from those who might otherwise sympathise with their cause. In an interview, the editorial chief of the radio station Ouaga FM in Ouagadougou explained that his station had initially been conducting interviews with the Burkinabé mutineers in 2011 and essentially gave them a voice to air their grievances: 'we talked [to the mutineers] before the big unrest but then there were rapes and lootings and shootings and we do not want to interact with them anymore'.[55] He claimed that the station did not want to appear supportive of the mutineers' more extreme behaviour. Other media sources followed suit. The Burkinabé government had also initially negotiated with the mutineers but drew the line when the series of mutinies grew increasingly violent. The government eventually countered them with force, killing at least six mutineers.

When a mutiny reaches a mass level, it also attracts opportunists who take advantage of the weak security situation. It then becomes difficult to determine if the perpetrators are civilians or soldiers, as both can wear civilian attire. When mutineers engage in hostage-taking, holding strategic locations or gathering in public locations, they are committing the acts in public and are generally unconcerned about hiding their identities. However, looting and random violence are more anonymous acts. It is common for mutineers to claim that some of the more criminal aspects associated with a mutiny are not the responsibility of their group. In interviews in Burkina Faso, numerous respondents (both civilian and military) talked of 'gangsters' who 'joined with the soldiers to steal'.[56]

In some cases, mutineers seem to acknowledge the negative effect that violence could have on their efforts and intentionally show they are unarmed. This is likely meant to deter a counter-attack as well as to avoid accusations of a coup attempt. A Burkinabé soldier described this tactic in a 1997 mutiny in which he was involved:

> Soldiers were given strict orders [by NCOs] to not go near the armoury, that anyone attempting to break into the armoury will be shot. We were told what to wear, basically the most simple of uniforms, no belts, no extra clothing, they wanted to give the signal that there was nothing to hide, everyone was unarmed.[57]

However, even when soldiers indicate that they are unarmed, their position in an organisation that has often been responsible for much insecurity in the region still gives an implicit threat of violence or instability. As a result, governments usually act with more expedition towards a mutiny than they would if members of the civil service or a business were taking the same action (as is often the case when mutinies coincide with civilian demonstrations).

The predictably unpredictable nature of mutinies

A common characteristic of mutinies in West and Central Africa is their fluid nature. Unlike coups, which can be executed in a matter of hours, mutinies are regularly drawn out events, lasting days, weeks or even months. Therefore, mutineers must be flexible and adaptable. A longer timeframe allows mutineers to anticipate how the government will respond and plan their countermoves. However, it also permits more individuals to join the revolt and regularly leads to a disjointed group, as further explained below.

Linked to the issue of fluidity within mutinies is their contagious nature. The potential for contagion has also been discussed in the coup literature, with the term 'coup contagion' used to describe a trend in which successful coups can trigger coups in neighbouring countries. However, the same only applies to a limited number of mutinies. The mutinies in Tanzania, Kenya and Uganda in 1964 serve as the strongest examples. However, a more convincing argument can be made that mutinies are internally contagious. Mutinies appear much more likely to spread within the borders of a country than to neighbouring countries. It is very common to see one unit start a mutiny and for others either to join in immediately or within a short period of time. Examples of incidents of an internal contagion include mutinies in Côte d'Ivoire (1990, 2000), Democratic Republic of Congo (1991), Republic of Congo (1997), Niger (2002) and Burkina Faso (2011).

Often the mutiny does not spread immediately, but instead after non-mutinying soldiers have observed the outcome of the mutiny. After a unit has successfully received their demands, either fully or partially, it is common to see other units copy the tactic. This trend can be seen in the mutinies in the Central African Republic in 1993. The initial mutiny involved the presidential guard, but five days after this mutiny was resolved the Régiment de Défense Opérationnelle du Territoire (RDOT) also mutinied. The RDOT made similar demands and sealed off the treasury in protest at their late payments.[58]

Mutinies are contagious because the grievances expressed by one unit often resonate with other units or individuals. Most of the earlier-mentioned demands, in particular over pay and housing, affect large sectors of the military. Concerns over promotion opportunities and corruption are also likely to be grievances seen across the armed forces. When a complaint is specific to a particular unit, it is less likely to lead to further mutinies. The mutinies in The Gambia in 1991 and 1992, as will be highlighted in Chapter 7, were particularly about the special pay promised from their deployment on a peacekeeping mission. The vast majority of their fellow Gambian soldiers did not go on the deployment or share in their grievances, and the mutiny did not spread to other units. A similar case involved a mutiny in Liberia in 1963 over specific complaints about the way officers had handled money contributed to a communal fund. These junior soldiers' complaints were specific to a particular process, quickly addressed by the headquarters (ultimately leading to the arrest of four officers and the base commander), and did not lead to similar incidents with other units.[59] It is important to note, however, that this dichotomy of broad grievances leading to contagions and specific grievances generally remaining contained is not always an easy separation. It is common for mutineers to list numerous complaints, some of which are shared by others. For example, soldiers may have grievances about lack of payment for a deployment that are specific to their unit but then blame the delay on corruption among higher ranks, which many others can relate to.

In rare cases, the fluidity of mutinies has resulted in them being diverted into a coup or other form of rebellion against the state. Mutinies give junior soldiers a level of control and power that the normal structure of the organisation has intentionally kept from them. Ambitious individuals, often junior officers, can see this as a prime opportunity to make a move to capture more power. Additionally, individual officers do not have to mobilise soldiers, as they already have a disgruntled audience to work with. The case of Sierra Leone in 1992, as detailed in Chapter 6, is one example where the rank-and-file soldiers wanted to mutiny over their pay and conditions but officers escalated the plan to a coup. In Abidjan in Côte d'Ivoire, soldiers took to the streets in 1999 in a mutiny over unpaid salaries and poor living conditions.[60] Negotiations between the mutineers and the government were reportedly called off when Robert Guéï, a former general who had been fired two years earlier, announced that President Henri Bédié had been removed and a ruling council formed with himself as the leader.[61] Reports from the time note that while the mutiny appeared to have been conducted by 'ordinary impoverished privates who were appalled by the deterioration in their living standards, the assumption of power by General Robert Guéï seems less spontaneous'.[62] Other reports openly questioned whether the general put the soldiers up to the task. In these scenarios, internal instability increased after the coup, and the military remained unsatisfied. When a mutiny escalates or leads directly to a coup, the original complaints of the soldiers are often sidelined in the need to focus on the broader task of developing a new political structure. This scenario will be further discussed in the case study of Sierra Leone.

It is not only military personnel who see opportunity in mutiny; politicians are also guilty of using a mutiny to advance their cause. Even if mutineers are not calling for political changes, they are still drawing attention to perceived problems in the military or political system. In doing so, they may expose a power vacuum that others can seek to fill. Similarly, it is common to see opposition leaders or parties use a mutiny as an opportunity to call for political change. Variations of this pattern occurred in the Central African Republic in 1996 and Burkina Faso in 2011.[63] The opportunities that mutinies can create or the divisions that they can expose at times lead to accusations that mutineers are directly encouraged to revolt by senior military or political leadership, as reports suggest was the case for Côte d'Ivoire in 1999. These allegations are reasonable in some cases but are the exception, not the norm. The vast majority of the cases examined in this book appear to have concerned junior soldiers acting without any political connections or influences. They often express a feeling of being marginalised and ignored by the political or military leadership. During interviews in the case study countries, I asked numerous soldiers whether there was any direct encouragement to mutiny from outside their unit and all answered variations of 'no'. Some even seemed to find the idea of being encouraged by officers or politicians amusing, and one soldier explained that it was because 'our officers never come down to talk to us' that they planned more extreme measures to get their message across.

Although mutinies typically rely on a set number of tactics, variations in the participants and potential reactions by those inside and outside the military mean that mutinies are often fluid and become increasingly unpredictable as they progress. It is not just a matter of mutineers attempting to make moves that are unpredictable to the government. Instead, it appears that the outcomes become unpredictable even to those involved. Earlier sections of this chapter identified patterns that could help observers anticipate what tactics mutineers are most likely to use, but the actions of the mutineers are only one piece of the puzzle. It is common to see other units and individuals, both military and civilian, become involved, and their roles and actions add to the volatility of a mutiny.

Determining success in a mutiny

In examining broader patterns of mutinies, a final issue to address is whether mutinies work. Are the demands of mutineers usually met? This is not an easy question to answer as mutinies often involve numerous participants making a variety of demands. An examination of the seventy one mutinies in this book indicates that most mutinies are at least partially successful. The government or the military hierarchy typically provides some concession, although often not the full demands. Both Hamby and Rose, each writing about Western

THE TYPICAL MUTINY

mutinies, argue that mutinies pay off in the long run for the majority of participants.[64] They believe that while a few may be punished, the conditions protested against are usually improved and the state reconsiders issues brought up by the mutineers. However, the data for West and Central Africa do not support this hypothesis. Mutinies in this region appear to follow the opposite pattern: they pay off in the short term, not necessarily in the long term.

The threatening nature of mutinies pressures a quick solution, and this usually comes in the form of a payment. Hierarchies often promise to look into soldiers' other complaints. However, there is little evidence to suggest that the more ingrained problems such as corruption, promotion procedures or favouritism are addressed after the mutiny. This pattern was seen in mutinies in Guinea in 2007 and 2008. In several mutinies in these two years, which spread throughout the country, soldiers were given bonuses, salary increases, increased transport allowances and rice at a reduced cost.[65] Yet requests to investigate senior officers for fraud were denied, and soldiers continued to claim that their superiors were living 'in opulence'.[66]

Some of the reluctance to address the underlying issues of mutinies is likely linked to the earlier discussion of the privileged place of senior officers in many African states. Taking action against this sector of the military could threaten the political leadership or state stability. Additionally, the broader grievances would likely take years of sustained effort to investigate the problems and determine ways to counter them. Mutinies rarely elicit that level of pressure. Lastly, even some of the more material demands are often challenged by chronic financial constraints in many countries in the region. While states may be willing to pay one-time bonuses to mutineers, sustaining salary increases, widespread promotions or new housing structures requires long-term financial commitments, which most states are unable or unwilling to make.

Support for the argument that mutinies are rarely a long-term fix can also be found in the list of mutinies in the previous chapter (Table 1). There are numerous examples of countries that experience mutinies over and over again with soldiers usually expressing similar grievances in each revolt. For example, Burkina Faso experienced six mutinies in a matter of eleven years, Niger had five in ten years, and soldiers in the Central African Republic rebelled six times in eight years. The persistent problems within the Burkinabé military, despite numerous mutinies, will be discussed in more detail in Chapter 8.

Another way to analyse whether mutinies are successful is to examine if and how mutineers are punished. Mutinies would likely be considered unsuccessful for those involved if the action resulted in the mutineers being dismissed from the military or jailed. Like many aspects of the military, punishments are often not a matter shared with the public, and trials are often conducted through courts martial (the internal military court system). However, there are also times when governments highlight the punishments, likely in the hope that it will serve as a deterrent for other soldiers. From the cases examined in this book, the most conclusive thing that can be said about the punishment of African mutineers is that there appears to be no clear pattern. African governments are not necessarily lenient on mutineers, as Hamby and Rose claim when discussing mutinies from a Western perspective.[67] It is also not the case that only ringleaders are punished, as they also suggest. There are numerous examples of harsh punishments that go beyond just the mutinying unit to others in the military and officers. For example, following a mutiny among Ghanaian troops, which involved a single unit, 125 soldiers were dismissed, six given jail terms, and the ringleader was sentenced to death (the sentence was later commuted to life in prison).[68] Following a mutiny in Niger in 2002, 268 soldiers were arrested, a number of whom spent eighteen months in prison. Similarly, the mutinies in Burkina Faso in 2011 resulted in the dismissal of 566 soldiers, 217 of whom faced criminal charges.[69] The Nigerian government demonstrated how seriously it viewed mutiny by sentencing sixty-six mutineers to death in 2014.[70] However, there are also plenty of examples, also across time, where mutineers received minimal or no punishment.

Although most mutinies do not lead to long-term advantages for soldiers and data are inconclusive on the chances of punishment, the continued presence of mutinies in the region suggests that soldiers believe they will be successful. As this chapter has demonstrated, mutinies are not a reckless action. Instead, there is likely some calculation of risks before soldiers decide to revolt. It is doubtful that soldiers would continue to mutiny if they did not believe the risk was worth the potential reward. The following chapter will reinforce the point that soldiers often calculate their chances of success before engaging in a mutiny by demonstrating that mutinies occur more often in regimes with some respect for democratic principles. Part of the explanation for this trend is that soldiers believe that these governments are more likely to be receptive to their grievances, and thus their probability of success is heightened.

Conclusion

In returning to the debate over whether there is such thing as a typical mutiny, this chapter has demonstrated that, although each mutiny is to some degree

THE TYPICAL MUTINY

unique, there are also particular aspects of mutinies that are common across states and time. Mutineers' grievances in the region generally concern issues surrounding their conditions of service, which can include material aspects (salary, housing, etc.), leadership and military procedures (promotions, relocations, etc.). Underlying the desire for improved conditions is often a sense of injustice over perceptions that their conditions are at extreme odds with the lifestyles of senior officers. This gap between the ranks has developed as a result of the military's unique role in African politics, both in colonial times and particularly after independence.

The perceptions of injustice that go along with a decision to mutiny are just as important to understanding a mutiny as the publicly declared grievances, but they are difficult to observe through media reporting. The less tangible aspects of mutinies will be discussed further through case studies using interviews with former mutineers. The publicly declared grievances generally have a clear solution, although the time it would take to implement the solution varies. For example, soldiers can be paid, unacceptable leaders can be fired and matters such as promotion criteria can be adapted; yet the grievances have often been brewing for a long time, generating a sense of distrust, disrespect and contempt, which is harder to remedy. This is an important trend in non-African mutinies as well. Lawrence James, studying British mutinies, writes, 'although the genesis of a mutiny could be attributed to trivial matters, the form and level of the resultant collective action could be completely disproportionate to the original case'.[71] Even if mutinies appear to be about pay disputes, it is often more accurate to view them as a sign of severe tensions within an armed force.

The data in this chapter have shown that mutineers typically use a limited number of tactics, which include public gatherings (often in proximity to decision-makers), firing weapons in the air, taking hostages and holding strategic locations. These tactics serve the purpose of publicly expressing dissatisfaction and forcing a dialogue with the leadership about their demands. This desire for attention to their cause is further achieved through the relatively new trend of mutineers directly engaging with the media. Despite a recurring pattern of tactics, mutinies are unpredictable in practice. In many cases, the cohesion needed for a mutiny proves to be very tenuous and dissolves as the mutiny spreads and gains more participants.

The threat of violence is the most valuable tool used by mutineers. Even when mutineers do not directly engage in violent actions, their position within an organisation that has the ability to cause widespread instability as well as a history of doing so causes alarm among both the political and military leadership. Although mutinies are often strengthened by threating to use violence, the actual use of violence is often their downfall. Violent acts, especially against civilians, are likely to isolate the mutineers and potentially trigger a counter-attack.

4

PUBLIC DISCOURSE, PROTESTS AND REVOLTS

When mutinies in West and Central Africa are examined chronologically, the most eye-catching trend is the dramatic increase in the 1990s. The spike in mutinies in this decade corresponded with what is often referred to as the democratisation period in Africa. This was a time of both turbulence and hope, in which authoritarian regimes quickly collapsed, the number of competitive elections increased and the average citizen attained more political rights. However, debates continue about whether the political reforms seen during the 1990s were successful and lasting.[1] The political changes during this period were a result of international pressures as well as local activism, in which many Africans across the continent were demanding reform. Richard Joseph refers to these events as the 'awakening process'.[2] Similarly, the rank-and-file soldiers in the region also seemed to be reawakened after decades of limited incidents of mutiny.

Eboe Hutchful argues that the democracy movement 'won the battle for civil society but lost the battle for the military'.[3] He laments the 'failure of the democracy movement to "capture" key sectors of the military'.[4] While militaries in the region overall were not active participants in progressing the movement, this chapter will show that in many ways soldiers were 'captured' by the movement's themes. Their rhetoric and demands often appeared to have been borrowed from civilian groups advocating greater democratic rights. Just as civil society rediscovered its popular voice, so too did the military, although the junior soldiers expressed theirs through mutinies.[5]

The mutineers' appropriation of the prevailing political rhetoric of the 1990s has some similarities to the ways militaries in the 1970s and 1980s often embraced socialist and Marxist themes.[6] The political language these military regimes used has been criticised as 'convenient ideological gloss',[7] and the same also applies to the way in which the mutineers used the democratic rhetoric of the 1990s. However, unlike coup leaders, who seek to project themselves as political leaders, mutineers are generally not instigating political change but are using popular political themes to discuss their own conditions in the military.

Part of the explanation for the overlap between civilian and military demands in the 1990s is that both were negatively affected by international economic changes at the time. This chapter begins by addressing these changes and will demonstrate the effects of shifts in Cold War relations on the region's militaries. The similarities between the civilian and military movements go beyond shared economic hardships, and the chapter shows ways in which mutineers appeared to have been inspired by the themes of the democratisation movement. They displayed awareness of the political landscape of the time by using popular discourse from the democratisation movement within their public statements. While this chapter focuses mainly on the 1990s, its lessons are not restricted to this time period. The last section of the chapter will look beyond the 1990s to demonstrate that mutinies most often occur in countries that display respect for civil liberties and political freedoms. Mutineers tend to view democratic leaders as more responsive, and they often use the political freedoms and civil liberties that are associated with democracies to their advantage.

The spike in mutinies in the 1990s is in stark contrast to the low number of reported mutinies in the 1970s and 1980s. In the 1970s and 1980s, many states in the region lacked press freedom, and regimes maintained tight control over the domestic sources of information and banned independent news outlets.[8] Mutinies are generally considered a threat and an embarrassment to the leadership, and thus state media outlets are less likely to publicise a mutiny. As a result, there may have been mutinies in the 1970s and 1980s that were put down quickly and never reported. 'Missing mutinies' is a possibility in all of the eras covered in this research, but they are most likely when independent reporting is absent.

Global trends lead to ground-level complaints

The 1980s were a financially difficult time for African states. By the beginning of the decade, 'virtually every African country was manifesting signs of acute economic distress, reflected in a mounting and unsustainable debt burden, a permanent trade deficit and an acute fiscal crisis which meant that the state was unable to maintain basic infrastructure or fund essential social services'.[9] International financial institutions and Western governments arrived at the conclusion that uncontrolled state expenditure was a primary cause of the economic crisis across the continent, and African states were pressured to accept Structural Adjustment Programmes (SAPs). SAPs required states to pursue economic reforms as stipulated by international institutions in order to receive loans.[10] A key aspect of the required reforms was a reduction in state expenditure in general and in the number of public sector employees specifically.[11] These programmes therefore threatened the interests of the military, which had grown substantially throughout the 1970s and into the 1980s. In particular,

> donors attempted to impose a predetermined ceiling (or 'acceptable level') on the military expenditures of the states. These attempts were directed especially at those states deemed to be engaged in 'excessive' or 'unproductive' expenditures on the military at the expense of the social sector and economic development.[12]

Although most states formally accepted SAPs, there were various ways in which they attempted to manoeuvre around full implementation of the required changes.[13] Wuyi Omitoogun explains that disagreements between African states and donors over what constituted appropriate military spending 'led to two unintended consequences: (a) the deliberate manipulation of military expenditure figures; and (b) the resort to off-budget spending, which further compounded the problem of public expenditure management'.[14] The general lack of transparency in military spending in many states combined with the intentional manipulation in relation to SAPs makes it difficult to assess military spending in the 1980s and 1990s.

Despite questions over the reliability of government statistics, there have been some attempts to examine trends in military spending across a number of decades. Nadir A.L. Mohammed, for example, has analysed the 'average levels of military expenditures, military burden, arms imports, relative size of the armed forces to total population, and the ratio of capital costs of total military spending' for thirteen African countries between 1963 and 1987. While acknowledging that there were variations between countries, he concludes that the previous mentioned indicators 'increased gradually in the 1960s, escalated sharply during the 1970s, reached a peak in the late 1970s, and displayed a significant reduction in the 1980s'.[15]

The Stockholm International Peace Research Institute's (SIPRI) database of military expenditure can be used to extend Mohammed's analysis into the

1990s and beyond. The database starts in 1988 and continues into 2017.[16] The figures show a steady decline in military expenditure from the late 1980s through the late 1990s across sub-Saharan Africa. During this period, military expenditure was the highest in 1988 when total military expenditure for sub-Saharan Africa was $12.2 billion and reached its lowest in 1996 with $8.2 billion.[17] The figures also decreased when examined as a proportion of GDP (from 3 per cent in 1990 to 2.6 per cent in 1998) and as a proportion of central government spending (from 11.8 per cent to 8.5 per cent).[18]

However, these reductions were disproportionate across Sub-Saharan Africa, with South Africa, Angola and Ethiopia accounting for the largest decreases in expenditure.[19] The decreases in these cases relate to settlements that were reached following periods in which states (and their international allies) deemed it necessary to maintain high military spending. Analysis of specific countries within West and Central Africa using the SIPRI database shows a varied picture, but the pattern of declining military spending from the late 1980s to the late 1990s is still a general trend in many states. For example, military spending in Burkina Faso was nearly halved between 1990 and 1996, while Guinea and Côte d'Ivoire saw decreases in military spending between 20 and 35 per cent in the early 1990s. There were exceptions to the trend, which can be explained through an examination of the political context of the time. The substantial increase in Sierra Leone's military spending during the 1990s, for example, can be attributed to its civil war. Unfortunately, many of the countries that are most mutiny-prone (Democratic Republic of Congo, Republic of Congo, Central African Republic, Guinea Bissau, Niger, Benin) have multiple years of missing data or no data at all, which makes it unfeasible to assess changes in their military spending.

In relation to decreased defence funding, the number of military personnel was reduced from the 1980s into the 1990s. The size of sub-Saharan African militaries had quadrupled between 1963 and 1979 but then fell by a third by the mid-1990s.[20] The data on military expenditure and manpower show that African militaries were at their prime, in terms of size and funding, during the 1970s, but were downsized into the late 1980s. For many militaries, spending reached its lowest level in the 1990s. Spending across the continent then increased again from 1999 onwards.

In order to understand the reasons behind the increasing number of mutinies in the 1990s, it is necessary to assess how the economic conditions presented above affected the average soldier. Military spending alone is not a strong indicator of whether a military is content, especially at the lower levels, as military spending does not necessarily equate to better conditions for soldiers.[21] However, by the mid-1990s, soldiers in Central African Republic, Chad, Côte d'Ivoire, Democratic Republic of Congo, The Gambia, Guinea, Niger, Republic of Congo and Sierra Leone had all publicly claimed that they had not been paid their salaries or other monetary dues. A lack of salary payments was paralleled in the civil service in numerous countries as well.[22] Many soldiers also complained about decreased standards of living within the military.

The fall in internal military spending is only one factor that contributed to the decline in military satisfaction in Africa in the late 1980s and into the 1990s; another important factor was the waning influence of the Soviet Union and, ultimately, the end of the Cold War. Throughout the Cold War, the United States and the Soviet Union vied for African state loyalty and offered military assistance as a key incentive. However, by 1985, the Soviet Union had begun to disengage from Africa, and the Western allies soon followed suit. By the end of the 1980s, both superpowers 'had abandoned Africa as a geostrategic outpost'.[23] The end of the Cold War also brought an end to much of the foreign military assistance and other perks that the military had become accustomed to, such as foreign military training. William Thom explains that training immediately following the Cold War was 'almost non-existent' for most African states.[24] This was due to both decreases in foreign military training and the reduced funds available for internal training.

African states had also benefited from military equipment as a result of Cold War partnerships; however, this similarly declined with the end of the Cold War. According to Howe, 'between 1988 and 1995 official transfers in sub-Saharan Africa declined from $4.27 billion to $270 million'.[25] This decline reflects the shift from official state-to-state transfers of expensive equipment (aircraft, tanks, etc.) to a more grey market of small arms sales. Although many of the more expensive weapons were unnecessary for the types of conflict most countries endured, the downgrade likely symbolised a loss of prestige to many in the military.

With pressure to cut military spending and reduced assistance from abroad, equipment and maintenance in the late 1980s was neglected.[26] The equipment and maintenance deficiencies as well as training shortfalls were not of immediate importance to most states in West and Central Africa at the time because most were not involved in conflict. However, this changed in the early 1990s when most of the members of the Economic Community of West African States (ECOWAS) became involved in the wars in Liberia and Sierra Leone and began contributing troops to other regional peace operations. The reduced manpower and inadequate training and equipment had a particularly negative effect on rank-and-file soldiers as they bore the brunt in regional conflicts, both within their own countries and as regional peacekeepers. Chapter 5 will further expand on the trend of mutinies linked to combat deployments.

One may question why soldiers began to mutiny in the 1990s if the conditions in their respective militaries had been in decline since the mid- to late 1980s.[27] It may be the case that conditions were not quite bad enough in the 1980s to trigger a mutiny. Although defence spending had decreased in the late 1980s, widespread accusations of non-payment did not begin until the early 1990s. Moreover, there was little indication that the largely authoritarian leaders of the 1970s and 1980s would make concessions to the mutineers, which could have served as a disincentive to mutiny. The reduced likelihood of mutinies under authoritarian regimes extends beyond this time period and will be further examined at the end of the chapter.

It is also likely that the Cold War relationships that were strong in the 1970s and present, although weakening, in the 1980s served as a deterrent for mutinies. During the Cold War, many African states relied on direct military support from their non-African allies. In West and Central Africa, France played an important role in assisting African leaders who were facing internal threats. In the first three decades of independence; France conducted three dozen military interventions in sixteen different countries in Africa to assist their leaders.[28] The consistent willingness of foreign nations to intervene on behalf of African leaders 'undoubtedly dampened the aspirations of some potential insurgents or invaders'.[29] It is also likely to have caused potential mutineers to rethink plans to revolt. Junior soldiers would have been aware that they would stand little chance against an attack by better-equipped and trained foreign soldiers.

The end of the Cold War also reduced the willingness of non-African states to intervene in African conflicts. France, which had once been quick to deploy its paratroopers to help its former colonies, ended many of its mutual defence agreements with African countries. Thus the French government told its key African ally, Félix Houphouët-Boigny—the President of Côte d'Ivoire—that he could no longer count on French military reinforcements to contain domestic unrest.[30] When Houphouët-Boigny tested this new arrangement during mutinies in the spring of 1990, France stood by its word and refused his request for military assistance in putting down the mutinies.[31] As a result, Houphouët-Boigny gave in to many of the mutineers' demands.

While the high likelihood of foreign intervention throughout the 1970s and 1980s may have served to deter mutinies from taking place, the lack of foreign intervention in the 1990s seems to have had the opposite effect. Without the possibility of foreign assistance, in the early 1990s African leaders were quick to acquiesce to soldiers' demands in order to avoid further instability, which was already growing with popular protests at the time.

Dual mobilisation

While economic trends and shifts in international relations were factors that led to more grievances among the military, the political mood of the time also played a part in the increased number of mutinies. The swift regime changes that took place in the 1990s, following decades of authoritarian leadership, can be attributed to both international and domestic factors. Structural adjustment programmes failed to provide a quick cure for the ailing economies, and as the Cold War came to an end, international institutions and Western governments concluded that the 'absence of democratic government and political accountability in Africa was a significant contributory factor in economic malaise'.[32] External donors began to introduce political conditionality to aid allocations in which recipient countries had to implement democratic reforms and demonstrate respect for human rights. Given the deteriorating economic situation on the continent as a whole, most states had little choice but to concede to political conditionality, at least to some degree. Political conditionality served as a warning for leaders who had grown accustomed to neglecting democratic principles and human rights, yet in practice it was often selectively enforced.[33]

By the late 1980s, the legitimacy of single-party systems was being challenged internationally and internally. Declining per capita income levels for the average African caused people to further question the existing authoritarian and military-led political systems. Shared economic hardships led to a 'coalescence of political participation by all levels of society from elite to mass level'.[34] One of the main ways in which this coalescence transpired was through mass protests.[35]

The mass protests, which initially centred on economic demands, eventually widened to include political reforms.[36] However, the protests often lacked a cohesive political agenda.[37] Chris Allen, Carolyn Baylies and Morris Szeftel note that while the popular calls for 'good governance' were often undefined, the movement can generally 'be seen to include such elements as the rule of law, the safeguarding of basic human rights—including the right to organize, freedom of expression and freedom of the press—and the presence of honest and efficient government'.[38] While mutineers in the 1990s did not directly demand government improvements in these same areas, the examples in the following section will show that issues such as rule of law and human rights were also expressed in mutinies. Closely linked to the calls for 'good governance' were demands for multiparty elections, and much emphasis in the civilian sector was placed on building the requisite democratic 'hardware', such as electoral institutions and political parties.[39] Mutineers did not champion the need for multiparty elections, and in some cases, such as Senegal, soldiers were not even allowed to vote in elections (until 2007). However, the topic of elections regularly became a part of mutineers' narratives during this period.

Additionally, during the 1990s, there were 'soundly based popular perceptions that those closely associated with government did not personally share the effects of economic decline and, through massive corruption of public office, actually prospered whilst the majority suffered'.[40] Like the complaints made in the civilian realm, mutineers also highlighted the large gap in wealth and lifestyle within a military context and attributed the large differences to corruption. As later examples will show, mutineers also made demands for accountability for their leadership. Lastly, like the civilian sector, mutinying soldiers saw that one way to rectify the situation was to pressure the leadership to make changes through a shared voice, and both groups mobilised, although in different fashions.

Both the civilian democratisation movement and the military mutinies also represent the desire for a reconfiguration of power dynamics. This is consistent with Robert Dahl's explanation of democratic institutions, or 'the processes by which ordinary citizens exert a relatively high degree of control over leaders'.[41] Although the civilian democratisation movement was often unclear in its specific political goals, there was a general sense of empowerment that involved 'citizens attaining a new measure of self-confidence and a wider scope of taking control of their own lives'.[42] Mutinies can also be seen to represent a high degree of empowerment from the lower ranks and a desire for more control of their lives, neither of which are normally inherent in military hierarchies. The similarities in the themes of the democratisation movement and the military mutinies should not be seen as a coincidence; instead, it is more likely that junior soldiers gained inspiration and ideas from the movement.

Several examples will help illustrate this overlap between themes in the democracy movement and the mutinies of the 1990s. The first is the case of Côte d'Ivoire, in which 'the economic crises of the 1980s that affected most African countries, created peculiar kinds of problems' for President

Houphouët-Boigny,[43] whose government had established a practice of paying farmers a higher price for the country's agricultural commodities, especially coffee and cocoa, than the price paid by most African governments.[44] When world prices for coffee and cocoa dropped and the international donor community demanded austerity measures, President Houphouët-Boigny reduced subsidies, imposed new taxes and eliminated many government jobs. However, the economic crisis did not stop lavish state expenditure, such as a basilica in Yamoussoukro at a cost of $300 million.[45] In February 1990, the government announced a general cut of public wages by up to 40 per cent and an 11 per cent rise in income taxes.[46] In response, students, utility workers, educational and professional associations, taxi-drivers, hospital staff and factory workers orchestrated strikes and street protests throughout the following months.[47] They called for both economic and political reforms.

Several months later, it was the military's turn to express its discontent. On 14 May, around 100 rank-and-file soldiers attempted to take over the state-run radio station. The radio staff resisted the attempt and helped arrange for a delegation of the soldiers to meet with the president. The president promised the mutineers increased salaries, better living conditions and reenlistment.[48] His willingness to give in to the soldiers' demands was likely due to an increased dependency on the military in the face of a growing civilian opposition movement. As previously mentioned, Houphouët-Boigny requested French military assistance but was denied the help. Air force members took note of the army's success, and two days after the army mutiny they staged their own revolt using more threatening tactics, with fifty air force members armed with semi-automatic weapons seizing the control tower and a terminal building of Abidjan International Airport. Similar to the army recruits, they were angry over low pay and poor living conditions. However, they also added grievances over corruption among the officer corps, claiming that their superiors docked their pay on a regular basis for little reason.[49] When the government agreed to meet with the airmen to discuss their complaints, the mutineers initially refused because one of the mediators was the defence minister. The mutineers called him a 'corrupt billionaire' and demanded his removal from the mediation process.[50]

The mutineers in Côte d'Ivoire were likely inspired by the actions of local civilian protesters who had been expressing their discontent for months before the mutiny. The civilian and military personnel shared similar economic grievances, as well as the belief that corruption or general government economic mismanagement was a cause of their hardship.

The Gambia provides another good example of the overlap between civilian movements and mutinies. In the early 1990s, The Gambia shared the burden of economic crisis seen throughout the continent, and growing dissatisfaction was expressed through public protests. President Dawda Jawara was considered an advocate of human and civil rights and was often applauded for the country's record of free and fair elections. However, by the 1990s, the Gambian press had become increasingly critical of his nearly thirty years in office. Newspapers ran numerous stories accusing the government of inaction, with frequent news articles questioning why The Gambia still had no university, for instance. Public awareness and resentment over corruption in The Gambia was undoubtedly at an all-time high by the early 1990s owing to several ongoing corruption scandals involving individuals close to Jawara.[51]

The frustrations over government inaction and corruption in the civilian sector were also mirrored in the military. Gambian soldiers returning from the Economic Community of West African States Monitoring Group (ECOMOG) mission to Liberia in 1991 and 1992 took to the streets when they did not receive their due pay. They accused their officers of being behind late payment and expressed objections to corruption in the officer corps. The mutineers also specifically called for the removal of the highest-ranking officer in the country, Colonel Ndow Njie. For these sixty junior soldiers, it was not enough to just receive their salary arrears; they also wanted someone to be held accountable for the delay. The mutineers took their complaints directly to President Jawara, who met the junior soldiers and conceded their demands.

The examples of the Ivoirian mutiny in 1990 and the Gambian mutiny in 1991 reveal a remarkable reconfiguration of power. In both incidents, the mutineers were rank-and-file soldiers and were able to engage directly with the head of state. In many states, it would have been inconceivable for junior ranks to take their complaints directly to the president and even more shocking for the president to 'obey' these junior ranks. However, leading into the 1990s, there were increasing expectations that governments would be responsive. Growing domestic opposition and changes to foreign relationships had placed political leaders in a more vulnerable position, one in which they were more likely to grant concessions to the military. The power shift can also be seen in the way that both groups of mutineers made accusations against the top individual in the military structure. They show the belief that even an individual in a high-ranking position should not be above the standard regulations, signalling a major shift from previous decades when 'big men' were clearly above the law.

It is significant that the mutinies in Côte d'Ivoire in 1990 and The Gambia in 1991 were the first time either country had experienced a mutiny. Therefore, it is unlikely that these soldiers had 'learned' to mutiny from other soldiers and more likely that they picked up on common ideas expressed in the civilian population, which in both cases had publicly protested just before the mutinies.

Borrowed scripts

It was not only the general concepts of the democratisation movement and mutinies that overlapped; there were also similarities in the rhetoric mutineers and civilians used. By the 1990s, soldiers seemed to have been aware that military rule had lost its popularity, and in public statements made during mutinies they attempted to distance themselves from authoritarian regimes. Soldiers in the Central African Republic in 1996, for example, declared that their mutiny was 'corporatist' and 'apolitical'. The mutineers' spokesman, a sergeant, explained to Radio France International (RFI): 'We made these demands from the barracks, but all to no avail. We have been forced to take to the streets. We have no intention of destabilizing the regime; President [Ange-Félix] Patassé was democratically elected.'[52]

In a separate statement, the spokesman urged the president 'to take measures and prove he is a politician worthy of his office.'[53] He implied that, to be 'worthy' of the position, the president must be responsive to their demands. Although the issues were not resolved and the mutinies continued for months, the soldiers continued to insist that their goals were not political. In an interview with RFI, Captain Anicet Saulet of the Central African Republic said:

It is not our intention to stage a coup d'état, I think that is a problem that [could have been] solved within a matter of hours. It was not for nothing that the army took to the streets three times in the space of eight months. It means that there is a problem and we want this problem solved.[54]

Here, the mutineers were suggesting that they could easily have conducted a coup if they had wanted to do so, but that they were more interested in working with the political and military leadership to resolve the problem.

In some ways, these statements may appear to be part of a history of African military personnel publicly commenting on politics.[55] However, in the above statements, the mutineers appear to want to signal a break from coup leaders and show their support for democratic leaders and the process that brought them to power, or at least express their neutrality. Still, owing to the mutineers' membership in an organisation that has caused many problems for politicians in the region, their actions can be interpreted as a veiled threat. The mutineers may have been implying that they were supportive of the political leadership at that moment but that their loyalty could be dependent on how their demands were handled.

The rhetoric of the mutineers in the 1990s also made use of other concepts drawn from the democratisation movement, such as justice, human rights and popular participation. The spokesman for the 1996 Central African Republic mutiny, for example, stated: 'We appeal to Amnesty International, and we agree to stop [the mutiny] this Friday evening.'[56] In this case, the soldiers were attempting to gain sympathy from a prominent international organisation by implying that their three-month pay delay was a human rights violation. While Amnesty International did not take up their cause, the soldiers' call for their assistance showed an awareness of the growing international dialogue surrounding human rights, creatively using the trend to their advantage. Another example involves Guinean mutineers in 1996, who seemed to be influenced by calls for participatory politics. The five-point agreement they eventually reached with the leadership contains standard requests such as supplying new barracks and pensions for soldiers, yet it also demands 'the right of soldiers to participate in the administration' of the military.[57]

In 1997, mutineers in the Central African Republic called for 'an end to any hampering of collective and individual liberties, in particular body searches, arrests and house searches'. This is an especially unusual request, as 'individual liberties' are to some degree forfeited when soldiers join the military. In particular, living spaces are often subject to inspection within a military context. These demands reflect the growing attention to civil liberties at the time. The comments also hint at an objection to arbitrary arrests and emphasise the importance of following due legal processes.

Despite the increasing use of rhetoric about justice and calls for accountability, mutineers did not want those standards to apply to their own actions. Mutineers in the 1990s appeared nervous about their post-mutiny prospects. This makes sense considering that the lack of mutinies in the 1970s and 1980s meant that soldiers had few precedents for how mutineers would be treated by the law. To rectify this uncertainty about their status following the mutiny, mutineers began demanding that they would not be held accountable for their actions when the mutiny ended. Soldiers in Central African Republic, Côte d'Ivoire and Guinea all made deals with the government that gave them immunity after their mutinies had ended. Similarly, we should not assume that mutineers' use of language regarding human rights and civil liberties actually translated into increased respect for human rights during this period. Instead, it seemed as if much of the democratic language demonstrated an awareness of what were considered respectable and legitimate reasons to protest.

In addition to borrowing rhetoric from the democratisation movement, in some cases mutineers also imitated the movement through their tactics. In 1991, for example, Gambian soldiers held a procession to State House, while in 1997 soldiers in Burkina Faso marched to the Defence ministry to make their complaints heard, both in very similar fashions to civilian protestors at the time. Mutineers in Burkina Faso in 1999 were reported to have chanted their demands, as is common during political protests.[58] In this particular case, soldiers would have had regular exposure to civilian political protests because the mutiny occurred during a series of intense civilian protests against the Compaoré regime. It also became common for mutineers to assign a spokesperson for the group who would represent their cause to higher authorities and the media. This is similar to the practice of political, student and trade union organisations that regularly used spokespersons to articulate the goals of their respective groups.

In response to the series of mutinies in the 1990s that borrowed the language and behaviour of civilian organisations, political leaders ultimately followed suit by using rhetoric emphasising the rule of law. In 1993, for example, President Mahamane Ousmane of Niger publicly reminded the mutineers that the army is not a political trade union and that they were obliged to obey the constitution.[59] Similarly, after months of ongoing mutinies, President Patassé of the Central African Republic expressed his frustration by stating that:

> The current rebellion is condemned by the country's entire population, respectful of the constitution, and through it, of the Republic's institutions. In my position as Supreme Chief of the Armed Forces, I could indeed have ordered military operations to bring this rebellion to an end, but it would have brought harm to the civilian population. Thus, I was patient. I issue two demands [to the mutineers]: lay down your arms immediately and unconditionally.[60]

He went on to state: 'I was not elected to shed the blood of Central Africans, whether they be from the north, south, east or west. I ask you to do nothing during these difficult times that might jeopardize national unity.'[61] In both of these examples, the presidents, much like the mutineers, drew on wider political themes of the time. President Ousmane did not personally order the mutineers to end their campaign but rather highlighted the importance of the constitution as a governing document. President Patassé similarly couched his authority within the context of having been popularly elected. He also drew on the need for the mutineers to respect the constitution and state institutions.

The importance of international organisations in the 1990s is revealed through statements made by President Patassé and mutineers in the Central African Republic in 1996 and 1997. Following the first series of mutinies in March 1996, Patassé issued the following statement: 'The army knows that in my negotiations with the IMF and World Bank I refused to reduce the number of soldiers in the army. However, I do understand them and that is why I am ready to go meet with them when calm returns, and calm is returning.'[62]

While Patassé sided with the military over the international financial organisations in this statement, seven months later his attitude seemed to have changed. In November 1996, he stated:

> I have been watching things. I have been patient, lenient, and at times sympathetic. But from now on, things will be different. Certain compatriots still feel the need to try to scuttle the forthcoming negotiations with the Bretton Woods institutions by brandishing the specter of a third mutiny. There will be no third mutiny and no one had better take such a risk.[63]

Here, President Patassé was clearly emphasising his concern that the mutinies could affect the country's negotiations with international organisations, while simultaneously implying that the soldiers were intentionally attempting to derail the process. Yet despite the president's hardened rhetoric, the mutinies only came to an end with the assistance of foreign troops and international negotiators. Among the final demands of the mutineers was the 'continued existence of the international follow-up committee'.[64]

In August 2002, Nigerien mutineers claimed that 'we are not politicians, we are soldiers'. On the surface, this assertion was true; however, the use of political rhetoric, which often drew on popular concepts, as well as the themes and tactics of the democratisation movement, politicised the mutinies even when their stated goals did not include political power. Similarly, political leaders often countered the mutineers with political language, as presented above. In this dialogue, the actors (both mutineers and politicians or military superiors) seemed to be speaking above the problem. Layers of references to constitutions, good governance, democracy, human rights, international organisations and so on have to be unveiled to get to the specific demands of the soldiers, which are generally similar to the grievances from other eras. The political manner in which mutineers discussed their grievances during the 1990s appeared to be a product of the time period and the dominance of similar rhetoric in the civilian sector.

The argument that mutineers were inspired by popular political themes of the time raises the question of why the military failed to join forces with the civilian movement. Given the earlier explanation of the military conditions in the 1980s and 1990s, it would be fair to assume that the military would be sympathetic to the democratisation movement. The military, especially its junior members, was suffering many of the same hardships as ordinary civilians, and many of the calls for greater political liberties and respect for human rights would also benefit members of the military. However, instead, and with a few notable exceptions such as Mali in 1991, the military often put down mass protests.

One explanation for why the military in most states did not become actively engaged in the democratisation movement is that there had been a 'virtual "privatization" of key military units by incumbent dictators'.[65] These militaries or units were directly loyal to the individual leaders. Michael Bratton and Nicolas Van de Walle expand on why this was the case by stating that:

> the armed forces often came to occupy a privileged position within the *ancien régime*. To keep the soldiers content and under some semblance of civilian control, rulers granted to individual officers and the military units a generous array of perks, privileges, and rewards, including access to rents and commercial ventures. Transitions from authoritarian rule threaten these benefits, not only because the greater transparency of a democratic regime may lead to pressures for the suspension of privileges, but also because the military must negotiate with a new and usually less sympathetic political elite.[66]

Hutchful argues that the reluctance of the military to align itself with the democratisation movement should be attributed to the movement's failure to produce a 'clearly thought-out and articulated military policy'.[67] He states how 'this strategy needed to separate the military *institution* clearly from the military *regime* and to avoid lumping the two together, as the democracy movement tended to do'.[68] By 'making wholesale attacks against the military', those who may have been sympathetic to the movement were driven 'into the arms of the regime'.[69] Although there were elements of the military that were not satisfied under the authoritarian regimes of the 1970s and 1980s, they did not have trust or confidence that their lot would be improved with the movement towards democracy. Instead, the junior soldiers seemed to instrumentalise many of the themes of the democratisation movement for their own campaigns.

Popular input in political decision-making and the ability to hold leadership accountable are generally viewed as standard practices in non-authoritarian regimes and non-military contexts. However, these same concepts can be considered radical within a military setting. Military hierarchies intentionally prohibit junior members from having a say in the decision-making process. In the military, junior members are responsive to the orders of senior members; very rarely would it ever be the opposite pattern. For junior soldiers to demand that their seniors respond to their requests is what Rose calls 'an unnatural and unsettling state for troops'.[70]

This raises questions about why popular civilian ideas, which are 'unnatural' in a military context, would permeate the military sector. Militaries usually implement policies to separate their members from wider civilian society, with soldiers typically being housed on bases and required to wear uniforms and adhere to grooming standards that help unify the individuals while separating them from civilians. In many militaries, the duties of a soldier would rarely require day-to-day interaction with civilians. However, the role of African militaries were often placed soldiers in direct contact with wider society on a daily basis, through tasks such as manning checkpoints. African militaries have often been closely linked to the head of state and his or her protection, and militaries regularly have a heavy presence in urban areas, particularly capital cities. Urban areas and capital cities are the forefront of civilian political protests, and many soldiers would have been exposed to popular grievances and actions. Lastly, it is very common for junior soldiers to live off base owing to military housing shortages, which means that these soldiers spent a lot of their time with civilians.

It is not only the employment duties and lifestyles that exposed soldiers to the themes of the democratisation movement; the avenues in which the messages were being spread also played a part. Democratic ideas were spread through mediums to which soldiers would likely be exposed. Religious organisations, for example, served as an important counterweight to the region's authoritarian regimes, with 'political sermons' becoming increasingly popular throughout the 1990s.[71] An increase in the ownership of shortwave radios, as well as the proliferation of private radio stations and newspapers, gave civilians and the military greater access to political messages than in previous decades, while also facilitating the spread of information across state borders.[72] Sections of the youth, both student organisations and unemployed urban youth, also served as important instigators for political reform. Paul Nugent explains how, in the 1990s, 'nothing symbolized the erosion of government support more than the open contempt displayed by youth towards figures and symbols of authority'.[73]

Owing to the military's role in internal security in many African states, soldiers are often viewed as symbols of an oppressive state apparatus by urban youth. Yet it is important to note that many of the junior soldiers themselves belonged to the same age group and were likely to have maintained personal relations with students or urban youth. Although militaries often attempt to separate soldiers from the civilian population, the reality is that a large number of soldiers are youths, living in urban areas, listening to radios and attending religious services in the same manner as much of the civilian population. It is unsurprising, therefore, that many of the popular sentiments regarding democracy that were being expressed in the civilian population would also be picked up by soldiers.

The loosely defined boundaries between junior ranks and the civilian population became particularly clear to me when I spent a few weeks travelling with a young Sierra Leonean soldier. We would discuss the plan for the day, and then he would decide whether or not to wear his uniform. If the plan involved travelling long distances, the uniform was desirable as it made moving through any checkpoints easier and allowed him to obtain the coveted front seat of the shared transport (which was usually offered to him when in uniform). However, on days in which there would be a lot of downtime away from base and no travel, he seemed to prefer to wear civilian attire, presumably because his actions would be subject to less scrutiny. This example demonstrates the way in which soldiers in the region can maintain a foot in both civilian and military worlds, often strategically utilising the different identities.

A similar pattern of links between junior soldiers and civilian society can be found in research on the Ghanaian military, which suggests that 'the further down the ladder of hierarchy one goes ... the more likely that organizational boundaries will be breached'.[74] One reason for this is that junior ranks are less likely to have a substantial investment in the military status quo.[75] As the previous chapter explained, the junior ranks often attempt to balance a relationship with the civilian sector and the military hierarchy. Their behaviour during the democratisation period clearly demonstrates this; they borrowed themes, rhetoric and tactics from civilians, but for the most part never fully joined the democratisation movement.

Freedom to mutiny

Although the economic situation and political climate of the 1990s may have created the perfect condition for mutinies, the link between civilian movements and mutinies is not restricted to this period. Just as the pressure for democratic reform did not end in the 1990s, nor did mutinies. An examination of the incidents of mutiny described in Chapter 2 in relation to the Freedom House 'Freedom in the World' index scores of the country at the time of the revolt reveals that 70 per cent occurred in states that were ranked as either 'free' or 'partially free'.[76] Specific country examples also indicate that mutinies generally occur more frequently in countries exhibiting a higher degree of respect for political rights and civil liberties.

Just as there were few mutinies under the authoritarian regimes that dominated the continent in the 1970s and 1980s, there have also been few mutinies in the authoritarian regimes that exist in the region today. For example, long-standing authoritarian regimes such as that in Equatorial Guinea have been entirely free from mutinies. The Gambia serves as a particularly interesting example of how authoritarian political systems may deter mutinies. The Gambia's political trajectory is almost the complete reverse of that of most states in the region. During the 1980s, when authoritarian regimes were common, The Gambia was one of the few considered to be democratic. Yet, as many states in the region increased civil liberties and adopted democratic political practices, The Gambia became more repressive. As of 2016, it was one of the few countries in West Africa to be labelled by Freedom House as 'not free'. Although The Gambia had a series of mutinies in the 1990s, as the government became increasingly repressive mutinies ceased. Nearly everyone I interviewed about the potential for a mutiny in The Gambia felt that it was very unlikely, as President Jammeh would surely have any mutineers severely disciplined. Political executions in 2012 (the first official executions in twenty-seven years), including executions of military members accused of plotting against Jammeh, served as a particular warning for the consequences of threatening state stability.[77] The repressive nature of the state is an important explanation for the lack of mutinies, but not the sole reason, as will be explained in Chapter 7.

The most recent mutinies on the continent also support the trend of mutinies occurring more often in states with democratic political systems. In 2011, for example, mutinies took place in Burkina Faso, which is ranked by Freedom House as 'partially free', and mutinies also took place in 2012 in Mali, which at the time was ranked as 'free'. Sierra Leone has made considerable gains in political rights and civil liberties since the official end of its civil war in 2002. In 2013, for the first time, the country was listed as 'free'. The increased political freedoms have not necessarily erased soldiers' grievances, and some soldiers interviewed in 2011 and 2012 warned that a future mutiny might be on the horizon. The interviewees explained how their confidence in the political and justice system increased their confidence in conducting a successful mutiny in the future. One soldier explained that he felt a mutiny would be successful under the current political leadership because 'There are accessible leaders who want to know, who have an interest, who will listen. They [senior officers] will be arrested and they will be jailed.'[78] This man clearly believed the government would be responsive to their concerns, a shift from attitudes about the government in the 1990s, as will be discussed in Chapter 6.

The pattern of mutinies occurring most often in states that have at least some respect for democratic principles is somewhat counterintuitive, given that it may seem more logical for soldiers to revolt under a repressive system; however, repressive systems generally serve to prohibit a successful mutiny. Mutinies require a leadership that is willing to listen and respond, which is more likely under a democratic than an authoritarian regime. Thus, in some ways mutinies represent a level of faith in the leadership to address grievances. When soldiers have no faith that a leader will respond or the political system is so fragmented that there is no one to hear the complaints (such as in the midst of the civil wars in Sierra Leone and Liberia), mutinies become a pointless endeavour.

However, it is not only the perception that democratic leaders are more responsive that makes soldiers in democratic countries more prone to mutinies, as the civil liberties often associated with democratic political systems also work to the advantage of mutineers. In particular, increased media freedoms provide soldiers, as well as civilians, with new tools to express their grievances. As previously mentioned, media in Africa in the 1970s and into the 1980s were often state-controlled.[79] During this period, the media was typically a 'one-way operation' with 'people being spoken to, not listened to'.[80] This started to change in the 1990s, as one country after another introduced legislation giving local press the freedoms it had lacked in previous decades.[81] The increased media freedoms were partially a result of the democratisation movement, but they were also used to place pressure on the leadership for further political reform. The new media freedoms allowed reporters (albeit not without risk) to 'reveal what [was] going on behind the well draped windows of public institutions'.[82] There was increased public scrutiny of political figures and government procedures, with growing attention to corruption.[83]

Not all states have progressed in an equal fashion towards increased media freedoms, yet, generally speaking, there has been an increase in the number of privatised media outlets and more access to international media since the 1990s. The increased privatisation of media sources as well as the introduction of new forms of media has resulted in more interactive media, allowing messages to move 'downwards, upwards, and sideways'.[84]

Mutineers began to use this more interactive media to work around their chain of command, and in some cases to connect with the international community and the civilian population. Before the 1990s, there were only a limited number of examples of mutineers making radio announcements. One of these was in the Democratic Republic of Congo in 1966 when soldiers attempted to take over the radio station. However, as media freedoms increased in the 1990s, soldiers increasingly turned to the media during mutinies, a trend that continues into the present time. There were also periods in which media outlets approached mutineers rather than the other way around. During mutinies in Burkina Faso in 2011, news outlets sought out mutineers for statements, a trend that will likely continue as international and local media organisations compete for new stories.

A pattern has now emerged where disgruntled soldiers will often provide their story to the media in the hope that the threat of mutiny will be sufficient to resolve their grievances. The previous chapter described a scenario in 2012 in which Nigerian soldiers contacted the media to threaten their leaders with a pending mutiny. Sierra Leonean soldiers used a similar tactic during their deployment to Somalia in 2013, as will be discussed further in Chapter 6.

In the reporting of mutinies in the 1960s through the 1980s, little, if any, attention was paid to civilian opinion. However, this began to change in the 1990s with the emergence of privatised media outlets that published opinion pieces and letters to the editor. This situation has in turn changed even more drastically in recent years with increasing internet access allowing nearly anyone with online connectivity to comment on events in a public forum.

Likely to the chagrin of the political and military leadership, the media often sided with the mutineers. Following a mutiny in Niger in 2002, for example, a local newspaper published the following:

> When the mutiny first occurred, it is crucial to ask Mr. President why salaries of soldiers have not been paid for a good five months. What does the government expect mutineers to live on and survive? True, mutiny is an offense everywhere. But why is mutiny an offense for soldiers and government officials' remissness and irresponsibility not an offense? This is the root of the problem.[85]

There was additional criticism within the media, civil society and opposition when the president of Niger, Mamadou Tandja, responded to the mutinies by declaring a state of emergency that restricted civil liberties and particularly press freedoms.[86] Journalists who reported on the story were arrested, attracting the attention of international media.[87] Niger's Constitutional Court ultimately ruled against Tandja and declared that he did not have the authority to impose the state of emergency.[88] In the meantime, activists continued to engage with the mutineers' cause by staging a sit-in in front of the Congress Palace in Niamey where the African Commission of Human and People's Rights was being held, to protest against the imprisonment of more than 200 mutineers who had been held in jail for nearly a year without trial.[89] In this case, the media were actively involved in publicising the mutiny and its aftermath, as well as critiquing the government's response. The mutiny took place over pay and living conditions, as well as complaints over particular officers; however, it eventually took on larger proportions when civilian organisations used the government response to question the powers of the president and the lack of civil liberties. Though the media attention may not have earned the soldiers the lower meal prices in the army dining halls that they had initially demanded, their plight did receive international attention, with Amnesty International declaring its concern over the government's actions.[90]

Similar media criticism of the government followed a mutiny in The Gambia in 1992. A private newspaper, *The Point*, claimed to represent the voice of the local population when it wrote:

> Without in any way seeking to prejudice the proceedings of the court-martial, it is to be said, as the public is already saying, that while the actions of the 35 privates is to be condemned, having regard to the kind of discipline expected from the army, it must also be pointed out that they should not have been given the chance for this repeat performance through nonpayment of any part of their allowance, however small.[91]

Foroyaa, another private newspaper, used the mutiny to criticise the People's Progressive Party (PPP) government: 'PPP does not respond to the rights and entitlements of its people. Urge citizens to vote them out of office in upcoming election.'[92] As in Niger, the mutiny became an example of government mismanagement in the eyes of the civilian opposition. The Gambia's government-run newspaper, *The Gambia Weekly*, did not report on the mutiny or mention any military indiscipline. Instead, the week after the mutiny, as if to counter the potentially negative media, the paper reported on plans for a military parade in which the president would provide medals to soldiers for 'long and dedicated service to the nation.'[93] The parade story was too mundane for any other news outlets to report. This contrast of public versus private media reporting of the same event helps show that without private media it is unlikely that mutinies would gain the attention the soldiers desire.

Thus increased press freedoms and access to media from the 1990s onwards have often worked to the mutineers' advantage. They began to use media outlets as a way to express their grievances, circumventing their chain of command and gaining wider attention for their cause. The increased attention also highlighted due legal processes for mutineers. However, with the increased presence and types of media, rarely does one actor (for example, the government or mutineers) fully control the flow of information. Instead, the more interactive style of media, which in some ways gives the mutineers a voice, also limits the ability of the mutineers to control their message. As the examples of Niger and The Gambia demonstrate, civilians have become increasingly involved in reporting on mutinies and providing their opinions about the event. While this can have advantages for the mutineers, it also makes it easier for their cause to be used by opposition political groups or others seeking to discredit the government or military leadership. The case study of Burkina Faso in Chapter 8 will discuss the ways in which media aimed at popular culture have also become engaged in telling the mutineers' story.

Conclusion

The mutinies of the 1990s can be used to gauge the impact that international economic and political changes had on rank-and-file soldiers while also demonstrating how they responded to these changes. In the 1990s, African soldiers were not immune to the political currents of the time, even if they were regularly seen as suppressing the movement towards democracy. Issues that were prominent in the civilian sector, such as corruption and demands for accountability, were also key themes in the mutinies of this period. Just as 'ordinary citizens' in the 1990s began to 'exert a high degree of control over leaders', so did rank-and-file soldiers through increased mutinies.[94] Mutineers also used similar rhetoric and tactics to the civilian actors who were pushing for democratic reform. The attitude of the military towards the democratisation movement is not one of complete support or disregard, but rather a more nuanced relationship. While the democracy movement may have 'lost the battle for the military', this chapter has shown that the movement was not lost on the rank-and-file soldiers.[95]

The importance of political context for mutineers is a pattern that extends beyond the 1990s. Mutineers need a responsive leadership if their mutiny is to be successful. Thus democratic leaders, who are typically more responsive than authoritarian leaders, make better negotiating partners for mutineers. Additionally, mutineers benefited from the democratization movement in the 1990s and the democratic reforms that have persisted in some states today. They were quick to use civil liberties, such as press freedoms, to their advantage to express their grievances.

5

THE PRICE OF HARDSHIP

DEPLOYMENTS AND PEACEKEEPING

One of the most significant international trends for African militaries since the Cold War has been the uptake in international peacekeeping. Between 1990 and 2009, around sixty different peacekeeping operations were deployed in Africa, and most African states have contributed troops to at least one peacekeeping mission.[1] These include missions led by the UN, regional organisations and sub-regional organisations. West and Central African states increasingly contributed troops to peacekeeping missions, and most states remain committed to various missions today. As of August 2016, nine of the top twenty-five troop- and police-contributing countries to UN missions were West and Central African states.[2] However at times, these deployments led to the emergence of grievances among the peacekeepers, which has in turn resulted in mutinies. This chapter will demonstrate how the increase in mutinies from the 1990s onwards can partially be attributed to increases in deployments throughout the region, particularly deployments on multinational missions.

These missions often have unintended consequences that can undermine the goals of peace operations.[3] Scholars and international organisations have brought attention to peacekeeper involvement in sexual exploitation and trading in conflict minerals, as well as arms trafficking, while studies on peacekeeping economies have noted rises in commodity prices and disparities of incomes related to peacekeeping missions.[4] Yet mutinies following deployments on peace operations have not received much attention.

Of the seventy-one mutinies listed in Chapter 2, seventeen, or 24 per cent of the dataset, involved grievances directly related to deployments. Twelve of these deployment-related cases involved deployments on multinational peace operations.[5] The pattern of mutinies following peacekeeping participation has occurred in nine West African countries (Benin, Burkina Faso, Chad, Côte d'Ivoire, The Gambia, Ghana, Guinea, Guinea Bissau and Nigeria), indicating that it is not simply the result of one country's policies. Mutinies have also followed missions led by the United Nations, the African Union (AU) and the Economic Community of West African States (ECOWAS), suggesting that the problems cannot be attributed to one funding or organisational body. While this book focuses specifically on West and Central Africa, the trend extends beyond this region. In 2009, for instance, Burundian troops mutinied over grievances related to their participation in the African Union Mission in Somalia (AMISOM).

This chapter begins by explaining why recently deployed troops may be especially prone to mutiny. This discussion is applicable to internal deployments, such as the mission by Nigerian troops deployed to counter Boko Haram within Nigeria, as well as international deployments. The latter part of the chapter will then focus specifically on multinational peace operations.

Military hierarchies typically involve 'implicit contracts' or 'social contracts' between soldiers and their superiors where 'in exchange for obedience, the chain of command will see to the needs of its personnel and ensure that they are well cared for'.[6] Being a soldier is often viewed as more than just a job, since it potentially involves high risks, lifestyle restrictions and is legally binding. In return, soldiers expect more than just pay. They often expect housing, subsidised food, uniforms, training and an acknowledgment of their sacrifices. If soldiers feel that their superiors are not fulfilling these expectations, they are more likely to renege on their obligation to obey orders from the chain of command. While this pattern applies to mutinies in general, this chapter will show why deployments in particular often alter the contract between soldiers and their superiors.

Like most contracts, the ones between soldiers and their chain of command shift depending on the workload. When stationed at home, both sides may be more lax about the agreement or find alternative ways to meet the demands. For example, it is common for West and Central African soldiers to take on small side jobs that their bosses overlook, or soldiers may be assigned to positions that could supplement their salaries (such as working at check points, where bribes are frequently given). When troops are deployed, the contract shifts as soldiers' expectations of what they are owed by the command increase along with the risks of the job. Deployment on multinational missions often further heightens soldiers' expectations as they are able to compare their conditions with those of soldiers from other states in the region. However, it is more difficult for superiors to 'take care of' soldiers on a deployment, owing in part to their increased needs (equipment, logistics, etc.), which do not necessarily coincide with increased funds. As this chapter will show, the hierarchy often fails to meet the heightened expectations of deployed soldiers, thus breaking the contract with the rank and file.

Risks, entitlements and respect

For states in West and Central Africa, international peace operations are the most likely type of deployment for soldiers. There is a wide spectrum of peace support operations, some of which occur in the midst of conflict, while others occur after a ceasefire has been reached.[7] However, the line between the various types of operations is often blurred, and mission mandates can change.[8] Most of the multinational missions described in this chapter involve operations to areas in which conflict was ongoing or where there was a high probability that the unit would encounter combat. This is part of a trend described in the Report of the Panel on United Nations Peace Operations (the Brahimi Report), published in 2000, which showed evidence that 'the current era of "complex" peacekeeping in civil-war-torn states has seen a drastic shift away from developed-country blue helmets—the standard practice during the Cold War—towards blue helmets supplied by third world states'.[9] Although this trend has been subject to criticism on the grounds that it has 'an unpleasant mercenary flavor, whereby rich countries appear to pay soldiers from very poor countries to undertake dangerous peacekeeping jobs', the pattern has not shifted since the report was issued.[10]

There is also a pattern in Africa in which regional peacekeepers are among the first to deploy to a conflict zone and later 'rehatted' into a more multinational and better-resourced (usually) UN mission.[11] This has occurred in Liberia, Sierra Leone, Côte d'Ivoire and most recently Mali. However, this trend has led to claims that 'Africans give the blood and the UN takes the glory.'[12] It is an unfortunate reality that African troops are involved in the most dangerous peacekeeping missions. Highly risky operations are of course not limited to international operations. Countries such as Nigeria and Mali have also experienced high troop casualties in deployment to counter threats within their borders. The intensity of the deployments in which many of the region's states are involved is an important issue because the risks of the mission are often part of the justification for deployment-related mutinies.

The heightened risks associated with deployments often lead to a heightened sense of entitlement. Soldiers on deployment or returned from deployment believe they are due more from the government or military hierarchy as a result of their experience. Soldiers with combat experience revise their criteria of what is acceptable pay, based on the risks involved. For example, a Sierra Leonean soldier involved in the mutiny plan of 1992 commented that 'the pay was very much low ... Soldiers just get 10,000 [leones] a month and you sacrifice your life for the nation.'[13] Similarly, a Gambian former soldier discussing the 1991 and 1992 mutinies described how 'soldiers felt that they were in Liberia risking their lives and still the amount of money they were expecting was not reaching them ... they were exposed to danger and ... they don't get the money they expected'.[14] Hence the problem was not only an issue of pay; rather, the issue of pay, when combined with the risks of the mission, made the situation unacceptable.

Similarly, when I asked a Sierra Leonean soldier about deployments to Darfur, he gave the following response: 'If I go to Sudan, I risk my life and only get $400, my life is worth more than that.'[15] For this individual, the bonus deployment pay was still not enough to justify the potential danger. As these examples show, danger is considered a chargeable experience, and the soldiers expect to be compensated for it.

Increased expectations following deployments are not unique to West or Central African militaries and parallels can be drawn in civilian jobs. Most military personnel that deploy, especially to a combat zone, expect supplemental pay (often called hazard pay). Similarly, even non-military personnel expect that added responsibilities in their employment would also come with additional pay or benefits. Soldiers in nearly any professional military count on appropriate provisions when deployed. Thus the demands made by deployed or post-deployed soldiers in this region are not necessarily unusual; what seems to cause the trend of mutinies in this region is the inability of governments to meet the expectations of deployed soldiers. States often lack the funding needed for the missions, or there is misappropriation of the funds (or both). This trend will be discussed more specifically in relation to multinational missions below.

The hardships and sacrifices of a deployment also lead to a sense of entitlement in a more abstract way. There seems to be an expectation that, as well as additional pay, soldiers who have deployed deserve increased respect for having endured the mission. The sense of pride around deployments was often expressed in everyday discussions with soldiers during field research. Both in formal interviews and in casual conversations, soldiers were very quick to talk about the deployments in which they had been involved. Guinean soldiers talked extensively about their experiences on the ECOMOG missions to Liberia and Sierra Leone, and likewise Malian soldiers openly discussed their time deployed to suppress the rebellion in the northern part of their country. On several occasions during interviews in Sierra Leone, soldiers made a point to show me physical scars from their deployments. One officer took his uniform shirt off to show me a particularly severe scar resulting from a bullet to the chest and subsequent surgery. He also directly used this experience to justify his involvement in overthrowing President Joseph Momoh in 1992 by explaining that the government did not take care of those wounded in battle. As far as he was concerned, the government had failed to fulfil its responsibility, thus breaking an implicit contract.

A heightened level of respect for veterans was also apparent in the language used by interviewees. When soldiers told me about their military colleagues, friends or relatives, they would often add descriptors about the individual's deployment experiences. For example, in Sierra Leone young soldiers would admiringly describe someone as 'battle-tested' or 'battle-hardened'.

My conversations with soldiers from across the region also indicated that there is a strong consensus among soldiers that those engaged in combat deserve better treatment. While I was conducting field research in West Africa in 2012, there were two coups in the region (in Mali and Guinea Bissau). In casual conversations with soldiers in Guinea and Sierra Leone, there was overwhelming support for the actions of the Malian soldiers. They commented that the Malian soldiers were justified in their actions because the government was not taking care of them in their fight against rebels in the northern part of the country. Interestingly, soldiers did not have the same sympathy for their counterparts in Guinea Bissau and made dismissive comments about how they were always 'acting up'. That the Malian solders' initial complaints were over deployment conditions seemed to win them sympathy among other West African soldiers.

The pride and respect associated with deployments is a trait that extends far beyond Africa. Militaries worldwide reward combat experiences with medals, ribbons or promotions. This universality of heightened respect for combat veterans can be linked to issues of honour, as described by Iliffe, who uses

Frank Henderson Stewart's definition of honour as a 'right to respect'.[16] Iliffe explains that groups determine the criteria for honour. Stratified groups typically experience vertical honour, in which special respect is awarded to those of superior rank.[17] Within a military context, the 'group' seems to largely agree that endurance of combat deployments is honourable and deserves heightened respect. Additionally, combat experiences often appear to give soldiers a heightened position within the vertical honour structure, even if they hold a seemingly junior rank.

When the hierarchy treats combat veterans poorly, it is viewed as a particular insult. Military interviewees implied that there was a level of tolerance when soldiers in the barracks are paid late, but it was not acceptable for combat veterans to be treated in the same way. Post-deployment mutinies can serve as a way to defend the honour soldiers feel they deserve.

Familiar complaints, new importance

Deployments require supplies, equipment and logistics that would not be necessary while stationed at home. These additional needs often fail to coincide with additional funding, and soldiers regularly claim that they have not received the required equipment. At the same time the deployment environment, often to remote locations, makes resupply challenging, especially for states that lack adequate aircraft and vehicles.

However, many of the deployment grievances related to supplies and equipment are not new; instead, old complaints take on a new level of importance when they occur in a deployment setting. Soldiers commonly grumble about not having equipment or uniforms while in the barracks, but these concerns become more significant when a soldier is deployed. Outdated equipment is of little relevance in the day-to-day lives of soldiers who do not need it to survive. Yet when in combat, outdated equipment or a lack of supplies such as ammunition can be the difference between life and death. The case study of a planned mutiny in Sierra Leone, detailed in the next chapter, will demonstrate this point. The mutiny was planned while the soldiers were deployed to counter rebel forces, and their complaints included lack of equipment, uniforms, boots, food and medical care and inconsistent pay. These were not necessarily new complaints; the government had long been neglecting the military. However, these issues had more severe consequences for the soldiers who were deployed. One soldier from the deployed unit explained that the group was 'demoralised every time we go to battle' owing to the lack of supplies and support.[18] The old complaints led to new complications on the ground for deployed soldiers (including casualties within the unit) and severely altered their attitudes towards the mission and their chain of command.

A lack of adequate equipment was also a key complaint of Nigerian mutineers in 2014. Rank-and-file soldiers tasked with countering Boko Haram in north-eastern Nigeria refused to fight because they had not been given proper weapons and ammunition. They argued that the senior commanders were 'sacrificing soldiers'.[19] In a court martial several months later, the soldiers were found guilty of mutiny and sentenced to death by firing squad, a conviction that has received widespread condemnation both within Nigeria and internationally.

Deployments can also expose inadequate military training. Similar to the concerns over equipment shortfalls, the lack of adequate training becomes increasingly important and apparent in the midst of a combat scenario. Combat situations can also reveal that the unit's ground leadership or other support elements such as intelligence lack proper training.

Insufficient training and support was a particular concern of soldiers during the ECOWAS Ceasefire Monitoring Group (ECOMOG) mission to Liberia in 1990–9. The ECOMOG deployment to Liberia was controversial, in part because of a broad mandate that included both peacekeeping and peace enforcement, which raised questions about the political motivations and legality of the mission.[20] It was also contested by several of the sixteen ECOWAS member states. Only six countries initially contributed troops to the mission, and of those six countries, five were Anglophone.[21] From the start, the mission was plagued with numerous practical complications, including inadequate equipment, intelligence and logistics.[22] For example, in its early stages, the mission lacked basic intelligence reports and maps.[23] After Action Reports (AARs) revealed that there was no standardised training across the contingents, which reduced their effectiveness as a force.[24] Interoperability among the troops was further challenged by the variety of equipment, training and shared languages.[25] There was also a lack of the most basic supplies, such as uniforms, boots and food.[26]

The equipment shortfalls, training inadequacies, interoperability challenges and chain of command confusion led to high casualty rates and demoralised troops.[27] There were an estimated 500 ECOMOG troop fatalities during the initial mission to Liberia.[28] As junior soldiers made up the bulk of the deployed units, inadequate preparation or support likely had the greatest effect on the rank-and-file soldiers. These grievances, along with the pay concerns described in the following section, led to several mutinies among the ECOMOG contingents.

Another common grievance among mutineers following deployments concerns lack of information about the mission. Similar to the above grievances, irregular communication between seniors and junior ranks is not a new concern, but it becomes a particular point of stress on deployment. For instance, soldiers have accused their hierarchies of misleading them about the required length of deployment. Chadian troops deployed to Mali as part of a UN stabilisation mission (MINUSMA) mutinied over their length of deployment in 2013, and Sierra Leonean troops on AMISOM publicly expressed dissatisfaction at having been deployed beyond their one-year contract.[29] The latter case was a unique situation, as the extended deployment was a result of the unexpected Ebola crisis.[30]

Similarly, a month's extension beyond their deployment contract was the central complaint of a mutiny threat by Nigerian troops deployed on the UN/AU mission to Darfur in 2012. The Nigerian soldiers' lengthy public statement reveals common themes of deployment-related mutinies. They expressed offence at their treatment in relation to their veteran status by saying that the extension represented the government's failure to pay 'respect to their men and women on tour of duty'.[31] The mutineers accused the government of treating them 'as if [they] are not humans' and threatened to 'create a scenario which will deter the ongoing peace process in Darfur' if they were not flown home by a given date.[32] Similarly to most deployment-related mutinies, they blamed their grievances on officer negligence and corruption. These West African examples are consistent with wider research on the psychology of international peacekeeping missions, which has shown that uncertainty in the length of deployment is one of the critical issues affecting stress levels among peacekeepers.[33]

Pay problems

In addition to grievances over equipment, training and the length of a deployment, pay is also a key complaint of most deployment-related mutinies. The pay grievances take on several different forms, the most basic being that soldiers simply have not received their due pay. At times, this is directly linked to the logistical problems, as hierarchies have claimed to have difficulties physically getting the due pay to soldiers.[34] Even when soldiers do receive their salaries, and allowances, it is common for those on deployment to view the amount as inadequate, particularly in relation to the deployment conditions. As noted above, the greater risks associated with deployments often lead to a heightened sense of entitlement in terms of pay. These two types of pay grievances are not mutually exclusive, and at times mutineers have claimed that their inadequate salaries are late.

A combination of the above pay grievances contributed to mutinies by returned ECOMOG soldiers in The Gambia in 1991 and 1992, the first mutinies the country had ever experienced. The mutineers claimed that they had not been paid their salaries and that the promised pay was not adequate given the hardships of the mission. In the words of one former soldier: 'soldiers on the ground must be paid better, they were facing war every day. They should be paid more. Why would anyone risk their life for that?'[35] Another Gambian military interviewee complained: 'they were in real war situations, so for them to not get paid was a real problem'.[36] Gambian soldiers who were in the military at the time explained that the action was as much about perceptions of disrespect towards the recently deployed soldiers as it was about pay.[37]

The Gambian soldiers placed the blame for their grievances on the senior hierarchy. One soldier explained that the deployment pay did not reach the soldiers because 'the senior officers were robbing them'.[38] Another Gambian interviewee expanded on this by claiming that 'the top brass got the [deployment] money and sliced it, only gave some to the soldiers'.[39] These accusations were difficult to verify, but they appeared to be widely believed by soldiers and furthered existing tensions that had been building between the ranks at the time. The claims by the peacekeepers were seen to represent and perpetuate growing distrust between the junior and senior ranks.

The grievances over ECOMOG pay were not unique to the Gambian contingent. It was common for ECOMOG soldiers in Liberia to go months without payment, and many remained uncompensated when they returned home. To some extent, the payment problem can be attributed to the context of the ECOMOG mission to Liberia. This venture occurred at a time when many states were experiencing severe internal economic constraints, as described in the previous chapter. The ECOWAS Standing Mediation Committee agreed 'that troops from participating countries were to be self-sufficient for the first thirty days, after which ECOWAS was to pick up the funding', but it was unable to do so.[40] ECOWAS's goal of collecting 50 million dollars in donations from African states and other international donors was not met, which resulted in incomplete funding for the new force.[41] This may explain why some troop-contributing countries, such as The Gambia, struggled to provide the extra deployment pay.

Some analysts attribute this lack of payment as the motivation for the widespread looting and theft by ECOMOG soldiers and have argued that 'more frequent payment of allowances would reduce the number of soldiers who loot little items.'[42] However, much of the looting went far beyond the need to survive, and the payment delays should only be seen as a partial explanation for this behaviour. Even if only a fraction of the ECOMOG soldiers were involved in looting, the organisation as a whole gained a poor reputation among Liberians who claimed that ECOMOG really stood for 'Every Car or Moving Object Gone.'[43] Some also speculate that the lack of financial and material support for the peacekeepers on the ground led some peacekeepers to work with the rebels they were supposed to be fighting.[44] The common perception that ECOMOG soldiers were collaborating with rebels increased the difficulty of the mission and further demoralised many of the participants.

Even in the later stages of the mission, when the conflict had received more international attention and monetary contributions, funding still remained a problem, often because of the complexity of the multinational, multi-organisational mission. For example, problems arose when ECOMIL soldiers were 'rehatted' into the UNMIL mission in 2003.[45] In 2004, soldiers from Guinea Bissau staged a mutiny demanding unpaid wages from their involvement in the ECOMIL/UNMIL mission. They accused their army chiefs of pocketing their peacekeeping payments, while the army chiefs accused the UN of not paying the salaries from the transition from ECOMIL to UNMIL.[46]

The emergence of complications in funding missions in which numerous nations and several international organisations are involved is hardly surprising. As noted, the ECOMOG Liberia mission was severely underfunded, but payment arrears are a regular challenge for UN missions as well.[47] However, soldiers are generally not sympathetic to funding difficulties at the organisational level. When they are not paid on time, they do not seem to question if the organisation is at fault, but rather blame their officers or others above them. This makes particular sense within a military chain of command, because officers are seen as being responsible for the care of those who work under them. This is significant because it means that delays in payments for multinational missions, regardless of who is at fault, have the potential to cause divisions and suspicions between the ranks of the contributing nation's military.

The problem with transparency

Compared with the earlier peace support operations led by ECOWAS, missions led by the UN generally provided better compensation to countries for troop contributions. However, this has not stopped African peacekeepers on these missions from engaging in mutinies. The grievances in these mutinies take on a slightly different angle than the pay grievances presented above and are related to the way peacekeeping pay is allocated.

There is no shortage of soldiers volunteering to go on UN missions in West and Central Africa, largely on account of the significantly increased pay compared with what they would make stationed at home. The lack of alternative economic opportunities in the region, especially for rank-and-file soldiers with limited advanced training or education, makes deployment on a multinational mission a coveted opportunity. The missions also provide an experience that could be valuable for future promotions or job opportunities. For some, the appeal of travelling or simply breaking the routine of life in the barracks may also be appealing.

During interviews with soldiers in West Africa, the desire to participate in UN peacekeeping missions was a regular topic of conversation. In discussions just weeks after the 2012 Malian coup, Sierra Leonean and Guinean troops continually brought up the potential for a multinational mission to Mali for which they could become involved. It became clear that instability in Mali was seen as a significant opportunity for neighbouring countries' troops. According to Kwesi Aning, in Ghana there is a 'perception among the troops that participating in peace operations is an irrefutable way to improve one's financial situation. Thus being selected to participate in such a force has become a major *raison d'être* for members of the GAF to stay in the forces.'[48] A report by the Kofi Annan International Peacekeeping Training Centre (KAIPTC) argues that Ghanaian soldiers are so keen to go on a multinational mission that even the possibility is enough to ensure military discipline. The report states that 'soldiers who are found HIV positive miss out on the extra income from peacekeeping missions and therefore make active efforts to prevent themselves from being infected'.[49] It credits peacekeeping missions (and particularly the pay incentive) as a reason for the military's low HIV rate.[50]

The income from peacekeeping missions has the potential to create long-term opportunities for the peacekeepers and their families. Returned peacekeepers 'who have managed to invest their peacekeeping funds profitably have subsequently purchased plots of land, built houses, purchased household goods and generally sent their children to better schools'.[51] Sierra Leonean peacekeepers told me how they had used their peacekeeping pay to buy motorbikes or cars that they would then hire out to taxi-drivers.[52] Thus entrepreneurial soldiers can often use the additional earnings to kick-start business opportunities.

It is not only soldiers and their families who benefit financially from involvement in multinational missions; the military as a whole also stands to gain. A report by the KAIPTC explains how this is the case for Ghanaian participation in UN operations:

> The Government ... is reimbursed for the ordinary contingent member with an amount of $1096 per month while for the specialist an amount of $1399 per month is reimbursed. Considering that the ordinary contingent member is paid $20 a day (making $600 a month for 30 days), while provision is made for catering and some of the other provisions under self-sustainment (not readily quantifiable), the country makes significant *profits* on each ordinary contingent member and specialist that it deploys on a UN mission.[53]

In addition to the financial benefits from personnel contributions, the United States, the United Kingdom, France and Canada (among others) offer training programmes to African militaries that contribute troops to multinational missions.[54] There are also lease reimbursement programmes, which enable African militaries to upgrade their equipment.[55]

This may seem like a win-win situation, as both individuals and the country benefit, but the discrepancy between what the UN reimburses the troop-contributing country and what individual soldiers receive has been a source of grievance among peacekeepers. The UN is transparent in its rate of compensation for troop-contributing countries. As of 2017: 'Countries volunteering uniformed personnel to peacekeeping operations are reimbursed by the UN at a standard rate, approved by the General Assembly, of a little over US$1,332 per soldier per month.'[56] Many African soldiers I spoke with, regardless of whether they had been on a UN mission or not, were more or less familiar with this figure.

However, the UN does not directly pay the salaries of the peacekeepers. That responsibility lies with the peacekeepers' home country, and the troop-contributing country is under no obligation to distribute the full funds to the troops.[57] The UN transparency contrasts with the lack of transparency usually found in the defence industry, where details of contracts, spending and individual pay are often not publicly available. Countries contributing troops to multinational missions justify paying peacekeepers less than the reimbursement stipulated by the UN by referring to the internal expenses involved in the deployment.

When it is not clear to soldiers what the additional money from multinational missions is being used for, they often assume that corruption is involved. Interviews with serving soldiers in Sierra Leone illustrate this point. One soldier discussing the country's involvement in the UNAMID mission explained that the peacekeepers 'are not happy, they are grumbling. 1,225 [US dollars] to country but we only get 400 [US dollars]. We do not know what the government is using the money for.'[58] In a separate interview, a soldier stated:

> If you think, they [the Sierra Leone government] are making something like one million, two million dollars over six months and they are not doing anything, not buying uniforms, not buying medicine for soldiers. They are not helping those that are representing us in Darfur. They are managing it poorly. If they don't change the system it [i.e. a mutiny] will happen.[59]

Another Sierra Leonean soldier speculated that the officers were benefiting from the missions by claiming that the officers' lifestyles could not be maintained on a regular salary.[60] The same complaints that were expressed in interviews in 2011–12 began to attract local attention in 2013 when a Sierra Leonean soldier deployed to Somalia called into a popular Sierra Leonean radio station to express the soldiers' anger.[61] In response to the peacekeepers' allegations that money was fraudulently being deducted from their pay, the Ministry of Defence produced a document detailing the ways the government was investing money earned from peacekeeping missions.[62]

Similar complaints were expressed to the press by Nigerian soldiers who had participated in MINUSMA in 2013. They argued that the government had not given them an explanation for why they only received part of what the UN pays for peacekeepers. They expressed their frustrations in relation to the dangers of the mission by stating: 'they have cheated us after we have risked our lives, left our families for seven months'.[63] Another interviewed soldier put forward the common accusation that officers were benefiting from the soldiers' hardships: 'it is sad our *ogas* are treating us like this and feeding fat on us on the field'.[64]

The grievances of peacekeepers extend beyond claims of officers pocketing parts of their salary, as soldiers have also argued that there is a lack of transparency in the selection of peacekeepers. The selection of peacekeepers is the responsibility of the troop-contributing country, not the UN. Soldiers in Sierra Leone alleged that, in order to be selected for a peacekeeping mission, they are expected to pay the assigning officers 'something like 10 per cent ... It is a mission, if you are fortunate to go they want you to give 10 per cent. If you don't do it they hold up your rank, they make you relinquish your appointment.'[65] Similar accusations were made in the Sierra Leone media in 2013.[66] Aning observed a comparable trend in Ghana, where 'different types of "protocol" facilities are extended by junior officers to their senior officers, either to get their duty tours extended or to be selected to participate in a peacekeeping operation as a whole'.[67] He notes a variety of different ways in which the protocols work, but the general trend is that those in a position to select who deploys often require compensation from those they send on a deployment. This practice extends far up the chain of command, and there is often a degree of corruption involved in the selection of units or branches of the military to be involved in the mission, not only the selection of individual peacekeepers.[68] During interviews with soldiers in Burkina Faso, none mentioned being required to pay to go on a mission, but they were adamant that the selection was based on personal relationships, not necessarily merit. Even an individual who was in an authoritative position within the military admitted 'if you do not know someone you will never get assigned to an important mission'.[69]

The perceived corruption within the selection process, and the soldiers' tendency to blame officers for late pay, are significant because it indicates a more systemic problem. The roots of the grievances over peacekeeping pay go deeper than issues of money. The perceived exploitative actions threaten to delegitimise the officer corps and their orders in the minds of the enlisted soldiers, which weakens the hierarchy.[70] The resentment and suspicion of the soldiers towards their superiors do not necessarily vanish when the soldiers receive their due pay. The case study of The Gambia in Chapter 7 will show how late payments for peacekeepers were seen as evidence of corruption among the officer corps. Even after the soldiers received their pay, doubts and suspicions persisted in the minds of enlisted soldiers about their officers, resulting in further instability within the armed forces.

Revealing the greener grass

Another important aspect of peacekeeping operations is the ability for soldiers to compare their conditions with those from other countries. On multinational peacekeeping operations, soldiers live and work together with foreign comrades, usually for extended periods of time. The individual soldiers perform the same job as their fellow peacekeepers under similar conditions, but all are paid by their home governments. However, the various countries contributing troops do not pay the same amount to the soldiers they deploy. The economic conditions and cost of living vary widely between countries in the region, and thus it could be expected that salaries would also vary. Those who are on the lower end of the pay scale often view the pay difference with contempt. Soldiers compare more than just pay when on multinational missions.

Differences between countries regarding uniforms, food, equipment, leadership styles and specific country military procedures, such as the way they handle casualties or schedule troop rotations, have also served as a basis for grievances among peacekeepers.

For many junior soldiers, a deployment on multinational missions is often the first time that they have been able to engage with colleagues from other countries. This may change as a result of increased regional exercises or joint training, often hosted by Western organisations such as United States Africa Command (AFRICOM). However, these exercises tend to be of a much shorter duration than peacekeeping deployments, and specialised training courses are often focused on NCOs and officers. The experience of extensive engagement with other African troops via peacekeeping brings new insights and makes some soldiers question their own conditions, particularly in comparison with others. This observation is consistent with the arguments made by academics in the 1960s and 1970s that African military officers often revised their view of their expectations and roles following exposure to a wide variety of military personnel and ideas by attending Western military academies.[71] Similar patterns occurred in pre-independence Africa as well. Collective action taken by members of the Tirailleurs Sénégalais following deployments abroad in the Second World War is one such example.[72]

The ECOMOG mission to Liberia serves as a good example of the ways that grievances can arise from the ability of troops to compare their treatment with contingents from other countries. As a sub-regionally led mission, it brought together numerous soldiers from countries in close geographic proximity and of similar socioeconomic status. The variations in pay among the ECOMOG soldiers were a consistent source of tension during and after the mission. ECOWAS had agreed on an operational allowance of 5 US dollars per day per deployed soldier, with each contributing country being responsible for paying their troops. However, there were 'noticeable differences both in the amount and pattern in which some contingents were paid'.[73] Soldiers from Sierra Leone claimed that, even when paid regularly, they were not receiving the agreed amount. Soldiers from Nigeria were known to go months with no pay, whereas other contingents received regular and full pay.[74] The differences were a key part of several mutinies that followed participation in ECOMOG. For example, a Gambian officer explained that one motivation for the 1991 and 1992 mutinies following the multinational mission in Liberia was that the soldiers 'believed they were being paid less than their counterparts from other countries'.[75]

Contributing countries on the ECOMOG mission were expected to supply their own soldiers with uniforms and equipment. The difference in uniforms was 'one of the most glaring aspects' of differentiation between the troops in ECOMOG. The Nigerian soldiers in particular were so poorly supplied and outfitted compared with the other soldiers that they often purchased uniforms from other contingents.[76] In Olonisakin's interviews, a Nigerian officer explained that it was 'disheartening to note that of all the contingents in Ops. Liberty the Nigerian contingent is the most badly turned out.'[77] A rank-and-file Nigerian soldier stated, 'When I arrived here [Liberia], a Guinean soldier was kind enough to give me one of his uniforms. Although it was a bigger size, it was better than what I had. Other countries do not have this problem of uniform.'[78]

In a military context, uniforms are much more than assigned clothing. Generally, military uniforms are seen as being earned, with individuals not allowed to wear the full uniform until passing a certain level of training. There are often strict protocols on how to wear uniforms, and those who wear their uniforms incorrectly face being disciplined. There is usually a high level of pride associated with military uniforms, and to be denied uniforms or to be given poor-quality uniforms is likely to be demoralising.

Insight into the conditions of other soldiers in the ECOMOG mission led to dissatisfaction in a variety of other areas. A former Gambian soldier argued that the Gambian contingent was undertrained compared with other West African soldiers, and that other countries were more prepared to deal with casualties.[79] Additionally, during the ECOMOG mission, Nigerian troops frequently complained that the Ghanaian troops were eating better than they.[80] Morale within the ECOMOG force further declined when the UN and the United States funded troops from East Africa to join an 'expanded' ECOMOG. These East African troops received three times the original ECOMOG pay, as well as better provisions.[81]

Within the UN, there has been some acknowledgement that the variations in peacekeeping pay can cause tensions. However, it is a politically sensitive topic because it is generally seen as a sovereign right for states to choose how they will use the UN reimbursement funds. The Senior Advisory Group for Rates of Reimbursement to Troop-Contributing Countries proposed that some of the welfare funds should be paid directly to the troops, not to the contributing countries. The UN General Assembly accepted this recommendation in 2013, but 'the sums involved are small: $2.76 per month per contingent member for Internet and $6.31 per month per contingent member for welfare'.[82] The vast majority of reimbursements for uniformed personnel, including the monthly per troop reimbursement rate, 'thus remain reserved for states to be allocated according to their internal policies'.[83]

Lastly, the introduction of new technologies has made it easier than ever for peacekeepers to stay in touch with other contingents during and after the deployment. This also makes it easier to continue to compare conditions with soldiers from other countries. In interviews with dozens of peacekeepers on the AMISOM mission, nearly all said they still had some level of contact with peacekeepers from other countries through social media accounts.[84] Soldiers explained that they had set up Facebook and WhatsApp groups to keep in touch with colleagues they had met on peacekeeping missions. When Sierra Leonean peacekeepers returned from AMISOM, rumours began to circulate within the battalion that the soldiers were due more than they had received. Numerous soldiers told me that they 'verified' that this was true by asking their Kenyan colleagues via social media what they were paid upon returning home. As noted earlier, a direct comparison of pay between different countries will usually uncover discrepancies due to the way peacekeeping is funded. Yet soldiers are often unaware of the nuances of peacekeeping pay. In this case, soldiers seemed to trust their foreign colleagues more than their superiors. Other soldiers also explained that they contacted their colleagues located at other bases using their mobile phones and WhatsApp accounts during the peacekeeping mission to find out about the 'R&R' (rest and recuperation) policies across different units.

Cohesion and division

Whereas the previous sections have described the types of grievances that often develop during deployments, it is also possible that the deployment setting contributes to the development of a mutiny by altering the dynamics of the unit. In the most basic sense, deployed soldiers are physically separated from the larger military organisation. Units may feel freer to discuss or plan a mutiny away from the watchful eyes of their senior hierarchy. Beyond the issue of distance from their home bases, deployments can lead to strong group cohesion.[85] During deployments, 'members are immediately known to each other and their actions are interdependent, mutually supporting, and reciprocal'.[86] Soldiers deployed together are in constant contact with each other, not only during intense combat situations but also during the long mundane downtime, which inevitably occurs on deployments. In more recent years, with the increase in peacekeeping missions, units will often spend months together before the deployment in preparatory training. These shared experiences of hardships as well as the consistent close proximity often create close interpersonal bonds between members of the unit that may be absent or weakened when stationed at home.

Military scholars regularly discuss cohesion in relation to its ability to create more efficient and motivated units. Anthony King claims that there is a common presumption that the close personal relationships formed within cohesive units 'generate good performances because it motivates the individual members to fight'.[87] However, he also draws on various studies that show a darker side to cohesion, one that can motivate individuals to take part in deviant behaviour. The close bonds can cause the group to subvert or ignore their authorities as well as their obligation to the organisation. Guy Siebold argues that highly cohesive units may be particularly likely to disobey orders when 'peer bonding is strong and bonding with leaders is poor'.[88] The deployment experience can increase peer bonding as well as the divisions between the deployed soldiers and their leadership based at home, increasing the likelihood of disobedience. King cites cases of Western mutinies involving French and Australian troops during the First World War and US troops during the Vietnam War among his various examples of deviant military behaviour among combat units.[89] African deployment-related mutinies, which are also likely to have been affected by increased group cohesion, can be added to this list of indiscipline.

Mutinies are a unique dynamic in that they often involve a strong bond within the group as well as a level of detachment from the larger organisation. Mutinies require trust within the group, as the group as a whole must have faith that the individuals will stick together during negotiations or a potential counter-attack. Shared deployment experiences may enhance this trust. However, in addition to the increased group cohesion, the experience may also lead to feelings of division, isolation and dissatisfaction in the larger military hierarchy. The division between those that have been deployed and those that have not also follows the rank structure, as combat deployments consist mostly of rank-and-file soldiers led by junior officers. This division builds on the often significant economic divisions between the junior ranks and senior officers in West Africa, as described in Chapters 2 and 3.

As noted earlier in this chapter, during interviews and casual conversations rank-and-file soldiers generally spoke highly of those that had been on deployments, particularly deployments that involved combat conditions. However, they also gave negative statements about senior officers who had no deployment experience. In the case of Sierra Leone, detailed in the next chapter, there seemed to be a type of alternative rank structure that revolved around combat experience.

Olonisakin arrived at a similar finding from her interviews with Nigerian peacekeepers following the ECOMOG mission to Liberia. According to Olonisakin, when the peacekeepers returned home, there was a strain between them and their fellow comrades. She notes that the peacekeepers'

> views were influenced largely by their experience during [peace] enforcement. Believing themselves to have been 'battle-tested' by the Liberian mission, many of them considered their contemporaries at home 'inexperienced.' Indeed, some considered themselves to be not only better soldiers than their own contemporaries, but also superior to many officers at home who had no experience in battle.[90]

This kind of 'unified division' may be particularly explosive when combined with the deployment selection process in some African states. For example, President Sani Abacha in Nigeria was accused of having used 'ECOMOG postings to get rid of troublesome units and officers'.[91] This pattern extends beyond Nigeria to other states with bloated militaries. Multinational missions can serve as a 'release valve' by stationing a portion of the military outside the country for a period of time.[92] This type of selection process is likely to be particularly risky in relation to mutinies, as soldiers who are already wary of the government or the military hierarchy may become further discontented by unfulfilled expectations from the mission.

Conclusion

The grievances soldiers express following deployments are similar to those in other mutinies in the dataset, as both involve complaints over conditions of service and feelings of perceived injustice. However, the deployment setting brings a heightened importance to the grievances. Many of the more vague complaints about military neglect take on a practical importance during deployments, as inadequate equipment or logistics on a deployment can threaten soldiers' lives. Soldiers also expect more pay owing to the increased hardships and risk involved in deployments. They also seem to find particular offence in delayed payments for combat veterans. While hierarchies may be able to fulfil the expectations of soldiers when based at home, the heightened expectations and complications that come with deployments often prove to be too much for the chain of command. The basic expectations of soldiers that they will be taken care of, as well as the heightened expectations of increased pay, are often unfulfilled and thus come to symbolise a break in the implicit contract between soldiers and their superiors. Disobedience through mutiny becomes easier to justify in light of the unfulfilled obligations of their leaders.

Deployments on multinational missions in particular create new avenues for perceptions of injustice. Soldiers are able to compare their situations directly with those from other countries. When they compare living conditions, pay, uniforms and equipment with their foreign colleagues, there are bound to be discrepancies. Soldiers often alter their views of their own conditions and treatment in comparison with others. Involvement in multinational missions is profitable for the contributing state and can lead to new opportunities for corruption or new opportunities to perceive corruption, especially when there is little transparency in how the added income is used.

A key theme in this book is how mutinies are often used as a form of communication between junior soldiers and their superiors. Yet this chapter has also shown that miscommunication can contribute to mutinies. Soldiers who mutiny following deployments often express resentment that they were misled about aspects of the deployment. Soldiers frequently complain that their pay is less than they anticipated or that their deployment tour was longer than expected. In these cases, clearer communication down the chain of command would reduce the tensions as many of the expectations (particularly in relation to pay) appear to be based on rumour rather than military guidance.

The number of multinational peace operations continues to increase and does not appear to have a near-term conclusion. Most UN missions and UN peacekeepers are located on the African continent, and added to these are missions by the African Union and sub-regional organisations.[93] As a result, there are numerous opportunities for African soldiers to be involved in multinational operations. My findings do not suggest that countries contributing to peacekeeping missions must brace themselves for a revolt upon their return. The number of peacekeeping troop contributions far outweighs the number of peacekeeping mutinies. However, the chapter has identified a number of common grievances that have sparked mutinies by peacekeepers from various states and provides lessons for those aiming to improve the effectiveness of international peace operations.

The pattern of deployment-related mutinies should not be seen as merely linked to the number of deployed troops. Instead, the deployment grievances build on existing tensions and suspicions between the senior and junior ranks in many militaries in the region. Deployments, and peacekeeping deployments in particular, may provide new avenues for material grievances, but the underlying accusations against the senior military hierarchy are part of a wider regional and historic narrative.

6

A COUP HIDDEN IN A MUTINY

CASE STUDY OF SIERRA LEONE

On the morning of 29 April 1992, around fifty soldiers entered the capital of Sierra Leone, Freetown, and staged a revolt against President Momoh. By mid-afternoon, the president had fled the city, and Sierra Leoneans found out they were now being ruled by a twenty-seven-year-old military captain. There is little agreement in the academic literature or media reporting on whether the action should be described as a coup or a mutiny. This chapter will provide new details on the events that day as well as how the plan to revolt developed. The case study presented in the chapter will show that the confusion over what to label the incident is understandable, as even the soldiers involved had different ideas of the goals of their actions. The rank-and-file soldiers believed they were headed to the capital to ask for payment arrears, while the officers had a more ambitious plan to overthrow the government. This case study builds on the discussion of the differences between coups and mutinies presented in Chapter 2.

A brief history of the role of the military in Sierra Leone leading up to the events in 1992 will help contextualise the soldiers' grievances. The ceremonial role of the Sierra Leone military and a culture of political and familial recruitment had disastrous effects when the military was tasked with countering the rebel force known as the Revolutionary United Front (RUF). The chapter will then examine the internal dynamics of a specific unit, the Tiger unit, as most of the individuals involved in the revolt were from this unit. The hardship conditions endured in the fight against the RUF both bonded this combat unit together and caused its members to resent their senior hierarchy and political leaders. Their complaints and suspicions crystallised into a plan for a mutiny and ultimately resulted in a coup. The 1992 revolt did not ease military tensions but rather created further divisions, which contributed to two more coups within five years.

It has been over twenty-five years since the 1992 revolt and much has changed; however, according to military interviewees, some sectors of the Sierra Leonean military still see a mutiny in their future. The last part of the chapter will describe more recent grievances and outline the ways in which soldiers have used various tactics to open a dialogue with the political and military leadership about their treatment. Some of the key complaints among current soldiers involve peacekeeping pay. Compared with most of its neighbours, Sierra Leone is a newcomer to peacekeeping operations. Just months into its involvement in the AMISOM mission, Sierra Leonean soldiers had already begun to express many of the common grievances among peacekeepers, as described in the previous chapter, and had threatened to revolt.

The shifting role of the military

By 1992, the Sierra Leone military was no stranger to political interventions. Between independence in 1961 and the events in 1992, the military had carried out two coups, a counter-coup and several other unsuccessful attempts or plots.[1] These coups and attempted coups often put senior officers in close contact with politicians, which shaped the development of the officer corps and affected general military recruitment.

In the early independence years, it was common for political elites to serve as patrons for individual army officers.[2] Furthermore, 'in order for the client, the army officer, to rise in the hierarchy of his own organization, it was necessary for him to acquire the benevolent support of a civilian mentor'.[3] Thomas Cox relates this patron–client relationship to the prevalence of coups, counter-coups and coup attempts because military personnel had a vested interest in having their patrons stay in power or come to power. The importance of these personalised links within the officer ranks undermined the integrity of the officer corps. Individual officers were seen as receiving promotions, appointments or material gains based on personal ties, rather than merit. The highly personal way in which benefits were received within the military also led to highly personalised rivalries within the officer corps.[4] Thus the officer corps in Sierra Leone did not have a strong professional code or apolitical identity. It was not a cohesive group and 'remained a "corps" in name only'.[5]

The mixed loyalties within the military were especially apparent during President Siaka Stevens' time in office between 1967 and 1985. Stevens' tumultuous relationship with the military started as soon as he was elected in 1967, given that he was immediately ousted by the military just hours after he was sworn into office. However, he was reinstated the following year when junior military members overthrew their seniors in what is popularly called the 'Sergeants' Revolt'. The junior soldiers announced that they had ousted their military superiors because 'the rank and file of the army and police have been ignored'.[6] 'Stevens seemed to take note of this complaint and initially rewarded the junior ranks of the military: the military budget increased by around one-third within two years of the 1968 revolt.[7] Even when the military handed control back to Stevens, the rank-and-file soldiers demanded that the officers remain in jail. Stevens acceded and most of the officers remained locked away for nine month to a year after the coup, at which point only a fraction were reinstated.[8] The junior ranks' insistence on keeping the officers in prison symbolised the distrust between the rank-and-file soldiers and the officer corps at the time. This same distrust among ranks would fuel the coups of the 1990s.

While Stevens was initially grateful for the support he received from the junior ranks, the honeymoon period had ended by 1971 when soldiers attacked Stevens' house in a coup attempt. Several of the perpetrators were the same individuals who had helped bring him to power just three years earlier.[9] A second attempt occurred three years later. Thirteen soldiers were executed for their involvement in these attacks and dozens more were arrested, establishing a strong precedent for future soldiers thinking of attempting a coup.[10]

As a result of these threats, Stevens began to turn away from the military in favour of the police and foreign military assistance, with his regime signing a defence agreement with Guinea whereby Guinean troops were sent to Freetown to guard Stevens against his own military. He also negotiated an agreement for Cuba to train a paramilitary force called the Internal Security Unit (ISU).[11] The ISU became the most cared for, as well as the most feared, part of the state's security apparatus and took on many of the missions previously given to the military.[12] From this point onwards, the Sierra Leone military took on a largely ceremonial role.[13] The size of the military was intentionally kept small and little funding was available for updating equipment or training. This marginalisation of the military severely affected the ability of the Sierra Leone army to counter rebel forces when they attacked in 1991.

At the same time that the vast majority of the military was cast aside, the top ranks had become more embedded in the political system. This culminated in Stevens' appointment of General Momoh to parliament in 1974.[14] While Stevens saw the military as a potential risk to his rule, he was also aware that the complete isolation of the military would increase this threat.

After seventeen years in power, Stevens stepped down in 1985 and left General Momoh to lead the All People's Congress (APC).[15] That same year, General Momoh won a general election in which he was the only candidate.[16] Momoh inherited a one-party state with a bankrupt treasury. Although once seen as a successful military leader, Momoh was largely viewed as an inept political leader with a blind loyalty to Stevens.[17] He did little to change his reputation or the inherent corruption that riddled state institutions. By 1990, Sierra Leone was ranked the poorest country in the world, despite the state's significant reserves of natural resources.[18]

By the late 1980s, Sierra Leone, like other states throughout the continent, was under pressure to reduce government spending, and as part of the austerity measures subsidies were cut.[19] This had a severe effect on the average citizen, as the price of fuel increased by 300 per cent and the cost of rice by 180 per cent between 1989 and 1990.[20] Civil servants and teachers often went unpaid, and by the early 1990s much of the professional class had left the country.[21] Around the same time, Momoh encountered growing internal and external pressures to end the one-party political system.[22] Student activist groups had become increasingly vocal in opposing Stevens and then Momoh. At least two of the officers (Lt Tom Nyuma and Lt Komba Mondeh) involved in the revolt in 1992 had been members of the activist group Pan African Union (PANAFU) and had participated in rallies before joining the army.[23] Additionally, nearly every newspaper edition from around 1989 to 1991 featured details of corruption and government incompetence, which further eroded the confidence of citizens in the government.[24] The frustrations of the civilian population were not lost on the soldiers involved in the 1992 coup, as they addressed many of these issues in their speeches explaining why they had taken power.[25]

It was against this backdrop of economic failure and deep-seated anger at government inefficiency and corruption that the RUF began its attack on Sierra Leone in 1991. The RUF was a rebel group led by Foday Sankoh, a former corporal in the Sierra Leone army who had been arrested and discharged from the military for his alleged involvement in the coup attempt against Stevens in 1971.[26] The RUF had links with the National Patriotic Front of Liberia (NPFL), led by Charles Taylor, but its goals were also specific to the conditions in Sierra Leone at the time.[27] When the RUF first attacked eastern Sierra Leone in March 1991, President Momoh sent Sierra Leonean military units to the east to counter the attacks. Few of the soldiers had any combat experience and most of the unit was expected to switch from a largely ceremonial force to a combat-capable unit almost overnight.

The Tigers are tested

The Tiger and Cobra units were among the first Sierra Leonean units tasked with countering the RUF. The experience of these soldiers against the RUF proved to be severely demoralising, and within a year of the beginning of the mission members of the groups led a revolt against the government. Most of those involved were from the Tiger unit, with a smaller number of Cobras.

By 1992, the army continued to 'serve as a major instrument of patrimonial favour'.[28] The officers of the Tiger unit were not immune to this system. For example, Captain Valentine Strasser, a leader in the Tiger unit, was brought into the military by a former APC minister, Thaimu Bangura.[29] However, not all clients in a patronage system are equal, and the leaders of the Tiger unit found themselves with much less political clout than their senior officers who had stronger ties to the ruling APC. The Tiger officers' assignment to the war front contrasted with the comfortable postings and fringe benefits that the more senior officers stationed in Freetown received. Furthermore, the government kept the military intentionally small (estimated at 3,000 to 4,000 personnel), and thus there was limited room for advancement.[30]

The small size of the military combined with limited employment opportunities also made joining as a rank-and-file soldier a coveted opportunity. Individuals who were enlisted in the military in the late 1980s explained that they were able to join because a family member or friend had given them a card.[31] In other words, individuals needed to know someone in the system or with ties to the system to be accepted. This furthered the trend of loyalties to individuals rather than the military institution or state. There was little adherence to the formal military hierarchy among both the enlisted and officer ranks.

Before 1991, most officers and rank-and-file soldiers had established some type of connection that had earned them a place in the military. However, this changed after the initial attacks by the RUF in 1991, when the government decided to increase the size of the armed forces. By the end of 1991, the military had grown to around 7,000 personnel.[32] Yet in the haste to boost personnel, the recruits were processed quickly and given minimal training before their assignments, and some of them were sent to join the Tiger unit. Many of the rank-and-file Tiger interviewees explained that they had only received basic training by the time the revolt had broken out, and one soldier even stated that he was still receiving his initial training when news broke of the rebel attack: 'So that day they gather us, distributed weapons to us, and that very day we deploy to Sangha. At that time, I [did not know much] about the army.'[33] Another soldier also highlighted the lack of proper training: 'at the time, I never knew my role. In 1991 to 1998 I never knew the roles of the Republic of Sierra Leone armed forces. It is only now that I know our roles and responsibilities.'[34] Many of these young soldiers' military experience was limited to this one unit. Their officers in the Tiger unit were the only military leadership they had ever worked under.

In many ways, this was a unit with few ties to the larger military structure, operating in a location and under conditions isolated from the rest of the military. The rank-and-file soldiers had a strong sense of loyalty to their unit's leadership, which seemed to develop around the hardship conditions. When asked about Captain Strasser's traits as a leader of the Tiger unit, one of his subordinates explained that he was a good commander 'because he had foresight, he used to encourage us in terms of difficulty, when we have casualty he sit around and sympathise with us. He used to take money from his pocket to buy marijuana, to motivate you.'[35] Another rank-and-file member of the unit recalled that Strasser 'was a good military leader because he always takes care of us, always tries to order equipment for us, have our rations on time'.[36] The enlisted soldiers described Lieutenant Solomon Musa, another leader of the unit, in similar terms via statements such as 'He cared about everybody, how they are doing.'[37] These remarks show that the enlisted soldiers' high esteem for their immediate supervisors was personal; they viewed their superiors as being responsible for their basic needs and in many ways their lives. No interviewee ever mentioned any particular military skills as a reason for their respect for their leaders.

The emphasis on the personal bonds with their officers stood in contrast to how many saw the senior hierarchy in Freetown, whom they had no contact and, no commonalities and no reason to trust. One rank-and-file soldier discussing the senior leadership stated: 'In those days we are having leaders who just do things on their own ... they never come down and see the ordinary soldier. You never see a commander.'[38] When the officers of the Tiger unit proposed a mutiny, it is likely that the rank-and-file soldiers saw the action less as an attack on the larger chain of command and more as an act of loyalty and solidarity to the only chain of command they really knew.

There was little difference in the background or qualifications of the junior officers and the enlisted soldiers serving under them. None of the officers or enlisted soldiers I spoke to had received any higher education at the time they joined the military. Several of the rank-and-file soldiers spoke of their personal relationships with the officers in the unit, whom they knew before joining the military. One rank-and-file soldier from the Tiger unit explained that an officer in the unit was, and still is, his 'very best friend'.[39] They were raised in the same region, joined the military together and have both served ever since. Despite their similar backgrounds, the officer had an older brother in the military, which helped facilitate his commission to the officer rank. These types of stories show that in many cases the distinctions between junior officers and enlisted were minimal in terms of background, education, age or experience.

The Tigers were not strictly an elite unit, but they had an honourable reputation within the military as one of the few 'battle-tested' units in Sierra Leone. In addition to distinguishing themselves by their combat experiences, members of the unit wore different scarves from the rest of the military as an expression of their unit's identity. One soldier fondly told me that, after the coup, all the civilian youth 'wanted to be a Tiger, everyone was wearing our muffler'.[40] However, the current military leadership may have realised that creating a separate identity within the military had negative effects and has since stopped using titles such as 'Tigers' and 'Cobras'. While on various bases in Sierra Leone, I was occasionally reprimanded by soldiers when asking if they had been a part of those units. One soldier told me 'we don't use those names anymore, they are divisive'.[41]

Members of the unit came from all parts of the country, although Freetown was the area most highly represented in the unit, a trait that made the soldiers especially popular among Freetown youth when they came to power. Their bond was thus not one based on shared ethnicity or regional background, but had instead been formed through shared experiences on deployment. Like most units deployed together, the Tigers spent large amounts of time together, both downtime and moments of danger, in an environment isolated from much of the hierarchy. Their group provides a strong example of the potential for increased unit cohesion as a result of deployments, as described in Chapter 5.

The strong group cohesion that formed within the Tigers was necessary for survival, as the decades of intentional neglect in updating the military quickly took its toll on the mission. The units on the eastern border did not have the weapons, equipment or training to engage adequately with the RUF. Even the commander of the Sierra Leone military at the time later admitted that the military and political leadership did not adequately prepare for the RUF rebellion:

> I will confess that at the time the rebels started in March 1991, we were really caught with our pants down. The strength of the army was small—a little above the colonial legacy—and arms and logistics inadequate, all a result of the economic difficulties the country had been enduring through over the years.[42]

Similarly, in testimony to the Truth and Reconciliation Commission in 2003, Brigadier (Ret.) Kellie Conteh explained that, at the time, the army was operating with less than 30 per cent of its transport needs and less than 20 per cent of its support equipment, and much essential equipment was simply non-existent.[43]

It had long been the government's policy to limit soldiers' access to ammunition, out of fear that they would use it in a coup attempt.[44] This policy is understandable in times of peace, but it was life-threatening in a time of war. Soldiers recall constantly being short of ammunition while battling the rebels. One soldier explained, 'When we were fighting we were only given twenty rounds, rebels were using hundreds a day.'[45] Another member of the unit similarly complained: 'Before 1992, we were not well catered for, you have twenty rounds, they only give you twenty rounds of ammunition to challenge a whole enemy who will come with everything they have.'[46]

Furthermore, the weapons issued were outdated and not conducive to the fight.[47] Media reports at the time note that the Sierra Leone soldiers, with bolt-action, breech-loading rifles, had no chance against the rebels armed with automatic weapons.[48] In the words of one officer in the unit, 'In 1991 when the war broke out, at that time the military was nothing to talk about. When we started with the RUF, soldiers are just using rifle, no AK47, no RPG, no mortar.'[49] There was also only a limited supply of vehicles, and soldiers lacked basics such as socks and boots.[50] As the conflict dragged on, there was irregular and inadequate resupply. Soldiers complained that their food rations were limited, with some stating that they often had no food. The units experienced several casualties, and little medical care was available for those that survived. In the words of Strasser, who was injured by shrapnel from rebel-fired mortars,[51] 'the worst part was there were no paramedics, no drugs, no blood.'[52]

Soldiers were clearly dismayed by the lack of adequate training, food, equipment and proper medical services. These grievances were compounded by the failure of the unit to be paid for months on end. Every soldier interviewed commented on the pay issue. Even when they were paid, the soldiers found the salary to be offensively low for the risks they were taking. These complaints demonstrate the altered expectations that often form on deployments.

The pay issue became especially incendiary when President Momoh publicly announced that his government was spending 1.2 billion leones a month (US $2 million) on rations and logistics for the war.[53] The stark contrast between Momoh's statement and the reality for the soldiers on the ground led many soldiers to believe that the money meant for them was actually being diverted into the pockets of the politicians and military leaders at the top. In their minds, not only were they suffering the hardships of war but others were profiting from it, which created a strong sense of injustice. This perception was mirrored in the civilian population, which was also expressing anger at government corruption.

From objections to actions

That the conditions on the eastern front were extremely difficult is beyond dispute, and the bitterness of the soldiers towards their situation was consequently understandable. However, nearly all published accounts fail to explain how the unit decided to take their complaints to the capital and how they executed their plan. These details are worth examining more closely, as they can help explain how a mutiny forms at a tactical level.

Many media and academic reports on the event of 29 April 1992 describe it as a mutiny or a protest.[54] The oft-told story is that the soldiers fighting on the eastern front were fed up with the conditions and decided to voice their complaints to the government in the form of a protest at State House.[55] Some accounts describe how the unit initially engaged in discussions with President Momoh before rebelling when the negotiations did not go in the soldiers' favour.[56]

The account I received while interviewing the soldiers is a more nuanced story. The officers leading the supposed mutiny assert that they never planned to negotiate with political leaders; from the start, their goal was to overthrow the government. However, the enlisted soldiers explained that they firmly believed they were going to the capital to protest over their pay and conditions. They were only told by the officers at the last minute that the order was to attack rather than mutiny.

The Tiger unit was based in Kailahun, while the Cobras were in Kenema, but the officers occasionally met at a bar near the Daru headquarters to discuss the war situation. It was over drinks at this local establishment that the officers hatched their plans.[57] In an interview, Strasser explained that he and the other officers had been discussing the coup for close to a year. When further questioned about the riskiness of such a plan, he replied, 'Yes, it was a problem, if it got out we would end in death. The ones that saw the problems first hand, that were deployed together, they could be trusted.'[58] Strasser's remarks suggest a close bond within the unit as a result of their time together in difficult conditions. Despite Strasser's statement about trusting those with whom he was deployed, the officers were cautious about allowing too many people to learn of the plan, in particular the rank-and-file soldiers. Hence, rather than revealing the true plan, the officers instead proposed a mutiny. They laid out their common grievances and suggested they all go together to Freetown to protest over their conditions and demand their overdue salaries.

When recounting the discussion proposing the mutiny, the rank-and-file soldiers seemed unsure of whether joining was a personal decision by each soldier or an order by officers. One soldier said 'it was not an order, just a conversation between everybody. And they say who wants to go and most of us say we are going.'[59] However, others explained that they were told to get in a truck (by Lt Tom Nyuma specifically) and only later found out where they were going.[60] Considering that the soldiers came from different units (Tigers and Cobras), it is possible that both stories are accurate. Several soldiers note that the only person to refuse, a fellow officer, was arrested on the spot. A corporal from the unit recounted that

> only one major ... in Kenema, refused to join. So he was arrested by the officers. He refused to join, he said soldiers don't strike, when soldiers strike is becomes coup. And that is why he refused to join, so he was arrested and loaded into the truck and came with us.[61]

It is unlikely that any of the rank-and-file soldiers would have refused to take part, and all the soldiers that were interviewed seemed to have supported the idea of a mutiny. That the arrested soldier was a major is significant, as it means he outranked the other officers present, thereby illustrating the bond between the enlisted soldiers and the junior officers (most lieutenants at the time). The rank-and-file soldiers appear to have supported the junior officers rather than the more senior officer.

When asked if they knew that the mission to Freetown was designed to overthrow the government, the enlisted soldiers all gave similar variations of 'no':

A COUP HIDDEN IN A MUTINY

Ration was low on the war front, salary was so small so this is why they say let's go to Freetown and arrest the officers. But we don't know it was a coup, later the mission changed.

Well initially we never knew what was going to happen. When we reached Freetown we were told 'gentlemen this is a life or death mission, be prepared to fight.' We did our best and we succeeded.

No, we did not know it was going to be a coup, we thought it would be a strike action.

We did not know any motive.

No, they don't tell us that. They don't inform anybody about a coup.

I was surprised! Because that was not the mission I heard about. I heard about the rations.

We were fighting, no proper medication, not enough rations, because of that the commanders organised that we would go to Freetown to ask for those.

At that time, our wives and relatives are staying down in Freetown and are not getting our rations, like rice. Salaries we are not getting in time. We decided we should come down and ask for those things. Not knowing that it was a coup to topple APC.

The officers confirm that they misled the enlisted soldiers. One officer explained: 'When we left Daru nobody knew what was the intention ... it was a hidden agenda to overthrow the APC government. They say they are going to demand salaries but actually the hidden intent behind the whole issue was to overthrow the government.'[62]

The disconnect between the account of the officers and those of the rank and file raises questions over whether the mission was an 'accidental' coup or whether the officers simply did not want to tell the rank and file the real intention. The officers insist that the latter is the case. It is possible that the officers were trying to save face by suggesting the event went exactly according to their plan. Still, the trajectory of the actions on 29 April, as described in the next section, does seem to suggest a plan beyond requesting payment arrears. Successful coups rely on secrecy, and it is possible that they were attempting to limit the number of people who knew of the plan.[63] Moreover, if the coup had failed, they could have claimed that their actions were just a mutiny, which is typically considered a lesser crime than a coup within a military court martial.

Despite misleading their subordinates, the proposed mutiny shows there was a level of trust between officers and the rank and file in this particular unit. Organising a mutiny could have meant arrests or worse for the officers if any soldier had informed the senior military hierarchy. Three days passed between the enlisted soldiers being informed of the plan to mutiny and the revolt itself, giving ample time for any of them to inform others. Furthermore, those that stayed in the east were also aware that their colleagues had gone to Freetown for the stated goal of making demands to the top military hierarchy.[64] Yet despite these soldiers knowing the plan and being aware of its illegality under military law, no one seems to have leaked the secret, as the soldiers stationed in Freetown admit to having been completely surprised. It is also possible that the lack of operational information leaks had to do with a lack of mobile phones and radios at the time. This type of secret would likely be harder to keep with today's technology.

Operation Mutiny becomes Operation Coup

Academic and media reporting tends to downplay the logistics involved in this operation, often stating that the soldiers simply marched to the capital. However, this is not accurate; nor would it have been possible for the soldiers to march the 250-mile distance. The top logistical concern was how to get from their location in eastern Sierra Leone to the capital, a long route made especially time-consuming given the poor road infrastructure. The soldiers were aware that their plan might not be supported by all of the military, and they were especially concerned about the checkpoints. A group of fifty soldiers arriving at any checkpoint would cause suspicion. They explained that some members of the unit travelled together in military vehicles and attire with a pre-prepared story that they were travelling to Freetown to report on the logistics concerns on the war front. Another version of the story was that they were travelling with their weapons to have them repaired in Freetown. Most of the men wore civilian clothes and travelled in stolen civilian vehicles in order to avoid raising the alarm.[65]

The unit met up on the outskirts of Freetown on 26 April. They had initially planned to conduct the revolt the next day, but they changed their plans upon realising that festivities were planned for Sierra Leone's independence day on 27 April. The officers rescheduled the mission for 29 April. This was one of the several points at which the soldiers seemed aware and concerned about how civilians would perceive their actions. Another example is that they conducted the attack early in the morning, when fewer people would be on the streets. There was also a strategic aspect to this decision, since fewer people meant less vehicle or foot traffic to obscure the routes and fewer people to notice irregular military movements.

A COUP HIDDEN IN A MUTINY

The responsibilities for securing vehicles and ammunition were divided between various officers. The plan involved capturing six key locations throughout the city. An officer from the unit explained: 'The first step was State House, the first attack was State House. The second Upgun Roundabout, the third site was the Pademba Road prison. The fourth site was the radio station, the fifth was the military headquarters, and the sixth was FBC [Fourah Bay College].'[66]

The soldiers never had to enact the full six steps, as the government was almost immediately toppled. However, the plan suggests that the officers were never intending to mutiny; they were geared for a full attack. True to their war experiences, the officers concocted a military plan that covered major strategic locations as well as a primary entry and exit point of the city.

Even upon entering Freetown on the morning of 29 April, the rank-and-file soldiers still thought they were going to hold a protest. They learned of the real plan as they approached State House. According to one rank-and-file soldier:

> To our surprise they tell us we are to attack State House. We start asking ourselves what are we here for. They tell us we are to ask for our rations and now they say we are to attack State House. But we are young soldiers and we work for our commanders.[67]

Several other soldiers provided similar accounts. The enlisted soldiers explained their surprise and fear at the sudden escalation in plans. When asked what he thought about the order to attack State House, one enlisted soldier said:

> I wanted to run away but there was no way ... I was a young soldier and it is a big thing, a coup. When someone says 'coup' I think 'AHHHH' [exclaiming surprise and fear], you see? But it was a command, if I ran away I would be arrested. It was do or die, you see?[68]

This soldier felt little concern over the plan to mutiny but found the coup idea much more serious and stressful, suggesting that there is a clear distinction between the two events in the eyes of soldiers.

Despite the surprise of the order, the soldiers obeyed and fired on State House and into the air. They also used rocket-propelled grenades. Media reports noted the weapons used during the attack and questioned whether the soldiers were really as ill-equipped as they claimed. However, soldiers interviewed alleged they acquired the better weapons upon arriving in Freetown. Everyone interviewed, including soldiers stationed in Freetown during the time, agreed that the attack came as a complete shock. A soldier involved in the attack recounts:

> We crawled right up to the main gate at State House. We fired, the town soldiers were not used to that sound, it was their first time to hear that weapon, so they started running. We chased them and seized them and distributed their ammunition. That is how we are able to capture State House that day.[69]

Another soldier put it more bluntly: 'The Freetown soldiers are cowards, that is how we are able to win.'[70] The language these soldiers used demonstrates the way in which the Tigers differentiated themselves from soldiers who had not deployed, a trait common in deployed units and a trend discussed in relation to honour in the previous chapter. Although they were all in the same organisation, the members of the Tiger unit called the other soldiers 'town soldiers' and discussed their inexperience with weapons and perceived lack of bravery.

There were small pockets of resistance, but most of the soldiers guarding State House did not stick around to fight. Even the respected SSD (formerly known as ISU) did not counter the attack.[71] By mid-afternoon on 29 April 1992, Captain Strasser came on the national radio and announced that President Momoh had been overthrown. This was the first time the majority of Sierra Leoneans had ever heard of Strasser. Although initially part of the Tigers, he had been moved to Freetown because of his injury on the warfront, and he did not travel with the troops from the east. Strasser was, however, involved in the early planning and possibly in coordination on the day of the attack.

In many ways, Strasser was an unlikely candidate to lead a coup. First, he was not the brains behind the plan, as explained by the officers involved. That title went to Lt 'Saj' Musa, who, in words of one soldier, was 'the whole machine behind it'; another soldier described Musa as 'the mastermind' behind the operation. Furthermore, Strasser did not have a distinctive educational background or any international experience (save for his time with ECOMOG in Liberia). He was never described as charismatic or eloquent. Strasser was not from a prominent family, and at twenty-seven years old he certainly did not have age on his side. Every individual, including Strasser, explained that the reason he was chosen as leader was his rank, which was the highest among the junior officers involved. Had they chosen a leader based on charisma, popularity or leadership skills, their choice would probably have been Musa (who became vice president under the military junta).[72] The adherence to military hierarchy in selecting the junta leader, and the obedience of the rank and file towards their immediate supervisors during the revolt, are examples of what Luckham calls the 'remarkable power of military norms in the midst of revolt'.[73] The soldiers were breaking many norms within military doctrine, but they did not seem comfortable acting outside of the chain of command within their own group.

In contrast to the media reports at the time, the soldiers never sat down with President Momoh to discuss their complaints; nor does it appear that the officers wanted to. According to one of the officers:

> President Momoh wanted to prey on the weak. We are from the warfront, we are battle-tested officers, we have tasted the bitterness of war. This is not a tribal mark [showing a large scar on his chest], this is a gun mark. For anything we do we will have to pay the price and the price will be life. So we don't have to compromise. When we enter the city we do not have to compromise on anything again.[74]

This statement reveals a heightened sense of entitlement based on the hardships endured in the combat mission against the RUF.

The plan as explained by the officers above, as well as Strasser's admission that it had been in the works for many months, counters popular media and academic accounts that claimed the revolt was accidental, spontaneous and disorganised.[75] It is possible to take a more cynical look at the officers' accounts and argue that they would be unlikely to admit that the coup had been an accident. However, if the officers are recreating the narrative, they have at least been consistent in doing so, as the story Strasser gave in the interview in 2011 is the same he told the media days after the event and similar to the accounts by other officers in the unit.[76]

'A change that changed little'[77]

The leaders of the revolt showed they were aware of the complaints within wider society and claimed their actions were largely in response to the call for change, rather than a response to their own poor conditions. This initially earned them a considerable amount of popularity, with Strasser attracting the nickname 'The Redeemer'. The one-party state had long fallen out of favour, and the young military officers were expected to bring new life to the system through their creation of the National Provisional Ruling Council (NPRC). Strasser's first speech to the public, made over the radio a day after the coup, used strong populist rhetoric and led many to compare him with other regional revolutionaries such as Flight Lieutenant Jerry Rawlings of Ghana or Captain Thomas Sankara of Burkina Faso.[78] However, these were comparisons he was never able to live up to, and the policies of the NPRC did not fulfil its promises of significant change.[79]

After the coup, many people idolised Strasser and other top members of the junta. Their style was imitated by youth throughout the country, and portraits of them were painted in the form of street art throughout the capital.[80] Although the enlisted soldiers had been deceived about the goal of the mission, none interviewed appeared bitter about it and several commented on feeling fortunate to have been involved in overthrowing Momoh. Several rank-and-file soldiers from the Tiger unit noted that they received immediate rewards for their involvement in the form of larger salaries and new postings in the capital. But this caused further divides in the military, as most of the top jobs and associated benefits went to the Tiger rank-and-file soldiers.[81] Thus a similar pattern that the Tigers had objected to was recreated when the NPRC came to power, only they were now the resented Freetown privileged.

Most members of the Tigers felt that their leadership had failed to make lasting changes for the military. One member of the unit stated: 'Some issues got better, some did not. Like one of the promises that was made by the NPRC was that they would provide accommodations for the soldiers, they were not able to.'[82] When asked about the benefits for the military after the NPRC came to power, a rank-and-file soldier responded:

> No benefits. Because they never succeeded. When they took office, they said the number one priority is to end the war and that was not done. The second one was to alleviate poverty, that was not done. The third is to bring the Sierra Leone army to standard welfare, in terms of training, logistics, and that was not achieved. So by this way, nothing was achieved.[83]

Although most soldiers agreed that they were disappointed with the lack of military changes made by the NPRC, they seemed less sure about whom to blame for the unfulfilled promises.[84] When soldiers talked about their grievances while in the east, they all pointed the finger at Momoh. Yet when similar grievances were expressed under the NPRC, they were often reluctant to blame their former unit leaders. Some were clear in stating that the decisions rested with Strasser, yet others continued to blame civilian politicians, alleging that 'Strasser was used by politicians.'[85] Another excused the junta's behaviour by stating 'it is because they are inexperienced. They are just junior military officers, none of them are graduates and they took some old politicians to advise them and they were given bad advice.'[86] Many of the soldiers noted their personal sacrifice during the mission to bring the NPRC to power and took the lack of continued benefits as an insult. Yet they still seemed reluctant to criticise one of their own. An interview with a rank-and-file member of the its exemplifies this point:

> Author: What were the benefits for your unit after the coup?
>
> Soldier: There were no benefits. In fact, Strasser deserted those that came to Freetown. Yes, he side-lined us. He side-lined us. Those that sacrificed their lives. We laid down our lives! But actually he was a good leader.
>
> Author: That seems contradictory to the statement about him side-lining you.
>
> Soldier: Well yes, but it was the other officers that were the problem. They failed to come down to our level and check. If he had come down and check, he would notice what was going on.[87]

With the politicians and older generation of officers out of the picture, the unit no longer had a common antagonist to rally against. When the revolt began, the unit was a cohesive group with shared complaints. When the coup proved successful, some members of the unit were among the most powerful in the country, while the majority were left with little to show for their efforts. These divisions took root and festered, and as the years of NRPC rule carried on, the officers began to turn on one another.

The RUF attacks, which members of the NPRC had experienced firsthand on the eastern border, continued and intensified under NPRC rule. In 1994, Strasser admitted that members of the military had contributed to the growing chaos, stating that around 20 per cent of the soldiers were disloyal.[88] The NPRC requested help from the UN and eventually hired outside private forces to assist, first the British-based Gurkha Security Guards (GSG) and later the South African-based Executive Outcomes (EO).[89] In 1996, Strasser's junta arrested him before forcing him out of the country. This internal coup was led by Lieutenant Maada Bio, one of the officers involved in carrying out the 1992 coup alongside Strasser. Bio gave in to popular demands for democratic elections, which brought an end to the NPRC after four years in power.[90]

The 1996 election was won by Ahmed Kabbah, who placed greater emphasis on using civilian militias to fight the rebels when it became clear that the military was failing at the job.[91] The largest among these civilian militias were the Kamajors, a group linked to traditional hunting guilds.[92] Kabbah expressed a clear distrust of the military, an extension of previous politicians' attitudes towards the military as well as a result of the behaviour of soldiers during NPRC rule. The military went from being the centre of power under the NPRC to fearing that the military as an institution would be disbanded and replaced with the civilian militias, which had become more institutionalised under the title Civilian Defence Force (CDF).[93] Furthermore, the militias and military were often in direct combat with each other.

It did not take long for the military to reassert its power, regaining control of the country just fourteen months after the election, this time through a coup led by two dozen heavily armed soldiers.[94] The anger and frustrations of the military were unleashed when the soldiers released prisoners from Pademba Road prison, who then ran rampant through the streets of Freetown alongside disgruntled military members.[95] Within a week of the coup, as many as 200 civilians had been killed.[96] Whereas the soldiers interviewed were generally comfortable, and in some ways even proud, when talking about the 1992 incident, the tone changed with the mention of 1997. None of the interviewees claimed any role in that event, and no one attempted to justify it. One officer passionately stated: 'If I want to be sincere within myself, I will pray to the almighty that that event would not be repeated. It was the worst we have ever seen. What we struggled for was lost ... everything was lost.'[97]

The new military leadership, under the title of the Armed Forces Revolutionary Council (AFRC), invited the RUF to join the military junta. The junta controlled the capital for the next eight months, until they were forced out by a combination of ECOMOG troops, Kamajors and loyal government soldiers.[98] Yet fighting continued, and the ensuing civil war did not come to an end until 2002.

Whereas there was a level of discipline and structure within the Tiger unit's revolt in 1992, by 1997 the military hierarchy had completely broken down. It is possible to see the 1992 events as setting the stage for what happened in 1997. The coup in 1992 created further division in the already-fractured military and further complicated the role of the military in the state. The NPRC failed to address the problems that had initially brought them to the capital. The breakdown of hierarchy, roles and order within the military, which began with the 1992 revolt, reached a climax in the 1997 coup.

A new military with new problems

In many ways, the revolt in 1992 was largely linked to the context of the unit, the political situation at the time and a military history in which official structures and procedures were often undermined by personal patronage systems. Much has since changed in Sierra Leone, yet soldiers today still see mutiny as a potential option for addressing their grievances.[99] Furthermore, the move towards democracy may actually have heightened the risk of mutiny in the country.

Following the end of the civil war in 2002, much internal and international attention was focused on restructuring and professionalising the military.[100] An important part of the restructuring of the armed forces involved integrating various elements of the military and rebel forces into one organisation. The programme has been considered a success story, and the soldiers themselves seemed proud of it. In the words of one officer involved in the events of 1992:

> Today if you are asking, you don't know who is RUF in the army. You don't know who is West Side in this army.[101] Today you don't know who is Kamajor in this army. You don't know who is old soldier. What they did was take the RUF and train them, they restructure, they say you are no longer RUF, you are a soldier. Anyone call you a Kamajor you may complain. West Side boys you are no longer West Side, you are soldiers. So today all of us are in this national army, there is no problem. We are all soldiers now so let bygones be bygones. We are all brothers.[102]

Nearly every soldier commented that the conditions in the military today were much better than those in 1992. However, the officer cited above may have been overly optimistic. In a number of other interviews, soldiers began to open up and express their belief that tensions were building below the surface. The most resounding complaint heard in interviews and during casual conversations was over accommodation, which was not particular to one specific base or region.[103] Those living in base accommodation generally found it to be below par; however, the bigger problem was the housing shortage. One officer estimated that 75 per cent of the soldiers, mostly rank and file, live outside the bases because of the shortage.[104] In other cases, several families are expected to live in what would normally be single-family occupancy accommodation on account of the shortages. Several junior soldiers living off base commented that they endure added expenses and time to get between home and work each day. Whereas the accommodation complaint on its own may not be enough to trigger a revolt, such widespread dissatisfaction could be used to further claims of military mismanagement.

In addition to the accommodation issue, soldiers also expressed grievances over corruption in the hierarchy. These accusations, which occasionally make their way into the local press, were also made during interviews. Soldiers explained that they brought their concerns directly to the government in 2009. One rank-and-file interviewee noted that a group of soldiers 'wrote a letter secretly with no names', informing the government of their accusations of corruption within the officer corps. This letter is confirmed in a leaked US embassy report, which states that the soldiers accused a government minister and other senior officers of promoting certain individuals on the basis of favouritism, as well as the theft of government resources and embezzlement of funds meant for the welfare of soldiers. The letter, which claimed to represent 850 officers and rank-and-file soldiers, ended with the following words: 'when all fails, please do not be surprised to see us seeking justice in our own way'. According to the embassy report, the defence minister dismissed the letter as 'just a bit of mischief', but the allegations created an uncomfortable atmosphere within the ministry.[105] A rank-and-file interviewee also noted that a delegation of soldiers met with the ministry of defence about the problems, but he insisted that the problems have persisted and soldiers are losing patience.

In 2010, the Sierra Leone military was deployed as part of the UNAMID mission in Darfur, the first peace operation the country had been involved in since the end of the civil war. Yet grievances quickly emerged about the deployment. Interviewed soldiers expressed frustrations about their payments, which they noted were less than the amount the UN reimburses the government. They further explained their anger at an informal system in which they claim soldiers are expected to pay roughly 10 per cent of their deployment salary from the mission to the chain of command as gratitude for assigning them to the mission. If they refused to pay, they alleged that they would be passed over for promotions or other opportunities in the future.

The primary complaint among these soldiers is pay-related; however, the concerns quickly took on the larger issue of corruption. The interviewees had calculated what they believed the government was making from the UN missions and explained that they did not know where that money was going. The soldiers accused the senior officers of 'not doing anything, not buying uniforms, not buying medicine for soldiers. They are not helping those that are representing us in Darfur.' They went on to explain that the top officers were driving cars that seemed beyond their salary range and questioned how they could afford to buy them. The implied answer was at the expense of the soldiers participating in the UN missions. Another soldier simply stated: 'They are taking the money and doing what they want with the money. They are enriching themselves.'

In March 2013, Sierra Leone sent a peacekeeping battalion to the AMISOM mission, the largest overseas military engagement that Sierra Leone has ever participated in.[106] Troops on this mission received more pay than the troops that had previously been deployed to Darfur. Yet soon into the deployment, familiar complaints developed. In October 2013, a weekend radio show aired a call from a soldier deployed on the AMISOM mission in Somalia.[107] This individual accused the government of 'fraudulently' reducing the peacekeepers' pay, alleged that Sierra Leonean soldiers were living 'precariously' on deployment without adequate supplies and food, and claimed that soldiers had to bribe officers to go on the mission.

Two soldiers interviewed together in 2012 explained that, if the ongoing problems within the military were not resolved, they 'sense something like a mutiny in the near future'. When asked who they felt was to blame for the payment problem, one soldier stated 'It is just the seniors [officers]. But the young ones will copy, maybe even they get worse. But if we set an example, we make them [junior officers] afraid that we will do the same to them.' Their plan involved arresting senior officers and bringing their complaints to the government. In the interview excerpt below, a rank-and-file soldier explains the goal:

> Soldier: There will be no violence. We just want to arrest those we suppose and hand them over. We want to expose them.
>
> Author: Expose them for what?
>
> Soldier: For embezzlement of government money. They are just eating this money. We want to expose them, to expose them so others do not do the same. If we do not do this in the future we will go back to where we came from. We will go back to war, back to revolutions. We do not go again to where we came from. But if you expose them, you bring them to justice, they punish them for that.

To these enlisted soldiers, there was more to gain from a mutiny than just pay. They believed a mutiny would discipline the officers and have a long-term impact. These soldiers never spoke of changing the system or promoting themselves. They actually seemed to have faith in the concept of military hierarchy and had a clear idea of how an officer 'should' behave. They were upset that the accused officers were not upholding the responsibilities of that position. Their statements support the idea proposed in past chapters that mutineers often see themselves as policing the officer corps.

The pending mutiny that soldiers discussed in interviews in 2011 and 2012 may have come closer to fruition in 2013. In August 2013, the government announced the arrest of a group of fourteen soldiers at the barracks in Makeni for plotting a mutiny.[108] Early reports of the incident suggested that the soldiers were planning to protest during President Ernest Koroma's visit to the region, while later charges alleged that the soldiers planned to kidnap or kill the president. The story of the soldiers arrested for mutiny and their trial received fairly regular coverage in local media as it dragged on for nearly two years. Sierra Leonean media raised concerns that the soldiers were being held incommunicado for the first several months after their arrest.[109] Similar reports followed in the international media, while human rights organisations also issued press releases detailing their concerns and urging the government to ensure a fair trial.[110]

The press freedoms in Sierra Leone allowed for attention to be drawn to the case, which may have ultimately placed pressure on the government to handle the trial in a more transparent manner. During the trial, the Sierra Leone government allowed journalists to attend, and local reporters live tweeted details from the courtroom. This is a sharp contrast to the secrecy of most mutiny trials and was likely one of the first cases of social media being used during a mutineer trial in Africa. In August 2015, courts acquitted the soldiers on the grounds that there was insufficient evidence. According to local defence lawyers, this was the first case in decades where soldiers had been acquitted of mutiny charges during a court martial in Sierra Leone.[111]

The tendency for soldiers to be increasingly vocal in expressing their grievances is concerning, particularly as it threatens to create divisions within the newly restructured force. However, in discussions with the soldiers, it was also clear that they had faith in the government to address the issues and a level of confidence in the justice system. One soldier explained that, if they were to mutiny, 'you must explain why you do this thing, and people will listen. There are accessible leaders who want to know, who have an interest, who will listen. They [senior officers] will be arrested and they will be jailed.' This remark suggests that soldiers' attitudes have changed since the events of 1992 and 1997, when soldiers had little faith that the government would respond to their requests. In those years, the government was the main target of military dissatisfaction, whereas with the soldiers interviewed above the government was seen as being able to provide a solution. This is a noteworthy shift, as it indicates that the military views the government as responsive and having legitimate authority over the military.

While soldiers appeared restless with the lack of tangible improvements, there is some evidence of the government being more responsive to their concerns, particularly in relation to peacekeeping. Although the defence minister argued that the AMISOM soldier's radio claims were 'unfounded' and 'unprofessional' and questioned whether the caller was even a soldier, he still provided a detailed response to each of the claims.[112] As the previous chapter explained, many of the peacekeepers' grievances appear to revolve around false expectations and uncertainty. The Ministry of Defence's efforts to bring clarity to the complex issues of funding for peacekeeping operations should consequently be seen as a positive step in reducing this uncertainty.

Another rank-and-file soldier also expressed a sense of faith in the government and justice system: 'if you kick the government out you are not going to address the problems appropriately, you are talking to the international community. But if you arrest the [military] leadership they [the government] will look at the problem and bring some of them to justice'. He believes that the government is capable of handling the various soldiers' complaints. He also suggests that, when a coup occurs, attention turns to international matters and the demands of the rank-and-file soldiers are ignored. These soldiers felt it was better to work within the system, rather than create a new one through a coup. This soldier confirms assessments made throughout this research that there are key differences between coups and mutinies. Soldiers see the two as different tactics to be used in different situations with different outcomes.

Conclusion

Although the grievances of the members of the Tiger unit in 1992 were specific to their own situation, they were also consistent with the larger pattern of mutinies. As in most mutinies in the region, their primary complaints were over material conditions, but these grievances were also closely linked to perceptions of injustice. The injustice involved the discrepancy between their own situation and the conditions of the senior leadership in Freetown, which had its roots in a long pattern of benefits awarded on the basis personal relationships rather than merit.

As is common with deployed units, the Tigers felt they were entitled to more from the hierarchy because of the difficult conditions they had faced. The decision to revolt, as well as their success in doing so, is likely due to increased group cohesion, which developed on deployment. The unit's rank-and-file soldiers expressed loyalty to their unit commanders, which appeared to be based on their personal contact with them during difficult combat situations. They demonstrated this loyalty as well as a level of discipline when they obeyed the order to attack State House, despite their expectations that the mission would simply be a protest. The case of the Tiger unit also demonstrates how internal revolts usually involve an interrelationship between cohesion and division. There was a sense of solidarity within the Tigers as a unit, yet there was also a sense of division from the larger hierarchy based in Freetown. While they acted cohesively as a group, their divergent understandings of the mission showed that the cohesion was limited.

Interviews with members of the Tiger unit, as well as with current soldiers, demonstrate that they view mutinies and coups as distinct actions. However, the distinction between the two events was clearer in discussions than in practice. This case study shows how the two forms of rebellion can become intertwined. Even though the rank-and-file soldiers unanimously believed they were going to conduct a mutiny, they very quickly shifted their action to a coup.

While current Sierra Leonean soldiers acknowledge that life in the military is much better than in previous decades, there was growing dissatisfaction with aspects of their conditions. The main complaints concern accommodation, peacekeeping missions and perceptions of corruption. Rank-and-file soldiers appeared to be frustrated with the lack of action on the part of the military hierarchy in response to their complaints, and in recent years they have attempted various tactics to work around their chain of command. Through letters to the government, radio interviews and even discussions with myself, they have attempted to bring wider attention to their cause. Soldiers have also considered mutinies as another way to communicate their message.

7

MUTINIES WITH UNINTENDED CONSEQUENCES

CASE STUDY OF THE GAMBIA

On the exact same day as Sierra Leonean soldiers and civilians were dancing in the streets in celebration of Momoh's downfall, Gambians were voting in the country's fifth general election. In 1992, these states were at opposite ends of the democratic spectrum, yet two years later both were under the control of a military council led by a junior officer. Whereas Sierra Leone's history of past military involvement in politics and emerging civil war made a mutiny or coup unsurprising, there had been no military revolts in The Gambia until 1991.

This chapter begins with a history of the Gambian military, which remains the youngest force in the region. Aspects of its unique development, often in collaboration with foreign military contingents, contributed to the complaints expressed by mutineers in 1991 and 1992. Both of the mutinies involved complaints over peacekeeping pay. Like many mutinies, the ones in The Gambia in 1991 and 1992 also involved accusations of corruption, particularly among the officer corps. These complaints resonated with many in the military, beyond those that had been deployed together. While the government addressed the pay issue, it failed to deal with the issue of corruption, which had created divisions between the junior ranks (including junior officers) and the senior officers. Rather than tackle these internal tensions, the government invited a Nigerian military contingent to take over the leadership of the military, which increased military dissatisfaction and ultimately contributed to a coup in 1994.

The leader of the 1994 coup, Yahya Jammeh, stayed in power for twenty-two years. Under his rule, civil liberties and human rights were curtailed, and the regime was widely considered authoritarian. The final part of the chapter shows how this reversal of democratisation in The Gambia under Jammeh's leadership made the country less likely to experience mutinies.

The reluctant creation of the Gambian armed forces

By 1981, The Gambia was one of only three West African states that had not experienced a coup attempt (alongside Cape Verde and Côte d'Ivoire).[1] President Jawara had ruled The Gambia since its independence from Britain in 1965. Despite his long tenure, The Gambia had held a series of multi-party elections considered free and fair. Jawara's People's Progressive Party (PPP) had always won a majority of seats, but opposition parties were also represented in the parliament. More radical political organisations espousing varied combinations of Marxism, socialism and Pan-Africanist beliefs (such as the Movement for Justice in Africa-MOJA and Gambia Revolutionary Socialist Party-GRSP) were present in The Gambia but were never considered a serious threat to the ruling party.[2] There had been no cases of deaths due to political violence, leading the country to be described as 'a sometimes lonely, outpost of political tranquility in a troubled area.'[3] Jawara had little reason to suspect his position was in danger when he travelled to Britain to attend the royal wedding of Prince Charles and Lady Diana Spencer in 1981. It was while he was abroad on this trip that the country experienced its first coup attempt. The Gambian coup attempt was unique for at least three reasons.

The first was that it was not carried out by the military. In fact, The Gambia had no military at the time. Since independence from Britain in 1965, law and order in The Gambia was the responsibility of the police and the Field Force. The Field Force had been formed out of the Gambian regiment of the Royal West African Frontier Force (RWAFF), which the British had created in the colonial period. At the time of the attempted coup, the Field Force and police combined had fewer than 600 personnel and both performed policing duties.[4]

Kukoi Samba Sanyang, a civilian who had been unsuccessful in previous attempts to run for political office, led the attempt to oust Jawara. Of the fifteen individuals initially involved, only four were in the Field Force. The remaining individuals varied in their educational background and professions. However, a number were taxi drivers, which resulted in the event being labelled 'the taxi driver coup'.[5]

The other two unique factors in the 1981 coup attempt are the length of the event and the level of violence and death it caused. After breaking into the Field Force armoury, the rebel elements released all prisoners from Mile Two prison and distributed rifles and ammunition to anyone they felt was on their side.[6] Rather than supporting the rebels, many who had acquired the weapons used them to attack others as part of their own personal vendettas, further undermining the efforts of the rebels who already lacked widespread support.[7] The coup-plotters also engaged in other measures that led to a loss of credibility, such as holding Jawara's wife and eight children hostage and threatening them live over the radio.[8] Sanyang and his co-conspirators soon lost control of the situation, and the plan to take Banjul was side-tracked by widespread looting, robbery and killing.[9] The Field Force was not quick to counter the rebels; instead, it remained neutral and waited for the dust to clear before choosing a side.

Within the first day of the coup attempt, Jawara requested the assistance of Senegal under a defence agreement that had been in place since 1965.[10] Senegal responded quickly and generously, sending in hundreds if not thousands of soldiers including airborne and sea-assault units.[11] The response was likely spurred by a fear of the movement spreading across the borders to Senegal. Within four days, the coup had been aborted, having cost the lives of thirty-three Senegalese soldiers and 500 Gambians, many of whom were civilians.[12]

A direct consequence of the coup attempt was the creation of the Gambian armed forces. Only a few months after the coup attempt, President Jawara and President Abdou Diouf of Senegal signed the Kaur Declaration leading to the creation of the Senegambia Confederation. This confederation aimed to integrate the Senegalese and Gambian security forces, as well as creating an economic and monetary union that would also serve to coordinate foreign policy.[13] In order to integrate the two countries' armed forces, The Gambia had to create a military.

It is important to note that Jawara had been in power for seventeen years before establishing a military. Before the coup attempt, he believed that The Gambia had no need for a military, and though he appeared supportive of the Senegambia Confederation, he never seemed fully comfortable with the idea of the Gambian armed forces. It is likely that Senegal exerted pressure on Jawara to create a military so that The Gambia would not rely on Senegal for security, as had been the case during the 1981 crisis. In an interview with the official state newspaper, Jawara acknowledged that he wanted to keep the military 'as small as possible'.[14] Throughout his time in office, he appeared reluctant to invest in the military and naive when it came to military matters.

The divisive effects of the Confederal Army

The Gambian National Army (GNA) was created in 1983–4 via a merger of the existing loyal members of the Field Force with new recruits. The new unit was set up and trained by a small British team. Around the same time, the Gambian National Gendarmerie (GNG), a force separate from the GNA, was established on the basis of a French military model and trained by the Senegalese.[15] Within five years of the coup attempt, Gambia went from having little more than a police force to a full military force comprising an army and gendarmerie alongside the police.

The use of British and French military models to create the Gambian armed forces led to confusion and an often-contentious relationship between the army and gendarmerie. Officers from each branch attended different forms of foreign training, which further intensified the divide between the GNA and GNG. Army officers under the British-styled system trained in the United Kingdom, the United States or occasionally Pakistan, whereas gendarmerie officers were sent for training in France, Morocco, Turkey or Senegal.[16] As a result, the two branches operated on the basis of different military doctrines, although both were part of the same military. This separation between the two branches gradually intensified into a rivalry.[17]

The Senegambia Confederal Agreement merged elements of the new Gambian armed forces with the Senegalese armed forces to create the Confederal Army. Two thirds of the Confederal Army was made up of Senegalese soldiers, with the remainder made up of Gambian soldiers with the ability to deploy anywhere within the Confederation.[18] The Gambian soldiers chosen for the Confederal Army were given the same pay grade as the Senegalese soldiers. Owing to the higher cost of living in Senegal, the amount was significantly higher than the normal pay rate for members of the Gambian military. This 'financial advantage made it the dream assignment of every Gambian soldier'.[19] However, it also meant there were disparities in pay within the new Gambian army, and soldiers 'complained of gross differences in income and privileges' as a result of the Confederal Army.[20] Furthermore, the Gambian military was unable to maintain this rate of pay when the Senegambia Confederation was eventually disbanded.

One former Confederal Army member explained that there was a degree of prestige involved with being in the unit. At the time, the Senegalese military had a longer history and higher standards for recruitment, and Gambian soldiers selected for the Confederal Army were supposed to match this standard.[21] However, former soldiers noted that in reality the best way to get chosen for the Confederal Army was to know one of the Gambian selecting officers. In an interview, a former Confederal Army soldier remarked that 'if it was not for corruption, I would not have been in the [Confederal] Army'. He explained that he did not meet the standard criteria, but he knew someone who assigned him a spot.[22] This favouritism, which began from the very start of the Gambian armed force's existence, is likely to have undermined the integrity of the officer corps. Furthermore, it weakened the hierarchical structures by providing privileges based on personal links rather than on rank or merit.

Even when the Gambian soldiers joined the Senegambia Confederate Army, they were junior to their Senegalese colleagues as a result of their newly appointed ranks. Owing to the vastly different size of the Gambian and Senegalese populations, Senegal also contributed more resources and troops.[23] Consequently, the Gambian military was always going to be in a subordinate position to the Senegalese military in the defence aspects of the Senegambia Confederation, and the key tasks of guarding the airport, port and Gambian president were given to Senegalese troops.[24] Political opposition parties claimed that the Confederation was a threat to national sovereignty and economically disadvantageous to Gambian citizens.[25]

Individuals who questioned the agreement did not have to wait long for the Confederation to come to an end, as the union was disbanded in 1989 following a dispute over the rotation of the confederal presidency.[26] In August 1989, Senegal removed all 300 troops from The Gambia without prior warning.[27] President Jawara explained that he only found out about the troop withdrawal when he arrived at work and saw that there were no presidential guards present.[28] The Senegalese defence minister justified the withdrawal by claiming that the Senegalese soldiers were needed to deal with an emerging issue on the border with Mauritania.[29] The Gambia in turn responded by initiating legal measures to dissolve the confederation.[30] Thus the Senegambia Confederation ended less than seven years after it was formed.

Most of the grand plans for the Confederation were never enacted (in particular the monetary union), and its demise did not have major repercussions for The Gambia's political or economic stability. However, the withdrawal of the Senegalese troops meant Jawara was finally dependent on his armed forces for both internal and external protection. This was the first time since the army's creation that it had not been under foreign leadership.

The Gambia's involvement in the Confederal Army, especially in the early stages of the military's existence, may have sown the initial seeds of discontent within the military. It created divisions within the armed forces by giving some soldiers more pay and prestige. In the words of one former soldier: 'We were seeing that some of us are treated better than others and that is very dangerous in the army.'[31] Additionally, junior soldiers alleged that the officer corps had engaged in corrupt practices during the selection of Confederal Army members. These accusations did not end with the termination of the Senegambia Confederation.

Dissatisfaction among the peacekeepers

At the same time as the Senegambia Confederation was being dissolved, the security situation in Liberia was deteriorating. As we saw in Chapter 5, ECOWAS, of which The Gambia is a member, decided to send a peacekeeping force to the country under the title ECOMOG. In August 1990, 150 Gambian soldiers were deployed to Monrovia, alongside Ghanaian, Nigerian, Guinean and Sierra Leonean troops.[32] This was the Gambian military's first involvement in a peace-support operation. The ECOMOG deployment was a controversial issue within The Gambia. Newspapers questioned the goal of the mission, and some military members expressed doubt over whether the military was adequately prepared.[33] However, similar to earning a spot in the Confederal Army, soldiers viewed an appointment to the ECOMOG mission as a potential way to earn money, since peacekeepers were paid a higher deployment salary. One former soldier explained that those who had not had an opportunity to be a part of the Confederal Army were compensated with appointments on the ECOMOG mission.[34] Although involvement in both the Confederal Army and ECOMOG resulted in additional pay, the ECOMOG mission involved direct combat and related hardships, whereas the Confederal Army did not. Those expecting easy additional pay from the ECOMOG mission were quickly disappointed.

The Gambian soldiers were involved in the first rounds of deployments on the ECOMOG Liberia mission, and thus the soldiers experienced the hardships that were particularly severe at the beginning of the mission. The ECOMOG involvement in Liberia was difficult and dangerous for even the experienced militaries in the region, and the Gambian military was further disadvantaged by its infancy. A former GNA commander explained that the Gambian peacekeeping unit was inexperienced and underprepared. He states that the army had 'never trained on its own, let alone participated in real armed conflict with its officers in charge. The British ... did everything for us ... So when C Company of 150 men including six of the best GNA officers were sent to Liberia, the timid command immediately collapsed.'[35]

In an interview, a Gambian former officer explained that the unit stood no chance against rebels who were trained and motivated to fight.[36] The most senior officer for the Gambian contingent was a captain, whereas all the other contingents had more experienced officers.[37]

During the initial deployment, two Gambian soldiers, Corporal Modou Bojang and Private Sama Jawo, were killed.[38] Five years later, in 1995, after the Jawara regime had been overthrown, President Jammeh approved a mission to retrieve the bodies of the two Gambian soldiers in Liberia.[39] After the bodies had been exhumed, a burial ceremony was held in Banjul. The government claimed that The Gambia was the only country to leave their dead in Liberia and that this had been a key cause of the previous mutinies.[40]

However, this appears to be a rewriting of history. There is no mention of soldiers being angry about the bodies of their colleagues being left in Liberia in the press at the time, and all interviewees were adamant that this had nothing to do with the mutinies. One former soldier explained that bringing the bodies home in 1995 was a 'psychological game to make the former regime look bad'.[41] Another stated that '[Jammeh] was in the army, he knows how to play with the emotions of the soldiers.'[42] Other soldiers said that members of the military are aware that if they are killed on the battlefield their bodies will be left there. They explained that this is not a practice unique to The Gambia but that 'great militaries throughout history have done the same during war'.[43] Rather than rectify an unresolved problem, the military junta was attempting to utilise the mutinies from past years to claim that the Jawara regime had been disrespectful to the military. However, as the interviewees' statements made clear, many soldiers saw through this.

The first Gambian ECOMOG contingent returned home on 13 April 1991. The soldiers were honoured with a ceremony, and another contingent of a similar size was sent to Liberia to replace the returned soldiers. Media coverage of the ceremony described how 'it was clear that Liberia was not a dinner party for them. Those known by our reporters had lost a lot of weight.'[44] Former soldiers noted the same, with one remarking that the returned soldiers looked like 'typical pictures of people from the third world', meaning that they looked malnourished.[45]

Less than a month after their return, the media in The Gambia started to report on pay issues within the unit. Newspapers reported that soldiers had only been paid part of their allowances for the later months in which they had been deployed and that they had received no compensation for the final month on the mission. The newspaper *Foroyaa* also questioned why the soldiers needed to tell their stories to the media to have their complaints reach official channels. It suggested instead that the government or military should have a mechanism in place to communicate with the soldiers over these issues.[46] These soldiers were at the forefront of the trend, described in Chapters 2 and 3, of soldiers taking their complaints to the media. Whereas many countries in the region were struggling to gain media freedoms in the early 1990s, The Gambia already had these rights, and soldiers used them.

The military leadership and the government did not pay heed to the grievances the soldiers expressed in the media. A month after the press had identified the pay issue, the soldiers had still not received their pay and the complaints escalated to a mutiny. On 13 June, two months after their return, the Gambian ECOMOG soldiers gathered in Yundum barracks to request a meeting with the commander of the armed forces, Colonel Ndow Njie.[47] Njie reportedly refused to meet the soldiers because of security concerns.[48] The next day, a small contingent of officers and NCOs, led by the British military advisor Lt Col. Jim Shaw, attempted to arrest the soldiers at Yundum barracks for organising a mutiny, but they were unsuccessful.[49] The ECOMOG soldiers took to the streets, arriving at State House in Banjul to express their dissatisfaction. There were around sixty soldiers involved in the mutiny, all sergeants or below.[50] President Jawara agreed to meet the soldiers and discuss their complaints.[51]

The government took the mutineers' complaints seriously and made some changes, although not necessarily ones designed to address the root causes of the mutiny. The mutineers were first and foremost asking for their back-pay from the peacekeeping mission.[52] They also requested improvements in accommodation, equipment and welfare.[53] However, according to Abdoulaye Saine, 'the motivation to mutiny ran deeper than just pay, there was widespread disapproval with the regime, in part due to increased corruption'.[54] This claim is consistent with the findings from my interviews with former soldiers, all of whom claimed that corruption was behind the non-payment. They did not believe the government's claim that the country did not have the money available, but rather thought that 'the senior officers were robbing them'. In the words of one former soldier, 'the top brass got the [deployment] money and sliced it, only gave some to the soldiers'. He further elaborated that the soldiers spoke to Nigerian soldiers while on the ECOMOG mission and found out that they were getting paid more than the Gambians.[55] The soldiers believed that the discrepancy between the Gambian and Nigerian pay proved that senior Gambian officers were taking part of their salaries: 'ECOMOG was not a Gambian contingent alone, it was ECOWAS ... how can a subregional force that is supposed to be recognised as an international organisation not have money to be paid?' One soldier explained that the perceived corruption demoralised the troops: 'a military should be proud, but there was too much corruption, too much nepotism'.[56]

President Jawara promised to pay the mutineers' owed allowances and to look into the other requests.[57] However, one former soldier says that paying the soldiers only justified the corruption accusations in the eyes of many in the military: 'if there was no money really, even if [the mutineers] were able to bring the sky down [the government] would not be able to get money but as soon as that happened they were paid the money. So where did that money come from?'[58] My interviewees believed that the immediate payment showed that the salary due had been available the whole time, and officers were simply not distributing it to the soldiers. Thus paying the soldiers so quickly only strengthened junior soldiers' perceptions of high-level corruption and incompetence. As the finance minister announced a pay increase for all members of the armed forces one month after the mutiny, it would appear that the government was aware of the resentment building within the ranks. The news outlet reporting the story expressed hope that the move would 'temper down the feelings that are running high'.[59] However, as will be discussed below, tempers continued to rise and dissatisfaction soon spread to the junior officers.

Initially, the soldiers that mutinied were asked to go on leave, but a later press release stated that they had been suspended on half pay until a full inquiry had taken place.[60] However, interviewees explained that members of the units were not actually dismissed from the military. Years after the event, Lt Col. Shaw (the British advisor who had pushed for the mutineers to be arrested) commented that he believed that the 1994 coup stemmed from the government's failure 'to take effective actions against the "dissenters" from ECOMOG'.[61]

The commanding officer (CO) of the GNA, Colonel Njie, was removed from his position shortly after the revolt, a move designed to demonstrate the severity with which the government viewed the revolt. However, this did not negatively affect Njie's career, as he was immediately given an ambassadorial position abroad.

Mutinies lead to a contentious caretaker

Less than a month after news of Njie's departure, the government announced that the Nigerian Army Training Assistance Group (NATAG) would soon be arriving in The Gambia to help train and equip the army. The NATAG arrangement was somewhat unusual in that the top Nigerian officer, Colonel (later promoted to Brigadier General) Abubakar Dada, was appointed CO of the GNA.

Soldiers recall being 'shocked' by the decision,[62] while media reports stated that the news of the NATAG arrangement 'came as a thunderbolt from the blue'.[63] The decision to bring in another foreign contingent was a controversial one from the start, and the idea of having the national military headed by a foreign officer was especially contentious. One local paper remarked: 'One can understand having foreign military advisors or trainers. Having a foreign military commander for a sovereign republic appears strange.' The same story then went on to list every individual in the Gambian military from the rank of captain and above, highlighting their long and decorated service, before raising the following question: 'Is the government telling us that none of these people are competent enough to head the army?'[64] The departure of Colonel Njie was due to the fact that he had lost the confidence of his men, yet Jawara did little to restore this confidence in the Gambian military leadership. By appointing Nigerian leaders, he was essentially confirming the shortcomings of the Gambian officers.

Although the government announced the NATAG plan almost immediately after the June 1991 mutiny, it took around nine months for the seventy-nine-member contingent to arrive.[65] In the meantime, The Gambia experienced a second mutiny. The second contingent from the ECOMOG mission returned from its deployment in December 1991. On 3 February 1992, thirty-five soldiers from the unit left Yundum barracks in a military vehicle around 9.00 a.m.[66] One account of the event claimed the soldiers had stolen weapons from the armoury and had fired shots in the air.[67] However, whether this actually happened is open to question, given that the published accounts of the court martial do not contain any charges of stealing or unlawfully discharging weapons.

The mutineers soon disembarked from the military vehicle, took over a bus and ordered the driver to head towards Banjul (a distance of roughly 30 kilometres). This bus hi-jacking by uniformed soldiers was apparently witnessed by many people during rush hour, and the news quickly spread and rumours grew. *The Point* newspaper claimed that 'before the truth emerged, there was chaos especially in the Serrekunda area where people stampeded to collect their kids from school and their wares from the market'.[68] Other media outlets reported similar reactions, with the streets being cleared out and shopkeepers locking up out of fear.[69] In reality, the event turned out to be much less dramatic than the local population had feared. The police and gendarmerie intercepted the soldiers at Denton Bridge, which connects Banjul to the mainland.[70] The thirty-five mutineers were arrested and court martialled.

The soldiers were making their way to Banjul to express their grievances over unpaid allowances from their ECOMOG deployment. A Gambian newspaper commented:

> If the people mistake the soldiers' demonstration for what it is not, it must be because nobody would have thought that they would be given a chance, through non-payment of allowances, for them to make a repeat performance of last year's march on the Presidency.[71]

In other words, why did the government not learn from the mutiny of the first ECOMOG contingent?

The actual amount of money that the soldiers were owed was relatively small. According to media reports, they were owed a balance of fifteen days' pay, totalling $45 each.[72] My interviewees explained that the material grievances were linked to perceived corruption among the officers, as had been the case in the previous mutiny. The soldiers felt they had been sent on a dangerous mission only to come back and have someone in their chain of command take their hard-earned money. In the words of one soldier: 'Let's say you are from the warfront, there is stress, you are making sacrifices of your life, this issue makes you very aggravated.'[73] Another former soldier explained that it was not just the ECOMOG soldiers who were upset about the non-payment; other soldiers and civilians thought it was disrespectful to refuse payment to soldiers who had fought for their country.[74] A former soldier stated: 'soldiers on the ground must be paid better, they were facing war every day. They should be paid more. Why would anyone go risk their life for that?' Another military interviewee explained that: 'they were in real war situations, so for them to not get paid was a real problem'.[75]

The mutineers' trial began on 25 February. Whereas the case of the 1991 mutineers was handled as an internal military affair, the 1992 mutineers were tried in public. Local media covered the court martial, and the judicial hall was packed to full capacity on the day of the trial. The soldiers were charged with eleven crimes, including breaking out of barracks, conduct contrary to good order, insubordination and wilfully obstructing police officers. The court martial, made up of three officers, deliberated for two days, eventually finding most of the soldiers guilty of at least one of the charges. The sentences varied from dismissals to fines.[76]

The third contingent of Gambian ECOMOG soldiers arrived home in July 1992, by which time NATAG was in The Gambia. The ECOMOG soldiers were paid their outstanding allowances immediately. At their reception ceremony, the new Nigerian CO of the GNA, Colonel Abubakar Dada, warned the troops that he would not tolerate any indiscipline within the unit and spoke at length about the importance of loyalty in the armed forces. An article in *The Point* described the speech as 'rude' and 'unfitting', arguing that the returned soldiers should be treated as decorated veterans rather than potential mutineers. It further criticised the implication that the mutinying soldiers were disloyal, stating that the soldiers should not be faulted for demanding what was promised to them. The article went on to condemn the government for 'expelling those experienced men from the army and having Nigerian troops in the country'.[77] The expression 'experienced men' presumably refers to the ECOMOG soldiers who were dismissed following the 1992 mutiny.

There were no further mutinies after NATAG arrived. Hence, it could be assumed that the grievances aired during the mutinies had been resolved with the decision to replace the senior Gambian leadership with Nigerian officers. Indeed, some media at the time congratulated the 'new military management team' on rectifying the problem.[78] However, in reality, replacing the top leadership did little to address the underlying problems in the military, in particular the problem of corruption and lack of trust in the leadership.

The unresolved problems grow

The mutineers did something that was unprecedented at the time in The Gambia; they publicly exposed the internal problems of the military. The complaints about deployment payments were specific to the ECOMOG soldiers, but their accusations of corruption and mismanagement resonated with others in the military, particularly junior officers, who explained how these problems had been festering for a very long period of time. One former soldier noted that, by 1992, corruption in the military was a 'cancer that had taken root and spread'.[79] Promotions were seen to be based on favouritism, which further eroded the soldiers' confidence in the hierarchy.[80] One former soldier stated that the senior officers 'did not have control and we did not respect them'.[81]

MUTINIES WITH UNINTENDED CONSEQUENCES

Senior officers were subject to a range of accusations, including involvement in profiting from items confiscated from illegal fishing operations, selling food meant for rank-and-file soldiers and bribing senior government officials.[82] Soldiers believed that senior military officers did not fear that their actions would be punished because they were closely aligned with politicians.[83]

In addition to these general complaints, there were also more specific grievances related to the NATAG presence. A former officer explains how 'the final straw was when the government reduced us to nonentities and brought in Nigerians to command and control us'.[84] Although enlisted soldiers had conducted the mutinies, the government decision to bring in NATAG most affected the officers. Gambian officers complained about the better accommodation, cars and pay the Nigerians received, as well as other fringe benefits such as free fuel.[85] The Gambians were not just envious of the Nigerians' material benefits; they felt that their presence was directly detrimental to their own careers. The Nigerians held all the highest positions, with no Gambians above the rank of major.[86] As such, the officers in particular felt that the Nigerians were thwarting their potential for advancement.

It appears that the junior officers were particularly offended by the Nigerian presence. The junior officers began to look down on the Gambian senior officers, believing they were either complacent or complicit in the system that they felt disadvantaged them. An individual who was a junior officer at the time said he and his cohort felt the senior Gambian officers were 'useless' and that there were serious internal tensions within the officer corps. He explained that because the junior officers worked most closely with the rank-and-file soldiers, their negative opinions of the senior officers spread to the enlisted ranks.[87]

The senior Gambian officers may not have been as concerned or vocal about the Nigerians because they were closer to retirement and perhaps not as worried about moving up the ladder. A Gambian academic and former member of the Jawara regime put forward a different explanation. He claimed that the difference between the junior and senior officers' reactions was due to a generational divide within the Gambian military. The junior officers had grown up in the 1960s and 1970s and were thus more exposed to radical politics than their predecessors. He argues that they were more politically conscious and less willing to stand by what they saw as major injustices within the force.[88] Abdoulaye Saine and Ebrima Ceesay arrive at similar conclusion, though they argue that the divide was not necessarily a product of exposure to radical politics, but of having been more educated than their seniors who grew up in the pre-independence years.[89]

The soldiers' negative response to the Nigerian presence under NATAG contrasts with the generally more accepting attitude towards the Senegalese presence under the Confederal Army agreement. By the time NATAG had arrived, the Gambian military no longer saw itself as inexperienced, especially after numerous deployments on foreign peace operations, and therefore less ready to accept of working alongside foreign troops within Gambian borders. A large part of the difference was cultural, as several former Gambian soldiers explained that the Senegalese and Gambians share many similarities in terms of indigenous languages, religion, history and culture. One soldier claimed that every Gambian has a relative that is Senegalese, and the Senegalese soldiers were seen as family.[90] This family metaphor did not seem to extend to Nigerians, however, who were instead viewed as foreigners. Lastly, under the Confederal Army, Senegalese and Gambian soldiers received the same pay and privileges. But this was not the case with NATAG. These complaints over foreign leadership are similar to the grievances expressed in mutinies seen in Kenya, Tanzania, Uganda and Zaire in the early 1960s. In these incidents, the foreigners were former colonial officers, but in all cases soldiers felt offended by the privileges and responsibilities being given to outsiders over the members of the national armed forces.

One other important aspect of the discontent among many Gambian military personnel at the time was the disbanding of the GNG. While the gendarmerie and army trained separately, they received more or less equal funding and served as a counterweight to each other.[91] It was the gendarmerie, for example, who countered the 1991 and 1992 mutinies among army members. However, in 1992 the government decided to disband the gendarmerie and merge the members into a unit within the police force called the Tactical Support Group (TSG).[92] For those personnel who were in the gendarmerie, this was an unpopular decision because the police received less funding and equipment than the army and was generally seen as less prestigious.[93] Soldiers blamed the decision to disband the gendarmerie on the Nigerians, who were advising the Gambian government on military matters at the time.[94] Furthermore, Gambian soldiers have retrospectively blamed the Nigerians for over-arming the GNA, introducing mortars, rocket-propelled grenades and heavy machine guns, whereas the force had previously made do with smaller rifles and handguns.[95] Numerous former soldiers argued that disbanding the gendarmerie meant that the 1994 coup was a foregone conclusion because there was no counterweight against the army.[96] The unequal strength of the army compared with the police came to a head in the showdown between the two forces on the day of the 1994 coup.

MUTINIES WITH UNINTENDED CONSEQUENCES

While tensions were rising within the military, the civilian population was similarly expressing its frustration with the situation. In the early 1990s, the media grew increasingly critical of Jawara and the PPP regime, which had been in power for nearly thirty years. Newspapers ran countless stories accusing the government of inaction, with news articles questioning why The Gambia still had no university.[97] Other articles called the PPP 'mere tax collectors', alongside pictures of rubbish piling up, and accused the government of failure to carry out even basic functions.[98] The criticism did not just come from the media; citizens of various sectors of society began to take to the streets to express their grievances. Market vendors took their complaints about government eviction notices to State House, taxi drivers held strikes for better facilities, women protested against water charges in Bakau by blockading a street, and high school students protested over exam changes.[99] Ongoing demonstrations in Brikama over the privatisation of the water supply grew increasingly large in the spring and summer of 1994, culminating in a march with an estimated 4,000 citizens, which turned violent when protestors clashed with the police (a rarity in The Gambia).[100]

Corruption also became a leading story in media in the early 1990s, with several high-level political corruption scandals being uncovered.[101] One government interviewee recalled how, in the early 1990s, 'the whole atmosphere had changed, everyone started talking about change, even myself, we weren't sure what type of change we just wanted a change'. He noted that the military and civilian population had a close relationship and that 'the military must have been aware of the grumblings of the civilians'.[102]

The third and final strike

The mutinies in 1991 and 1992 had given Jawara two warnings of the problems within the military, but more drastic measures were taken on the third revolt, which occurred on 22 July 1994.[103] In the months leading up to July 1994, it appears coups were on many people's minds. In his autobiography, President Jawara claims that rumours had been circulating of a pending coup, and this was confirmed by the former soldiers I interviewed. The local media reported extensively on neighbouring coups, in particular the 1992 coup in Sierra Leone, and even ran a story just weeks before the Gambia coup titled 'How Safe Are Our Leaders?'[104] However, few people would have guessed this particular timing for a revolt because there was a bilateral exercise with the US Navy scheduled to take place in and around Banjul. Announcements were made in the newspapers and radio to alert residents to the exercise and warn people not to be alarmed by the increase in uniformed soldiers on the streets.[105] Conducting the coup at the same time as a planned exercise, with American and Nigerian troops present in the country, led some soldiers who were there on the day to claim it was a brilliant plan, while others believe it was careless and suicidal.[106]

On the morning of 22 July, President Jawara was at his office in State House when he received a report that there were accounts of a coup plot, but the intelligence service deemed it just more rumours.[107] Less than an hour later, his aide de camp arrived and announced that armed soldiers were on their way to State House. They reportedly far outnumbered and out-armed the small contingent of presidential guards at State House that day. Advisors recommended that Jawara and his family leave immediately, and the American ambassador offered to allow the president and his family refuge on the navy ship that was anchored in Banjul port as part of the exercise. In Jawara's autobiography, he makes a rather surprising admission by stating that this 'was the first time I heard anything of a warship in our port'. He later goes on to say:

> It was strange that in all the official messages I had received daily from Banjul, my Vice President and Minister of Defence had not mentioned to me that he and our security chiefs had given permission for anything as massive as a joint GNA and US Navy training exercise, complete with a warship. I thought if the armed forces of another sovereign nation were going to engage with our national army in any kind of bilateral exercise, it would have been important enough for the head of state and commander-in-chief of the armed forces of the host country, at home or abroad, to be informed of such an engagement.[108]

This statement reveals just how disconnected Jawara was from the workings of his own military.

Jawara followed the advice to vacate State House and boarded the US ship. When word got out that there was a group of armed soldiers heading towards Banjul, confusion ensued within the armed forces, partly because people were uncertain if this was part of the exercise. The TSG from the police force was deployed to stop the soldiers from reaching Banjul. There was a standoff between the TSG and the soldiers near the Denton Bridge (the same location where mutineers were stopped in 1992). However, the police put up little opposition when it was confirmed that the soldiers were far better armed. Thus, with little internal resistance and a president who had already fled, the soldiers had no trouble taking over the state. The whole affair was over by midday, with no one injured. The event ultimately marked 'the demise of the longest continuously surviving multiparty democracy in Africa' at the time, as well as unseating the continent's longest-serving national leader.[109] The soldiers made the obligatory announcement over the radio that the constitution was suspended and a curfew was now in place. The announcement listed 'rampant corruption and the retrogressive nature of the country' as the cause of the coup.[110]

The BBC interviewed Jawara while he was still on the US ship and asked why he thought the military had overthrown him. He replied that he had heard complaints about salary, corruption and 'bad food in the barracks' and urged the soldiers to discuss the problems with him as their commander-in-chief.[111] Jawara also quickly learned that he could not count on international support. Although the US military was docked in the port, Washington did not give permission for the US Navy to intervene. Senegal also refused to come to his aid as it had in the 1981 coup attempt, instead offering Jawara asylum in Dakar. Furthermore, the Nigerian contingent, whom Jawara had trusted with his own protection and running the Gambian military, did not act to stop the coup. Numerous rumours continue about whether any of these three foreign powers were involved in planning or executing the coup, but there is little evidence to support such theories.

That Jawara left immediately, before the soldiers even reached Banjul, makes it difficult to establish whether the initial plan was to arrive at State House to make demands or to arrive at State House with the aim of taking over the state. Most of the military officers and police I spoke with noted that the event was led by officers and that the participants were heavily armed, thus suggesting that 'these soldiers were not going to just make a complaint'. In many ways, the scenario in Banjul in 1994 was similar to that of Freetown in 1992, as described in the previous chapter.

Lieutenant Yahya Jammeh was announced as the head of the new ruling council, named the Armed Forces Provisional Ruling Council (AFPRC). According to an officer involved in the events, this name was chosen based on Valentine Strasser's military junta (named the National Provisional Ruling Council/NPRC), which the Gambian officers admired.[112] The AFPRC looked similar to the NPRC in Sierra Leone in terms of the members' age (AFPRC members ranged from twenty-five to thirty years of age), and they had also received little by way of advanced education or international experience.[113] The Gambia's AFPRC was even more junior in rank than Sierra Leone's NPRC, consisting of one lieutenant (Yahya Jammeh) and three 2nd lieutenants (Sana Sabally, Edward Singhateh and Sadibou Hydara).

The junior ranks' anger at their senior officers, which was highlighted during the 1991 and 1992 mutinies, was acted upon by these junior officers. The few senior officers who were either loyal enough or bold enough to stand by while the junior soldiers rebelled were rounded up and arrested. A senior officer at the time stated that he was 'shocked' to learn that a sergeant was in charge of the arrested senior officers.[114] Another former soldier also noted the officers' surprise at bearing the brunt of the enlisted anger but claimed this should not have come as a shock given the history of mutinies and complaints about officers' behaviour.[115] In the months and years following the coup, nearly all officers from the rank of captain and above were retired, many after being detained and some having died or been killed in prison.[116]

Reporting at the time, and assessments written years after the event, claim that the coup was an extension of the previous complaints over non-payment of the ECOMOG mission.[117] However, this seems to be a misrepresentation of the events. None of the key soldiers in the 22 July coup were part of the ECOMOG deployments.[118] In fact, most of those that orchestrated the coup were on the opposing side in the mutinies. Singhateh was one of the soldiers that put down the mutiny on the Denton Bridge in 1992.[119] Sabally had the unfortunate luck of being on duty at Yundum barracks when the ECOMOG soldiers started the mutiny in 1992. He was investigated for involvement but found not guilty.[120] Jammeh was in the gendarmerie at the time and in charge of the military police, and thus he was also involved in restraining the mutineers who were arrested by the gendarmerie.[121] Furthermore, although the soldiers who overthrew the government did make complaints about pay when they came to power, they never claimed it was payment from the ECOMOG mission. In the AFPRC's first press conference, a journalist specifically asked if the soldiers' grievances were related to the Liberia mission, which Jammeh denied.[122]

The 1994 coup should not be seen as a direct continuation of the 1991 and 1992 mutinies; instead, the mutinies should be seen as an early warning of the growing discontent that eventually fuelled the coup. The previous mutinies may also have played a role in the 1994 coup in terms of logistics. The assistant general of police operations admits that when he received intelligence about soldiers making their way to Banjul on 22 July, he believed it was just 'another mutiny within the military'.[123] The vice president reportedly gave a similar account to the American ambassador, claiming that the disturbance was just another demonstration. Since the top levels of the military and civilian hierarchies saw the event as a 'mere' mutiny rather than a coup, this will almost certainly have given the rebellious soldiers more time to prepare. The government and military did not respond as forcefully or quickly as they could have done.

Potential problems below the surface

In the twenty-two years that Jammeh served as president, there were some tangible improvements in the country, such as the creation of a national university and improvements to roads and infrastructure. However, the overall economic conditions worsened under the Jammeh regime, particularly in the latter part of his rule. He was considered an authoritarian leader by most measures and international indexes. In 2014, for example, Freedom House moved The Gambia to its lowest category, 'not free', in terms of civil and political liberties. Human rights were regularly and violently abused, with numerous well-researched reports by international human rights organisations documenting torture, forced disappearances and unlawful killings by government and paramilitary forces. These abuses regularly targeted journalists and opposition figures, but government officials and military personnel deemed disloyal were also victims.

The military remained mutiny-free during Jammeh's time in office. One might assume that this was because the military was well taken care of by the Jammeh regime. This narrative was put forward by soldiers in Banjul, who only had positive things to say about their commander-in-chief. One soldier claimed: 'we are extremely happy about what he [Jammeh] is doing for the armed forces, he is one of us, you know what we say, once a soldier always a soldier, everyone is happy'.[124] While this individual may indeed be content with the current situation, it is unlikely he could have given a different response, given that the interview took place at the military headquarters in Banjul, just blocks from State House. My interviews with soldiers in The Gambia uncovered some valuable information about past mutinies, but individuals did not appear comfortable discussing the current state of affairs. This point was driven home by one officer telling me I could only ask questions to him and his men about events under the Jawara regime; any question about the Jammeh regime was off limits.

However, individuals who had recently left the military as well as some interviewees who still worked in the Gambian government were adamant that there were still widespread tensions within the Gambian armed forces. According to one individual who has long been working for the government in The Gambia:

'from the surface the military appears calm but inside it is not'. He went on to state: 'Gambians are very nervous at the moment, everyone is expecting a coup but no one will talk about it, some are wishing it, some are dreading it.'[125]

Under Jammeh's rule, there was a great deal of volatility within the military. Positions and promotions in the armed forces tended to depend on allegiance to Jammeh, and key positions in the military were typically appointed to those most loyal to the regime. There are numerous examples of promotions involving jumping ranks (even being promoted from enlisted to officer ranks) rather than progressing gradually through the standard rank structure.[126] However, just as soldiers were often quickly promoted, demotions were also a regular occurrence. Those accused of disloyalty could find themselves dismissed, jailed and in some cases even executed. Several interviewees in The Gambia joked that there was an extra battalion behind the bars of Mile Two prison. The manipulation of the rank structure likely created an intentional sense of insecurity within the military. The system involved a murky network of informants within the security services, which kept soldiers wary and on edge.

There were also widespread accusations that Jammeh favoured his ethnic group, the Jola, for positions within the military, particularly at the senior levels.[127] The favouritism is alleged to have continued down the chain of command, with claims that Jola junior ranks received disproportionate opportunities for assignments overseas, such as positions on peacekeeping missions.[128] The Jola are a small ethnic group in The Gambia, with 2003 estimates suggesting that they make up around 11 per cent of the population.[129] Ethnic preferences for key jobs and opportunities are suspected to have created internal divisions and resentment in the military between Jola and non-Jola.[130]

Claims of discontent within the armed forces under Jammeh are not mere speculation; coup plots and attempts were reportedly uncovered in 1995, 1996, 1997, 2000, 2003, 2006, 2009 and 2014. This list likely includes both imagined attempts, which served as a way for Jammeh to purge potential opposition, but also genuine threats to Jammeh's position from within the armed forces. The 2006 plot is a clear example of the latter. The plot allegedly involved both the Chief of Defence Staff, Colonel Ndure Cham, and the director of the national intelligence agency, Daba Mareneh, symbolising divisions and dissatisfaction at the top levels of the hierarchy. While Colonel Ndure Cham escaped at the time, Mareneh along with at least four military personnel accused of involvement were allegedly executed while other accused were given prison sentences and, reportedly, tortured.[131] The most recent coup attempt, in 2014, involved an attack on State House led by the former commander of the national guards,

Lt Col. (Ret.) Lamin Sanneh, and other members of the Gambian diaspora. Sanneh and three other former members of the Gambian armed forces were killed by soldiers loyal to Jammeh during the attempt.[132] While Jammeh labelled the incident a 'terrorist attack' by foreign dissidents, suspicion of involvement by members of the military led to arrests and courts martial of Gambian soldiers.[133] Along with the military detentions, dozens of civilians were also arrested, including members of Sanneh's family.[134]

The aftermath of these events was indicative of the general pattern of mass arrests and disappearances of military personnel (and at times civilian) that usually followed allegations of coup-plotting or coup attempts in The Gambia. The lack of transparency in the trials of the accused coup-plotters, the manipulation of 'confessions' and/or a lack of trials completely (at times due to quick executions or the unexplained disappearance of the accused) makes it difficult to unravel the truths from allegations, rumours and half-truths concerning the plans to oust Jammeh.

In discussions, most former Gambian soldiers and officers, government employees and Gambian academics attributed the lack of mutinies to the climate of fear in The Gambia under Jammeh. They insisted that there were widespread grievances in the armed forces, but felt that soldiers would deem a mutiny to be too dangerous. Some commented that Jammeh would never listen to junior soldiers and would label any demonstration a coup attempt and charge soldiers with the most serious offence. This supports the theory proposed in Chapter 3 that mutinies are less likely under authoritarian regimes. Mutinies require a reasonable chance that the government will respond and negotiate. Authoritarian leaders like Jammeh are less likely to engage in a dialogue about potential grievances. Interviewees emphasised how the risk would be far too high, often citing examples of executions and forced disappearances in the armed forces to make the point. Evidence of the brutal way Jammeh has dealt with opposition figures, journalists or others critical of his leadership also suggests that he would have been unlikely to allow public criticism from members of the military.

Conclusion

The mutinies in The Gambia in 1991 and 1992 were initially triggered by salary complaints, but underlying these grievances were accusations of corruption, mismanagement and a general distrust of the senior ranks in the hierarchy. Although the mutineers may have been the first to voice these complaints publicly, many of the issues had deep roots and resonated with larger sectors of the military. The government viewed the mutinies as a pay dispute and largely treated them as such, a common perception of mutinies and one this book attempts to dispel. The government addressed the deployment pay issue but did not appropriately handle the more systemic issues. Little was done to professionalise the Gambian military leadership or address the accusations of inherent favouritism, nepotism and corruption.

The arrival of the NATAG contingent at the invitation of the Gambian government following the first round of mutinies further exacerbated the problems, as the Nigerian officers were seen as another hindrance to career advancement, particularly by the junior officers. Whereas the 1991 and 1992 mutinies were limited to enlisted ranks from a specific unit, the response to the mutiny brought a wider range of personnel into the camp of disgruntled soldiers. The dissatisfaction of the junior ranks under NATAG leadership ultimately led to the 1994 coup. The case of the mutinies in The Gambia demonstrates how mutinies can often have unintended consequences. What was at the time viewed as simply a call for pay (and a fairly modest call at that) contributed to a cycle of events that drastically changed the country.

The ECOMOG soldiers in The Gambia are similar to the Tiger unit in Sierra Leone, both in their complaints and their deployment experiences. The cohesion needed for a mutiny was likely developed during the shared deployment experience to Liberia. The Gambian soldiers returned with a heightened view of their own role and worth within the military, a trend discussed in Chapter 5. The Gambian mutinies also serve to confirm that mutinies are often used as a means of communication. In 1991, soldiers initially attempted to open a dialogue with the government by bringing their complaints to the media. When that failed, they unsuccessfully attempted to pressure a meeting with senior leadership, yet their cause would ultimately only receive attention with the march on State House. In following their course, the mutineers were helped by the prevailing freedoms in The Gambia at the time, which allowed for generally free reporting on the story and a fair trial for the mutineers. The absence of similar freedoms and a neglect for human rights in The Gambia under Jammeh contributed to the lack of mutinies during his regime. Thus despite widespread signs of discontent within the armed forces, there was little indication that Jammeh would negotiate with the soldiers, making mutiny an overly risky action for soldiers.

In 2016 Jammeh lost the presidential election to opposition candidate, Adama Barrow. Yet, Jammeh only left office under the threat of a forceful removal by an ECOWAS military contingent. One of the many challenges that Barrow has faced is the inheritance of a military that was based on personal loyalty and links to Jammeh. In the first few months of Barrow's tenure, there have been mass desertions in the armed forces and threats of mutinies. At Barrow's request, ECOWAS has agreed to keep troops in The Gambia in the near-term to ensure a peaceful transition. However, significant military reform will likely be needed to maintain stability in the post-Jammeh era.

8

AN ESCALATING CYCLE OF MUTINIES

CASE STUDY OF BURKINA FASO

In October 2014, the President of Burkina Faso, Blaise Compaoré, who had already been in office for twenty-seven years, proposed a constitutional amendment to extend presidential term limits. In response, hundreds of thousands of Burkinabé took to the streets in protest. The wild card in this tense situation was the military, as it was unclear if the armed forces would side with Compaoré or the masses of demonstrators. As this chapter will demonstrate, the uncertainty surrounding where the military would stand is related to the armed forces' complex role and history in Burkina Faso.

The response of the state security services to the growing protests was inconsistent. At the National Assembly building, security forces retreated when the crowds of demonstrators arrived. Their inaction seemed to suggest they supported the protest or at least were unwilling to counter it. Yet at demonstrations near the Presidential Palace, the presidential guards opened fire on unarmed civilians, killing between nineteen and thirty-three demonstrators.[1] Confusion within the armed forces over how to respond to the situation was further seen at the highest levels of the hierarchy when two different officers declared themselves head of state after it became clear that Compaoré had resigned.[2] Following international pressure for a civilian to lead the transition, Michel Kafando was selected as president, while Lt Col. Yacouba Isaac Zida, deputy chief of the presidential guards, was appointed prime minister until the elections scheduled to take place in October 2015.

SOLDIERS IN REVOLT

The events in Burkina Faso in October 2014 were a remarkable example of mass democratic mobilisation. Yet for many in Burkina Faso, or those following Burkinabé history, the revolution did not come as a shock. Just three years earlier, similar widespread demonstrations had taken place throughout the country that foreshadowed the events of 2014. Alongside these 2011 protests were the most widespread military mutinies the country had ever seen.

This chapter focuses on the mass mutinies in 2011. A brief history of revolts in Burkina Faso will show that while the crisis of 2011 was exceptional in size and thus severity, it followed a pattern of previous similar incidents. An examination of the civilian demonstrations that took place in Burkina Faso in 2011 will set the stage for the military mutinies and illustrate how many of the themes expressed in the civilian protests overlapped with military complaints. The chapter will then chronicle the 2011 mutinies, outlining the various ways in which the government attempted to quell the rebellion, which it finally succeeded in doing after more than two months.

The large number of participants, their claims and their history of mutinying suggest there were significant tensions within the Burkinabé military structure. Aside to other violent mass mutinies, as described in Chapter 3, the Burkinabé soldiers were loosely united in anger and shared frustration, rather than unified around a specific goal or experience. The mutinies were so widespread that sectors of the military that did not participate became the exception. The two main groups not involved, the officer corps and the gendarmerie, will be examined in order to assess why these sectors did not join with their rebellious colleagues. The analysis of mutinies in Burkina Faso will also highlight the complex relationship between soldiers and civilians in Burkina Faso.

A temporary civilian–military union

When the editorial chief of a major radio station in Ouagadougou exclaimed that 'Our country is the champion of the coup d'état', this was very far from an exaggeration.[3] Burkina Faso holds the record for the most successful coups in all of sub-Saharan Africa, which is no small feat given the competition. In addition to seven successful coups, two failed coup attempts and at least six recorded coup plots, the Burkinabé military has also had its fair share of mutinies.[4]

Until 2011, the most well-known mutiny in Burkina Faso occurred in the southern city of Pô in 1983. The incident was sparked by the arrest of Captain Thomas Sankara, a highly popular revolutionary officer, on charges of treason.[5] Upon hearing of his arrest, the soldiers in Pô, led by Sankara's close friend Captain Blaise Compaoré, took control of the city, including police and customs stations and cut telephone communication to the capital. The mutineers set up roadblocks, and for over two weeks the soldiers had complete control of the city. Reports from the time claimed the atmosphere was tense, but there does not appear to have been any violence. The soldiers were clear in their demands: they wanted the unconditional release of their comrade Captain Sankara.[6]

At the same time that the commandos were mutinying in Pô, students throughout the country were protesting on the streets for Sankara's release.[7] The government eventually gave in and released Sankara, although they still kept him under house arrest. However, this did not prove to be the end of the matter, as tension continued between the government and Sankara, along with his many followers (both military and civilian). Less than two months after the Pô mutiny, the military overthrew President Jean-Baptiste Ouédraogo (who had come to power in a coup just a year earlier) and established a ruling council called the Conseil National de la Révolution (CNR), led by Sankara.[8] Civilian involvement in demanding the release of Sankara and later supporting the coup led Sankara to claim that the overthrow of Ouedraogo was a popular revolution, not an ordinary military coup.[9]

The civilian population and the military developed a close relationship during this period, which can help explain the crisis in 2011, as will be discussed later in the chapter. Even before gaining political power, Sankara made efforts to break down the barriers between the civilians and the military, causing an 'unheard of change of attitude'.[10] When he was in charge of the commando unit in Pô, for example, soldiers were encouraged to integrate with civilians. They assisted with the local harvesting, had joint football teams and formed an orchestra together.[11] Sankara's integration of civilians and military personnel was more than just a social assimilation. This young, charismatic leader espoused ideas that mixed populism, Marxism–Leninism, pan-Africanism and nationalism, similar to the ideas of Jerry Rawlings in Ghana at the time.[12] His calls for class equality along with basic provisions such as 'food, clean drinking water, clothes, housing, schools, and health' made him highly popular among the masses in Burkina Faso, which was at the time ranked as the third poorest country in the world.[13] He had a particularly strong following among the youth, a popularity that persists in Burkina Faso today.

Unlike Strasser and Jammeh, who also espoused populist ideas, Sankara proved his campaign was not only rhetoric, which increased his popularity, particularly among the lower economic classes. He sought to distance the government from anything that symbolised excess, even auctioning the government's fleet of Mercedes and readjusting government salaries so that ministers and public servants all received the same salary. He did not exempt himself from the policy and collected the same wages as other civil servants. Even as head of state, he ate alongside the rank-and-file soldiers in the mess hall.[14]

Sankara and the CNR tried to change the way the population viewed the military, as well as the way in which the military viewed its own role in the country. Being in the military was a core aspect of Sankara's public image. He wore military fatigues at nearly all times, even to engagements abroad. The image of him in a red military beret has become iconic, seen on T-shirts and stickers throughout the region and beyond. Sankara's appearance was not simply a matter of attire; it signalled the military as an essential part of the revolutionary ideas he espoused. Whereas the military in Burkina Faso (and elsewhere in the region) was traditionally seen as an extension of an often unpopular regime, Sankara argued that the armed forces should instead be seen and treated as a 'component of the people':[15]

> the new soldier must live and suffer among the people to which he belongs. The days of the free-spending army are over. From now on, besides handling arms, the army will work in the fields and raise cattle, sheep and poultry. It will build schools and health clinics and ensure their functioning.[16]

This plan was meant to 'produce a new mentality within the army' and remind soldiers how ordinary Burkinabé live and work.[17] Most military leaders who come to power in coups make attempts to win the military over with added equipment or increased salaries, but to some extent Sankara actually 'demoted' the military to civilian roles. Furthermore, during this period the military became 'juniorised', giving unprecedented power and influence to the junior ranks. The grievances shared between civilians and military as well as the empowerment of junior ranks over their seniors are traits seen in the 2011 mutinies.

Sankara and the CNR had plenty of critics at home and abroad, and the implementation of their programme did not always go according to plan. Many of the ambitious ideas Sankara had championed never came to fruition, and sections of the military were responsible for killing the revolutionary spirit, both figuratively and literally. In 1987, less than four years after coming to power, Sankara was assassinated. It is widely believed that Compaoré, Sankara's closest ally, was responsible for ordering the assassination.[18] With the death of Sankara, Compaoré became president, a position he held until 2014. By the time of his death, Sankara had come under criticism for using repressive techniques to suppress the opposition. The harmonious civilian–military relationship that Sankara had initially envisioned did not last.

A tested tactic

Compaoré won a series of elections in 1991, 1998, 2005 and 2010. However, these victories should not be seen as reflecting his popularity in the country. During this time, there were widespread restrictions on opposition parties, and voter turnout in presidential elections was relatively low. Voter turnout in the 2010 election, for example, was 54 per cent, down from 57 per cent in 2005.[19] Despite Compaoré's military background and his history of leading military upheavals (both the mutiny in 1982 and coups in 1983 and 1987), he was unable to keep the military satisfied. Soldiers in Burkina Faso have used mutinies as a means of expressing their dissatisfaction on a fairly regular basis since the late 1990s.

In July 1999, soldiers who had returned from the Central African Republic after participating in the MINURCA peacekeeping mission staged a protest over unpaid mission subsidies.[20] The mutineers also claimed that they received $230 a month on the mission, while their counterparts from Mali made $610, and therefore calculated that the government owed them (collectively) $20 million in back-pay.[21] This is consistent with patterns discussed in Chapter 5, in which dissatisfaction following peacekeeping deployments is often related to the ability of the soldiers to compare their conditions and pay with those from other countries.

The protest quickly spread beyond the peacekeepers to other garrisons throughout the country, with the soldiers joining the protests, adding their own complaints about living allowances. They also made specific demands for the government to return the sums that had been deducted from their salary to pay for new accommodation because the housing had never been built, accusing the senior officers of embezzling the funds that were meant for the housing project.[22] During the mutiny, the soldiers kidnapped Colonel Kouamé Lougué, a member of the Joint Chiefs of Staff.[23] NCOs were used as liaisons between the protesting soldiers and the military hierarchy, and the soldiers were paid at least part of the amount they demanded.[24] The 1999 revolts were similar to the events in 2011 because they occurred amid ongoing civilian demonstrations over the suspected murder of the journalist Norbert Zongo by government forces.[25]

Burkinabé soldiers also mutinied in 2003, 2006, and 2007. The incident in 2006 was the most serious. In December 2006, a police officer shot and killed a soldier. In response, the soldiers attacked police stations (some of which were set on fire) and freed over 600 prisoners from jail. As a result, the ECOWAS heads of state summit scheduled for Ouagadougou that week was postponed. A week after the incident began, 'a first meeting took place between soldiers and the MoD [Ministry of Defence]. Surprisingly, instead of complaining about their fellow deceased, they demanded for improvement of accommodation, welfare allowances and dressing.'[26] As will be discussed below, this escalation of demands also characterised the 2011 mutinies.

The Burkinabé Colonel Honoré Lucien Nombre argues that the soldiers were never penalised for participating in these events and no serious assessments were carried out to determine the root causes of the mutinies. In a report he wrote in 2008, Nombre expressed concern about the indiscipline within the military and argued that a major military restructuring was needed to address the problem.[27] However, it does not appear that significant changes were made in the military even after numerous demonstrations and mutinies. In order to resolve the tense relationship between the army and police, the Ministry of Defence announced a plan to move the urban military bases further outside of towns. The ministry believed this would separate the soldiers from their rivals, the police, and reduce the chances of another altercation between the two. However, in practice this angered the soldiers who wanted to remain close to their families in town. The soldiers then added this housing issue to their complaints about military retirement age and demonstrated in October 2007. A commission was set up, led by President Compaoré's brother, to negotiate between the soldiers and senior military leadership, which eventually resulted in the mutineers receiving some of their demands.[28] The events in 2011 should be viewed in the context of these series of mutinies. Soldiers were likely emboldened by the immediate material success of their past revolts but also still dissatisfied that the larger issues, such as corruption, had not been addressed.

Familiar dissatisfaction reignited

The 2011 military mutinies were directly preceded by and overlapped with the largest civilian demonstrations seen in Burkina Faso since at least 1998–9.[29] During interviews in Burkina Faso, locals referred to the mutinies and civilian demonstrations collectively as the '2011 crisis'. The civilian side of this crisis began with protests following the arrest and death of a student named Justin Zongo in Koudougou in late February 2011.[30] The government issued an official statement claiming that Zongo had died in custody of meningitis, yet rumours quickly spread that he had been beaten to death by the police. Students throughout the country were outraged that no one was charged with Zongo's death. Within two weeks, the protests had spread to dozens of cities throughout the country.

As the protests escalated, so did the scope of the grievances. The protests were no longer just about the perceived injustice of the Zongo case but about other suspected murders that had not been resolved. Chrysogone Zougmoré, president of Burkina Faso's main human rights organisation, the Mouvement Burkinabé des Droits de l'Homme et des Peuples (MBDHP), said that the crisis had resulted from years of injustice.[31] Bassolma Bazié, secretary general of the confederation of trade unions, CGT-B, explained that the death of Zongo in police custody was not a one-off event but rather the latest in a series of suspicious deaths over a number of decades, for which many held the government responsible.[32] Other infamous examples he cited were the deaths of Sankara in 1987, the medical student and activist Dabo Boukary in 1990 and the director of the newspaper *L'indépendént*, Norbert Zongo, in 1998.[33] In the words of Hamidou Idogo, editor-in-chief of *Journal du Jeudi*: 'here in our country we don't trust authorities anymore. There is crime in every domain and no justice.'[34] For many interviewees, like Idogo, the crisis of 2011 was first and foremost an issue of justice and human rights.

In addition to the issue of justice, labour unions, civil society groups and individuals began to protest over the high cost of living and low wages, grievances shared by many people across the country. The demonstrations grew in size and spread throughout Burkina Faso, with various groups expressing loosely related complaints. Cotton growers in Bobo Dioulasso protested at the low cotton prices, students in Koudougou took to the streets over police repression, teachers in Gaoua demanded higher living allowances and unions in Ouagadougou organised a march calling for an increase in public sector salaries.[35] Although the specific requests differed, they all shared and expressed feelings of dissatisfaction with the state of affairs in Burkina Faso.

Tensions rose along with the grievances, and the protests gradually became violent. Heavy-handed police responses led to civilian injuries and deaths, further incensing the protestors. Police stations, government buildings and the ruling party headquarters were vandalised and some set on fire by angry mobs. The targets of destruction were a clear indication that the demonstrators placed the blame on the government. This was confirmed in my interviews. When asked to explain the cause of the crisis, one journalist said, 'the crisis is complex but to say it simply, the explanation is bad governance'.[36] The media drew attention to the fact that Compaoré had been in power since 1987 and implied that it was time for a leadership change, calling the events a 'crisis of confidence'.[37]

The military enters the scene

The situation in Burkina Faso deteriorated even further when, after a month of civilian protests, the military started their own demonstrations. The initial cause of the military mutinies was not directly related to the initial cause of the civilian crisis, although both groups shared complaints about the justice system. Just as the civilian demonstrations quickly added grievances and participants, so did the military demonstration. As the mutinies grew, one trait that remained consistent was that all participants were among the enlisted ranks.[38]

The initial mutiny was sparked by soldiers' objections to a court ruling. A group of five junior soldiers based in Ouagadougou had been arrested after allegedly beating and publicly humiliating a (civilian) man they accused of being too forward with the wife of a deployed soldier. When the soldiers were given sentences ranging from fifteen to eighteen months in prison, their fellow soldiers took to the streets, firing their weapons in the air and eventually looting local shops in protest at the sentencing.

In interviews, Burkinabé soldiers explained that there were two reasons why this unit was angry about the sentencing. The first is that they simply felt it was not deserved. They commented that the soldiers felt they were defending the honour of their colleague's wife, and claimed that any respectable man would agree with them. The second reason, which one source called 'the most important reason', was that the rank-and-file soldiers felt they were being unfairly punished because of their low rank.[39] One interviewee explained, 'the guys had assumed that the higher officers would speak out on their behalf and they did not'.[40] Another stated: 'they were angry at their senior officers for not stepping in'.[41] From these statements, it is clear that the military is accustomed to being above the law. This is confirmed in a leaked US embassy cable from 2009.[42] The cable reports a series of nine military tribunals involving eleven military personnel who were tried publicly with the press in attendance. However, most of the cases involved driving offences, with one case of 'desertion during times of peace'.[43] The cable concludes that the 'Burkinabé military has been put on notice ... the soldiers are being told that they no longer benefit from total immunity',[44] thereby suggesting that it was unusual for soldiers to be held accountable for even small offences.

AN ESCALATING CYCLE OF MUTINIES

Soldiers argued that the mutineers were not only resentful that they were punished but also alleged that officers had done much worse in the past without having been charged.[45] Several different military sources told a story about an officer who had shot his wife and was simply moved to another base rather than charged with a criminal offence. Here, the mutinying soldiers were making similar accusations as the civilians in claiming that the law was selective. The soldiers never explicitly mentioned being inspired by the Zongo case, but the movement likely fuelled the accusations of inequality within the legal system. It became easier for the soldiers to claim their case was mishandled when there was a public outcry about the poor state of the Burkinabé justice system.

It is also likely that the arrested soldiers were particularly offended by having been detained by the police. One military source explained, 'it would be almost unheard of for a police officer to arrest someone in the military, even a junior member'.[46] There is a long rivalry between the military and police, as highlighted in the open conflict between the two groups in 2006.

In an effort to resolve the mutiny, the authorities released the arrested soldiers. However, this angered the members of the justice department, who went on strike to protest. Traders and shop-owners whose merchandise had been looted or destroyed by the mutineers also began to demonstrate. At this point, 'the regime was faced with a multipronged protest which included the movement against impunity, traders, the justice department, and the army'.[47] Before the government could resolve the problem, a separate mutiny broke out in Fada N'Gourma, around 200 kilometres east of Ouagadougou.

Much like the Ouagadougou mutiny, which occurred just a week earlier, the soldiers in Fada N'Gourma were protesting against a court ruling. In this case, the arrested soldier had been convicted of raping a minor. The residents of Fada N'Gourma, who had undoubtedly read the reports of the destruction caused in the Ouagadougou mutiny, immediately closed their shops and left the streets.[48] The soldiers fired weapons into the air and intimidated authorities into releasing their arrested comrade.[49] Professor Salif Yonaba argued that the release of the soldiers in Ouagadougou and Fada N'Gourma was a major setback for the rights of the Burkinabé people.[50] Overruling the decision of the justice department because of the unruly behaviour of junior soldiers further delegitimised the government, which was viewed as extending the pattern of impunity for military personnel. It confirmed that the law was selective, justifying the civilian accusations about the Zongo case and other previous unresolved crimes.

Although the initial demands of the soldiers from the 32nd Infantry Commando Regiment in Fada N'Gourma were met, on the following day (29 March) they rebelled again. This time, they fired a rocket at the courthouse.[51] The next day, soldiers in Gaoua and Ouagadougou mutinied.[52] Whereas the first round of mutinies in Ouagadougou involved random attacks on shops and traders, the second round was more targeted. This time, soldiers vandalised the houses of the mayor of Ouagadougou and the defence minister. In response, the government imposed a curfew, and President Compaoré agreed to meet with the discontented soldiers and civilians.[53] Despite the meetings, which were mediated by religious and traditional leaders, another large strike took place on 8 April, involving traders, civil society groups, political opposition supporters and students.[54]

After two weeks of relative calm in the military, Compaoré faced the most serious threat of his presidency on 14 April when his elite presidential guards (the Régiment de Sécurité Présidentiel, or RSP) revolted. This was the first time the unit had been involved in a mutiny.[55] The unit claimed the protest was over payment and housing allowances. The mutiny quickly spread to soldiers based at Camp Lamizana in western Ouagadougou.[56] There was also widespread looting, as well as car thefts and reports of rape.[57] The chaotic atmosphere made it difficult to tell if the crimes were committed by military personnel or civilians; however, it appears both sectors took part. Media outlets shut down, adding to residents' anxiety as they did not know what was going on.

President Compaoré's response reflects the severity of the situation he faced. Within a day of the RSP revolt, he had left the capital and had taken refuge in his hometown of Ziniaré, 30 kilometres north of the capital.[58] Just a day later, Compaoré dissolved the government, appointed a new cabinet and prime minister, replaced the chiefs of staff of the army, air force and police, and named himself minister of defence.

Compaoré quickly gave into the demands of the RSP, leading an RSP spokesperson to publicly reaffirm the unit's loyalty to the president. The spokesperson apologised for the damage the RSP had caused and called on other units to adhere to military discipline.[59] However, rather than calm the situation, the government response only seemed to inspire other units. Media reports quoted soldiers stating that they wanted their pay and bonuses to be equivalent to those given to members of the RSP.[60] Soldiers in Tenkodogo, Kaya, and Pô imitated earlier mutinies by firing weapons in the air, looting shops, seizing private vehicles and attacking the houses of senior officers.[61] The mutiny at Pô had symbolic significance, as this was the same base from which Compaoré had launched his mutiny in 1983.

The mutiny not only spread within the military but quickly infected the police force as well.[62] By the end of April, the Republican Guards had also joined the trend.[63] Thus, within a month of the initial Ouagadougou mutiny, nearly every branch of the security sector within every region of the country had taken part in a mutiny. The sole exception was the gendarmerie, as will be discussed later in the chapter.

During this month of mutinies, civilians also began taking to the streets in a continuation of the protests over Zongo's death, yet the demands of the protestors had now increased, with them calling for economic and political change. At times, civilians and military seemed united in their calls for increased wages, but in other incidents civilians directly protested against damage caused by the mutinies and criticised the government for not controlling the armed forces. Distrust continued to characterise the relationship between the various actors involved in the crisis—students, opposition groups, unions, military—thereby prohibiting coordination, even though they shared many of the same goals.[64]

On 28 April, two months after the turmoil had started, the newly appointed prime minister announced a series of changes in response to the demands of the civilians and the military. Key changes included the elimination of the development tax, reduction in the salary tax and salary increases in the public sector, as well as promises to charge any senior officials accused of being involved in corruption. However, these changes only affected a minority of the population and did little for the bulk of the people who made their living from agriculture.[65] Still, it did represent a government response to the civilian demands, and the widespread protests became more sporadic.[66]

Mutiny finale

Although the government seemed to have made progress on the civilian front, the military continued to express dissatisfaction with the situation. New mutinies broke out in Pô, Kaya, Dori, Tenkodogo, Dedougou and Koupela in May.[67] It is difficult to tell how exactly each of these mutinies were resolved, but it is likely that agreements were reached over salary issues or other material complaints.

After months of mutinies, the situation reached a breaking point at the beginning of June when soldiers in Bobo Dioulasso joined the revolt. Bobo Dioulasso, Burkina Faso's second largest city, is home to the country's second largest military base (the largest in both cases being Ouagadougou). The city has a sizeable university student population and a reputation as a rebellious town.[68] After three days, Compaoré sent members of the RSP, the Dedougou paratroopers and gendarmerie to 'forcibly disarm' the mutineers.[69] Officially, six mutineers and one civilian (a girl caught in the crossfire) were killed in the attack. However, according to military sources, the number of military casualties was much higher.[70] Following the attack, the government announced the dismissal of 566 soldiers, 217 of whom were charged with a criminal offence.[71]

What is unusual about the Burkina Faso mutinies is not that they ended in violence, but that the government refrained from using violence for so long. There are few cases in West Africa in which mutinies have continued for such a long period before being forcibly put down. One explanation for this is that the government wanted to use all possible methods before resorting to force. One military interviewee explained that peaceful negotiation is 'the Burkinabé way'.[72] Burkina Faso does not have a history of civil war or armed rebellions, and most previous coups and mutinies have been relatively peaceful. However, the massive scale of the mutinies was also likely a reason why Compaoré was reluctant to use physical force against the mutineers. With nearly every sector of the security apparatus expressing their dissatisfaction, there was no guarantee that his orders would be carried out. Soldiers throughout the country expressed more loyalty towards each other than to their commanding officers or the head of state.

This was the first time that mutinies in Burkina Faso had been forcibly suppressed. Whereas concessions were the norm in previous mutinies, Compaoré may have set a new precedent, indicating a less tolerant attitude towards mutinies. However, there were widespread concerns and rumours that the hundreds of police and soldiers removed from their position after the mutiny could create instability in the future. These concerns came predominately from youth and students, although several professionals also mentioned them. Comments about this potential threat include:

> The dismissing of so many soldiers can bring about insecurity. In the countryside I heard there is some [former soldiers] with bad intentions.
>
> Former soldiers become thieves, we all know someone who is victim of them, they will not hesitate to attack this country.
>
> I met one of them [a former soldier] out drinking, it is scary, they have a lot of training.
>
> Those that were arrested, we do not know what they are planning. They can come back. In the past they were shooting in the air but what if this time they shoot people.

AN ESCALATING CYCLE OF MUTINIES

Soldiers also expressed their concern over the dismissals by circulating pamphlets in the barracks in 2012. One of the pamphlets called for the release and reintegration of 'all dismissed soldiers'.[73] Another denounced arbitrary dismissals, specifically noting that some of the dismissed soldiers were not in Burkina Faso at the time of the mutiny.[74] The government did not reconsider the case of these dismissed soldiers, but the group renewed their claims to be reinstated after the fall of Compaoré, as will be further discussed at the end of the chapter.

There is not enough information to suggest that there was an increase in crime related to the dismissed security personnel. However, the rumours suggested doubts that the government could adequately counter a rebellion or wave of crime. Despite Compaoré remaining in power through the mutinies and protests, the 'crisis of confidence' still seemed to be exerting a strong hold on the population.

While the assault on the Bobo Dioulasso mutineers put an end to the 2011 mutinies, doing so may have led to unintended consequences. The International Crisis Group found that: 'The RSP's role in the repression of the Bobo Dioulasso mutiny has widened the gap between the presidential guard and the rest of the military, all the more so because RSP personnel who participated in the mutinies have not been punished.'[75]

Similarly, a Burkinabé professor argued that using one branch of the military against another has the potential to divide the force and to cause long-term resentment. He claims that the incident in Bobo Dioulasso has produced an accumulation of 'problems for a future crisis'.[76] These problems came to a head in 2014 and 2015, as will be discussed at the end of the chapter.

Depth of the grievances

As opposed to the earlier case studies in which soldiers were fairly clear about their grievances, the massive scale of the Burkina Faso mutinies made it difficult to identify what the soldiers actually wanted from the revolt. Media reported that the mutinies had been sparked by the government's failure to pay the soldiers; however, all the soldiers I spoke with stated that this was not the case. They instead claimed that one of their main grievances concerned the more complex issue of living allowances. Soldiers are entitled to a salary and a living allowance, and the living allowance is easier to manipulate.[77] The living allowance goes towards housing and food, which is often provided by the military and not paid in full. Soldiers believed that they should have been receiving more food and of a higher quality, as well as housing in accordance with the amount deducted from their salary as a living allowance. They also alleged that senior officers were taking part of this allowance for their own purposes.[78]

However, military respondents often seemed unconvinced that pay or living allowances were the primary motives. One military source argued that the soldiers were simply frustrated with the government and were seeking to take advantage of the government's weak position during the ongoing protests by demanding items such as uniforms, boots, and belts that they would not normally have mutinied over.[79]

Interviewees seemed to find it difficult to pinpoint the precise cause of the 2011 mutinies, yet, when asked the more general question of 'why has there been so much indiscipline within the military?', they quickly gave detailed responses. Most of the responses emphasised pervasive corruption and favouritism within the military. Numerous respondents, both civilian and military, stated that the problems begun with the recruitment process, which they claimed had become very personalised. One military source went into great detail about a concept within the Burkinabé military called 'Command Lists':

> So say the military is recruiting 500 individuals. The head of the army will get to submit ten names, then the regional commander submits ten, then the base commander, and so on, even down to the local chief. These individuals are hand-selected based on their affiliation and do not have to pass the other requirements, such as the physical tests. But those that have no affiliation must pass strict tests. Then when they get to basic training, the trainers know who is from the list, they are concerned about being too harsh on those that were selected by top officers. So those individuals get a pass again, while the others are treated very poorly. Everyone understands the system and it creates major divides from the start.[80]

Other military sources made similar accusations, with one stating that 'rich people send their sons and daughters to the military and no one can bother them'.[81] Another soldier remarked that 'officers can bring their children into the military, this is a problem because their superiors are afraid to discipline them because they are the sons of their boss'.[82] Yet another soldier pointed to 'favouritism in recruiting, they don't see who is best, they select sons of officers'.[83]

The recruitment issue has become particularly important in recent years, as Burkina Faso expanded the number of military recruits by 2,000 between 2008 and 2011.[84] This is a substantial number, as the Burkinabé military as of 2011 numbered between 7,000 and 8,000 (not including the gendarmerie).[85] Considering the mutinies consisted nearly entirely of junior rank-and-file soldiers, it is likely that many were recruited within the last few years. The increased recruitment was partially due to an aging force; however, it was also a response to Burkina Faso's increased involvement in peacekeeping missions. UN data shows a sharp increase in Burkina Faso's peacekeeping troop contributions in 2009, with a steady increase ever since. As of January 2017, Burkina Faso had 2,530 troops deployed on peacekeeping missions, most on MINUSMA (Mali) and UNAMID (Darfur).[86]

Soldiers also complained about the promotion process, with one military source expressing his anger that he was passed over for officer training in favour of others who were well connected but less qualified.[87] Another raised specific concerns about the way individuals were selected for deployments. He complained that peacekeepers were chosen from among the senior officers' friends and relatives, and that even with a strong military record and twenty-six years of service, he has never had the opportunity to be sent on deployment.[88] Another military source also confirmed the importance of being well connected for career advancement: 'if you do not know someone, you will never be assigned to an important mission'.[89] With Burkina Faso increasing its contributions to foreign missions, this is a concern that will likely continue if the hierarchy does not address it.

Underlying these complaints is distrust towards officers whom the junior soldiers viewed as endorsing and perpetuating a system that they perceive as based on favouritism. In interviews, it was often unclear if they were referring to the officer corps as a whole or the senior officers specifically. When I asked one enlisted soldier if he was referring to the senior officers or all officers, he responded 'some individual superiors are good, but as a group there are too many problems'.[90] Interviewees did not hold back when criticising senior officers. One soldier, speaking about the senior officers, stated:

> officers are taking advantage of their positions, driving big cars, living in big houses in Ouaga 2000 always going on foreign training opportunities, gaining more profit while the others are living like normal Burkinabé. The juniors work the most and gain the least, while the officers work the least and gain the most, it should be the opposite. This creates a lot of frustration for privates and NCOs.[91]

A junior soldier believed that most individuals got to a senior position through means other than merit, and that there is no respect for the senior officers among the rank and file as a result.[92] The officers appeared to recognise that they had no control over their subordinates. When I asked soldiers where the officers were while the rank and file took to the streets, answers included 'hiding' and 'they ran away'. No one indicated that the individual officers attempted to regain their authority.

In addition to allegations of corruption and favouritism, some interviewees also felt that the indiscipline seen in the mutinies was a result of poor training. One military source specifically stated that part of the military training should involve education about the role of the military: 'you have people that are trained and armed but not educated, they have no idea what being in the military means'.[93] In his opinion, soldiers need to be taught that the role of a soldier is to protect the citizens. The International Crisis Group has also highlighted problems in training. They note that, on average, there is one officer and two NCOs to train 200 new recruits, suggesting that training is likely to be of a very poor quality.[94]

A final contributing cause of the 2011 revolt, and previous mutinies, was the lack of communication within the military. Colonel Nombre highlights the 'communication gap between the bottom and the summit of the military' as a main cause of the 2006 mutinies.[95] To some extent, this communication gap is intentional, as the pattern of internal revolts has created a culture of secrecy within the military. Information is spread more often through rumours than via official channels. Soldiers confirmed this by explaining that most of the news they received during the mutinies came from mobile phone calls to their colleagues at other bases.[96] The International Crisis Group has also criticised the problems in communication: 'the rank and file rarely voice their day-to-day problems or express their discontent and so the administration never deals with even the most trivial issues, such as food quality'.[97] Insufficient communication contributed to soldiers' dissatisfaction, and the act of mutiny served as a remedy for this problem, with soldiers using the mutinies to express their myriad frustrations.

The exceptionally uninterested sectors

With such widespread participation in the mutinies, sectors of the military that did not become involved were the exception. The main exceptions include officers and the gendarmerie.

During the crisis, media speculation that a coup was about to take place proved premature.[98] Although the mutinies crippled the capital, at no point did the military attempt to oust President Compaoré. Interviewees, both civilian and military, were unanimous in stating that the soldiers had not sought to overthrow the president. The following is a sample of these responses:

> The soldiers could have easily taken over but they didn't, their goals were not about political gains.
>
> As a military man, I can tell you these soldiers had no political ambitions.

AN ESCALATING CYCLE OF MUTINIES

This was not a well-planned or organised event, our soldiers know how to do a coup and this was no coup.

That they did not move to take control of the state was not due to an inability to do so. There were numerous times throughout the months of mutinies that a coup seemed possible, if not probable. However, the mutineers were nearly all rank-and-file soldiers who had little interest in taking political power and did not appear to have a recognised leader.[99] The lack of leadership and organisation was likely a result of the geographic dispersal of the mutinies and the lack of a specific and shared goal.

One junior soldier claimed that 'if there were officers involved there would still be problems now',[100] implying that there would have been a coup or coup attempt. While it is not unheard of for a coup attempt to be orchestrated from the enlisted ranks, it is rare, and a successful coup by enlisted soldiers is particularly rare. None of my interviewees gave a direct explanation for the officers' refusal to become involved. However, the descriptions above about the perceptions of the officer corps and their relationship with the rank and file are likely to be part of the reason. The mutineers were frustrated over a system they believed favoured officers or others with connections to the political leadership, and it goes without saying that the officers are unlikely to have wanted to change this system. Similarly, as many officers have links to political leaders, there may have been little motivation to conduct a coup.

If officers had decided to make a move for political control, it is unlikely that they would have been able to capitalise on the discontent of the rank and file. In the cases of Sierra Leone in 1992 and The Gambia in 1994, the junior officers were able to utilise the frustrations of their subordinates, but in both cases this was due to their direct links with the individuals involved. While enlisted ranks and junior officers appeared united in the 1980s in Burkina Faso, there is little indication of a similar bond in 2011. The explanation of military discontent, as set out in the previous section, as well as the actions during the mutinies, demonstrates a divide between the enlisted ranks and officers. It is a divide that goes beyond the expected divisions in military hierarchies and is one that became antagonistic.

As noted earlier, the gendarmerie was the only security branch that did not mutiny.[101] This was not the first time that the gendarmerie had remained loyal in the face of growing mutinies. For example, when police and soldiers took to the streets in 2006, the gendarmerie did not take part. As a result, the gendarmerie was tasked with leading a commission to look at ways to reduce the possibility of similar incidents in the future.[102] Part of the explanation for this loyalty may have to do with the role of the gendarmerie in former French colonies in West Africa. The gendarmerie serves as a military police force, and often has a double affiliation with the Ministry of the Interior and the Ministry of Defence. The gendarmerie's continued existence into post-colonial times is often considered controversial because it is seen 'to represent the continuation of a military presence in domestic security and therefore legitimise the involvement of the armed forces in internal security matters'.[103]

A military source in Burkina Faso explained that gendarmes receive different, and superior, training from the army, air force and police.[104] Essentially, members of the gendarmerie receive training as soldiers and police officers by attending both traditional military training and courses on internal laws and domestic matters. As a result, the interviewee believed the gendarmes to be more conscious of their roles and responsibilities. Furthermore, gendarmes have the authority to arrest members of the military and the police. Another source believed that, because the gendarmes have a unique role in overseeing the discipline of the other security services, the gendarmerie leadership is much stricter than is the case in the other security services.[105] When I asked a military interviewee if pay was a factor in the difference in discipline between the military and gendarmerie, he did not seem to think it was a primary cause. He explained that the gendarmes were paid a 'little more' than the military overall, but he also noted that this was a hard distinction to make because the pay for both groups varied based on their duties.[106]

The unique and flexible role of the gendarmerie, as well as its arrest authority, has meant that the gendarmerie in many former French colonies have become closely linked to the ruling regimes.[107] Burkinabé interviewees explained that recruitment for the gendarmerie is more stringent than for the other services, a trend consistent with other gendarmeries.[108] Discussing Francophone Africa in general, Niagalé Bagayoko claims that 'The gendarmes generally enjoy a better reputation than the other security forces: they appear to be a disciplined corps respectful of hierarchy.'[109] This is consistent with remarks made by two Burkinabé sources, who explained that there is more respect for gendarmerie leadership among the rank and file, a trait that was demonstrated during the mutinies. While army units throughout the country were rebelling against their leadership, the gendarmes stayed loyal to theirs. Several individuals noted that Djibril Bassolé was previously in charge of the gendarmerie and used this to make the argument that the gendarmes have strong and respectable leaders. Bassolé served as the foreign minister of Burkina Faso and was a highly visible individual within the international community for his involvement in numerous conflict mediations, most recently between Malian rebels and the Malian government. He ran for the president in 2015, a decision that caused controversy given his links with the Compaoré regime.

The divisions between those that mutinied and those that did not reflect the divisions within an organisation and between organisations. Variations in daily conditions, training and the history of different sectors of the armed forces help explain the variations in their likelihood to revolt.

New changes replicate old patterns

In the midst of the military revolts, Compaoré ordered the largest political shake up in his then twenty-four years in power by dissolving the government and appointing a new prime minsiter and cabinet and thirteen new regional governors. While on the surface this seems significant, in reality many of the same old political hands were simply reshuffled. For example, of the twenty-nine-member 'new' cabinet, thirteen had been part of the previous cabinet.[110] This sleight of hand did not go unnoticed. One interviewee stated: 'Both the old and new government is here to preserve the role of Blaise Compaoré. So is there a change? Yes, but it is just as bad as before.'[111] Compaoré also appointed himself to the position of defence minister, a move that gave him even more power than he had before the crisis.

Compaoré made similar changes within the defence sector by dismissing the chiefs of staff of the army, air force and police (the chief of the gendarmerie kept his job owing to the gendarmes' loyalty during the mutinies). Although sources claimed that the army chief of staff had been particularly unpopular, his removal failed to placate the mutinying soldiers.[112] Furthermore, a military officer explained that the 'fired' senior officers were simply rotated into a different offices rather than actually being removed.[113] Military interviewees acknowledged that some immediate benefits resulted from the mutinies. Junior soldiers reported that their salaries had increased (along with the salaries paid to civil servants) and that some of the food issues had been resolved. The request to allow soldiers to purchase their own food, rather than have it provided by the military, was also granted.

Another major change to come out of the mutinies, and one not expected by the soldiers, was the firing of hundreds of soldiers and police. Although the number of rebellious soldiers removed from service was high, it was by no means all of those who had been involved in the mutinies. The dismissals were likely intended to serve as a lesson for those contemplating a future mutiny as much as for punishment of those involved.

A Burkinabé military source also noted how the government had implemented measures to make it physically more difficult for soldiers to mutiny, or at least to cause such widespread violence. There was a concern over how easily soldiers throughout the country were able to access ammunition. In response, ammunition storage became more centralised, with most ammunition being secured at one base rather than spread throughout a number of smaller bases and outposts. He claims that although soldiers still carried guns, few had any ammunition.[114]

High-level personnel changes, mass dismissals and increased payments to soldiers did not address the systemic problems within the military. In the words of one military source, 'the problem is deeper than just removing a person; it is the same structures, the same people and the same philosophy'.[115] Another enlisted soldier noted how 'there is still a part of the army that cannot be touched', suggesting that the elite units (i.e. the presidential guards) were still above the law.[116] The indiscipline and lack of respect for military authority resulting from perceptions of corruption and favouritism will be much harder to fix. When I asked my military sources what changes they would like to see, one responded 'a new generation of officers', while another remarked 'we need new blood'.

There was some indication that the government and the military leadership were considering more sustained changes following the mutinies. An annual conference to discuss ongoing concerns within the military was established and at least two iterations have been held (in September 2012 and 2013).[117] The theme for the first annual military conference was communication, which reinforces complaints heard during interviews about poor internal communication within the military.[118]

During interviews in 2012, members of the military and civilians revealed a strong sense that the crisis in 2011 had not been fully resolved and more tension was yet to come. Despite acknowledging improvements, most civilian respondents did not think the reforms had gone far enough. Many noted that after the initial decreases in food prices had crept back up and there had not been changes in employment opportunities. University students were particularly vocal about the need for more change. In an acrimonious debate on campus in 2012, students loudly applauded and cheered the statement that the 2011 reforms were 'just a manipulation by the government to keep us quiet, we are only seeing our banks, our food, if we want real change we must look beyond that, all the government did was lower the price of rice and we are satisfied, we must go beyond this'. Another participant declared 'we cannot talk about change when the same head is dictating the same body', implying that it was time for the president to leave office.[119] In interviews, some individuals made statements such as 'to be sincere, this is just the beginning' and 'the crisis is not behind us, it is in front of us'.[120] A source within the Burkinabé military described the series of mutinies since the 1990s and pointed out that, with each successive demonstration, the military had become more violent. He said he was worried that this would be devastating for the country if the pattern continued.[121] Several other interviewees shared this opinion, with responses such as 'next time it will be worse' and 'if it happens again I think it will be a full revolution'.

Memory of the mutinies continues

Much of the destruction and violence the mutineers had caused came at the expense of the civilian population. There were dozens of injured civilians, numerous reported rapes, and extensive damage to shops and private residences. The local media ran pictures of soldiers wielding heavy weapons on the streets, civilians with bloody injuries caused by soldiers, and shops trashed by mutineers.

Between those that experienced the mutinies first hand and those that heard of them through the extensive local media coverage, it would be easy to conclude that the mutinies severely damaged the civil–military relationship in Burkina Faso. However, interviewees portrayed the events in a more nuanced way. Numerous civilian interviewees expressed the opinion that, although the violence by the military was wrong, they were forced into the situation because they had no other way to express their complaints. A sample of such comments includes:

> They [soldiers] should be able to strike, our government does not allow the soldiers to strike.
>
> We are a democratic country, it is unfair that they [soldiers] cannot participate.
>
> Those soldiers, they were fighting to claim their rights too, even a soldier needs to take care of his family, the hierarchy is the problem.

Many felt that the military was poorly treated. A Burkinabé professor stated that he was not surprised by what had happened because 'those guys are abused, have no rights, they have bad living conditions, it is all they can do'.[122] Another academic stated: 'all Burkinabé should be treated equal but the military are often treated badly and they don't have their rights'. He added that their actions should be condemned and they should have brought their case to the judge, but that 'All this happened because the military does not trust the justice system of Burkina Faso'.[123] Despite nearly every civilian interviewee stating that they were shocked and concerned by the violence unleashed by the mutinying soldiers, they were sympathetic to the causes and placed the overall blame on the government.

A number of civilian respondents also sought to deny any wrongdoings by the military. One civilian expressed the belief that criminals took advantage of the chaotic situation to steal and cause damage, for which the military was later blamed. Another stated that 'some gangsters spoiled the name of our military'.

The complex relationship between the civilian population and the military in Burkina Faso has been portrayed in the country's popular culture. Less than a year after the mutinies, there was both a play and a film released about the event. This fictionalised account, titled *Le Foulard Noir* (The black headscarf), was showing nightly at variously cinemas throughout the country in the spring of 2012, indicating that the mutiny was of widespread interest in Burkina Faso and that the story had commercial value.

The government actively endorsed *Le Foulard Noir*, and the film received partial funding from the office of the president.[124] Leading military officers as well as the prime minister were in attendance at the premiere, and announcements about the screening were posted on the official government webpage.[125] The film was later shown at military barracks throughout Burkina Faso as well.

The film follows a family in Ouagadougou, portraying how the mutinies affected their lives. Despite the government funding, the film does not censor what took place during the mutinies. It graphically depicts civilians being killed by stray bullets from the weapons of mutineers, and soldiers raping women. However, not all of the military are portrayed as perpetrators. *Le Foulard Noir* also paints a complicated picture of the relationship between the military and civilians. For example, there is a scene where soldiers visit the family of a civilian killed in the mutiny to offer condolences and another where soldiers explain that they also have relatives who have been victimised in the rebellion. At the end of the film, there are pictures of the actual destruction caused by the mutinies throughout the country.

While the film gives a realistic account of aspects of the mutinies, it is largely void of the context of the mutinies. The film focuses solely on the military revolts, not the wider civilian protests, which may have touched on sensitive political issues. In the portrayal of the revolts, it is unclear why the soldiers are rebelling. Speaking about the film, the then Prime Minister Luc Adolphe

Tiao explained that everyone objected to the violence that took place but the important part of the film was the ending, in which forgiveness dominated.[126] Boubacar Diallo, the film's director, claimed that the film was meant to expose the 'ugliness' of the events and to allow society to 'reflect together'.[127] He explained that the film was intended to help the younger generation raise its level of civic consciousness.[128]

Whereas it is common for leaders to try to hide mutinies or at least not publicise them, Compaoré did almost the opposite by supporting the film's production. This may have been a sensible move, as it created an open dialogue about the events. However, the overall message seemed to be forgiveness of the individuals involved, rather than an inquiry into the larger issues that had motivated the revolts. In this sense, the film seemed to reflect the government's attitude towards the events.

In February 2013, nearly two years after the mutinies, a popular Burkinabé rap group called Waga3000 put out a music video that also recreated the mutinies. Whereas *Le Foulard Noir* appears to have been marketed mostly within Burkina Faso, Waga3000 has wider appeal. The group tours internationally, and its music and videos can be purchased digitally on many major music sites. The song in question, titled 'Voir sombrer ses fils',[129] takes on a more political tone than *Le Foulard Noir*, criticising both leaders and soldiers. The song focuses on the issue of injustice, and one of the two rappers is wearing a shirt with Norbert Zongo's name on it. Similar to *Le Foulard Noir*, the military is not portrayed as one-dimensional. In some parts, soldiers are shown attacking civilians, and one scene implies rape, yet a final scene shows a soldier and a civilian embracing.

The complex way that the mutinies were portrayed in popular media is consistent with the way the former mutineers view themselves. In April 2015, four years after the mutinies, a group of former mutineers who had been fired following the revolt staged a press conference.[130] They asked the transitional government to reinstate them to their former positions in the military. They admitted that members of the military were involved in destruction during the mutinies and apologised to the country. Yet they also explained that they objected to the government's portrayal of them as criminals, both in the local press and internationally. They noted that there had never been a complete investigation into each individual's role in the revolts despite the mass dismissals of serving personnel. They argued that the dismissals were selective, favouring some soldiers over others. These claims are remarkably similar to those that sparked the mutinies and the civilian protests in the first place. They alleged that the justice system is marred with inequalities and that there is a lack of transparency in decision-making. Their claims mirror many of the complaints heard in interviews regarding favouritism within the military. The former mutineers also attempted to contextualise what was often seen as military indiscipline as part of wider expressions of dissatisfaction with the Compaoré regime.

With the fall of Compaoré, there have been more frank discussions about the role of the military in Burkina Faso. The primary concerns aired in these discussions revolved around the RSP, which was accused of abuses, including killing protestors, during the 2014 demonstrations against Compaoré. The RSP was directly linked to the past president, and many have argued that the unit was no longer needed. The Commission for National Reconciliation and Reform, established under the transitional government, called the presidential guards an 'army within an army' and recommended disbanding them.[131] Their report suggested giving the role of presidential security to the police and gendarmes.[132] Given the elite status, higher pay and general immunity that the RSP has long enjoyed, it is no surprise that it vocally rejected the idea of becoming part of the 'regular' security forces.

The RSP moved from a vocal rejection to physical action in September 2015 when it stormed a government meeting and took the interim president, prime minister and members of parliament hostage. The attack took place only two days after the report from the Commission for National Reconciliation and Reform had been published. The coup leader, General Gilbert Diendéré, stated that the action was designed to 'prevent the disruption of Burkina Faso due to the insecurity looming during pre-elections'. However, this is unlikely to have been the real motive. The direct threat of disbanding the RSP was probably a key driver for the unit to attempt to oust the transitional government and replace it with a leader more friendly to their cause.

The same divides between the army and the RSP that were visible during 2011 were seen in an extreme form when the regular army sent units from around the country to the capital and threatened to attack if the RSP did not hand power back to the transitional government. The army appeared to gain popular support for countering the RSP, who were seen as Compaoré loyalists by many. After nearly a week in power, the RSP retreated, General Diendéré stepped down and interim President Kafando returned to office. However, this did not placate the unions, who continued to hold general strikes demanding that the RSP be disbanded and held accountable for its crimes. Within just a few days of Kafando's return to office, the government announced that the RSP would be disarmed and disbanded. Again, the RSP objected and there were several standoffs and violent altercations between the RSP and the army. Yet tensions eased over the following week, and the process of integrating the 800-member RSP into the regular army began.[133]

The case of Burkina Faso in general, and the events of 2014–15 in particular, serve as an important reminder that militaries are not homogeneous organisations and more detailed work on the various divisions within the security sector can further our understanding of how they operate or fail to operate effectively.

Conclusion

In the cases of Sierra Leone and The Gambia, specific incidents (war conditions in Sierra Leone and peacekeeping non-payment in The Gambia) unveiled larger concerns within the military. However, in Burkina Faso, there was no singular issue that triggered the 2011 mutinies. There was no indication that soldiers were paid irregularly; nor were there specific concerns over deployment pay or any immediate changes to military regulations. It took relatively little to lead hundreds, if not thousands, of soldiers throughout the country into acts of indiscipline and criminality, suggesting severe problems within the military.

The 2011 mutinies in Burkina Faso help further the argument that mutinies need to be viewed as being about more than demands for material concessions. Soldiers were inspired to revolt, in part by a sense of injustice towards a system they believed to be corrupt and based on favouritism. These problems were deeply ingrained in the military and affected recruitment, promotions and deployments. The perception of corruption led to a lack of authority and legitimacy among the officers in the eyes of their subordinates. The division among the ranks was demonstrated during the mutinies, in which only rank-and-file soldiers participated. The mutineers also conducted targeted attacks on several high-ranking officers' residences. While the mutinies in Burkina Faso were part of a history of revolts, the government response in 2011 was unprecedented. The mass dismissals following the mutinies set an example for soldiers contemplating future mutinies; however, much more will need to be done to restore confidence and respect between the ranks and their officers.

The sense of injustice among the soldiers mirrored that of the civilian demonstrations, and it is likely that soldiers drew some inspiration for their revolt from the ongoing civilian protests. This link between mutinies and civilian protests is part of a pattern in the region, as explained in Chapters 3 and 4. The two sectors did not work together during the crisis, despite putting forward similar demands. The rank-and-file soldiers and non-elite civilians shared mutual concerns over the cost of living, and both felt that their struggles were the consequence of a hierarchy that did not represent their interests. The mutinies in Burkina Faso remained a theme of discussion among the civilian population because they were not seen as a purely military matter. The mutineers' actions had severe consequences for the civilian population, but they were seen by many as being a part of a wider struggle.

9

AN ALTERED VIEW OF MUTINIES

This book's analysis of mutinies in Africa since the independence era challenges the notion that the revolts were an internal military matter, best studied by military historians. Unlike the more familiar historical cases of Western naval or battlefield mutinies, in Africa mutinies tend to take place at home bases, often in populated cities. Mutineers' grievances are often influenced by many of the same political currents as those of the civilian population and reflect wider frustrations concerning underdevelopment in the region. This overlap clearly indicates that soldiers are members of wider society, and their links to the general civilian population are often the strongest at the junior levels. My interviews with mutineers found that their complaints extend far beyond material grievances and regularly centre on disparities and suspicions between the ranks. These tensions are not limited to disagreements or personal enmity between individuals but are structural and can be found across the region since independence. The divisions between the ranks have systemic roots in the often-political role militaries have taken or have been rewarded in African states. This trend has led to officers regularly being among the most elite in any given country, a sharp contrast to the lifestyles and positions of the junior ranks.

Just as the history of African militaries and African politics is important in comprehending mutinies, a narrow focus on the study of militaries has likely contributed to a neglect and a misperception of mutinies. A heavy emphasis on coups in Africa and the officer corps within academia has led to the assumption that mutinies are almost always precursors to coups. Yet this book's examination of mutinies and the junior ranks has shown that enlisted soldiers often have different goals from their superiors and use different strategies to achieve them. This book has called for mutiny to be viewed as its own phenomenon. In doing so, we gain a more nuanced understanding of the military as an organisation and the various ways its members challenge as well as uphold authority.

Just as mutineers have been influenced by the political landscape, so too have they shaped it. The threat of violence and acts of violence that occur during mutinies have challenged both political and military leaders, spurred social unrest, led to civilian casualties, threatened peacekeeping efforts and, in extreme cases, resulted in international interventions. Thus a better understanding of mutinies is relevant beyond the study of militaries.

Future of mutinies in West and Central Africa

The data in this study, along with the summary of historical studies of mutinies presented in Chapter 1, demonstrate that mutiny is a remarkably durable tactic. It is a tactic that has been used by militaries throughout the globe for centuries and shows no signs of ceasing in West and Central Africa in the near term. Although the conditions for mutinies are in some ways unique to each country's history and military, there are also mutiny trends that span across the region. These patterns can help to anticipate when there is a heightened chance of mutiny in the future.

Chapters 5, 6 and 7 highlighted a trend whereby mutinies follow deployments, with particular emphasis on peacekeeping deployments. Peacekeeping missions have been widely supported by many African states for a variety of reasons including financial benefits, experience for the troops, to relieve a bloated military or as a gesture of goodwill. However, these deployments can lead to increased grievances. There are several reasons for this. The first is that soldiers on deployment have increased expectations because of the heightened danger of the mission. Soldiers expect the hierarchy to provide them with proper equipment, logistics and adequate leadership, which would be less necessary while stationed at home. However, limited funding and the logistical complications of deployments often mean that hierarchies are incapable of meeting these heightened expectations. Secondly, the significant pay increases that are earned on deployments lead to new complications, with soldiers claiming that the competition to participate in peacekeeping missions has created new avenues for corruption and favouritism. Thirdly, the multinational environment allows soldiers to compare their conditions with soldiers from other countries. The way the UN funds peace operations allows for easy comparison between the peacekeepers. The UN is transparent in their process of compensating every country with the same amount per peacekeeper; however, each country does not pay its peacekeepers the same salary. Soldiers from countries that pay on the low end of the scale often speculate about why they receive less than other soldiers performing the same duties. These grievances over pay are likely perpetuated by a lack of official communication from some of the individual contributing countries and their troops. Soldiers in Sierra Leone, for example, have publicly complained that they do not understand what the surplus money from UN peacekeeping is used for.

While many of the deployment-related mutinies are unique to the deployment setting, like other mutinies in the region they primarily involve grievances over pay and conditions of service. Significantly, mutineers on deployments also typically place the blame on their officers (as opposed to the funding institutions or politicians). Therefore, below the surface of claims of unpaid deployment salary are growing divides and resentments between the ranks, which have the potential to cause additional problems, even if the mutineers receive their material demands.

Mutiny has been a durable tactic because it is an adaptable one. This book has examined mutinies over a fifty-five-year period, during which time some of the tactics commonly used by mutineers have changed. Soldiers have consistently used tactics that gain the attention of the military or political hierarchy. However, new technological advances, as well as improvements in freedoms of speech and media in many states, have allowed soldiers new opportunities to communicate their concerns. From the 1990s onwards, mutineers have used the media more often, and in recent years social media have gained traction within the military. These new forums are particularly conducive to the desire of mutineers to spread the message about their grievances far and fast. Given the young age of many mutineers and increased internet access throughout the continent, future mutineers will likely turn increasingly to social media and new technologies as a means to communicate, both to their colleagues and to superiors. The interconnectedness of mainstream media and social media creates the ability for mutineers' grievances and actions to be projected on an international stage. In many cases, this can create further pressure for superiors to respond, as well as placing further scrutiny on the mutineers. This trend of a wider reach for junior soldiers could also be valuable for researchers into mutinies or militaries in general, as it would provide more insight into the internal workings of the state security organisations, which have always been highly secretive.

Technologies such as mobile phones will continue to pose new challenges to governments attempting to quell mutinies, as they make it much easier for soldiers to spread information quickly. Interviewed soldiers in Burkina Faso, for example, explained that mutineers in 2011 called their peers at other bases to find out what deal they had struck with the government. They explained that there were units that mutinied a second time after they had already reached an agreement with the government because they found out, or at least heard rumours, that other units had received a better deal.[1] New technologies also make it increasingly important for military hierarchies to communicate effectively with the junior ranks to alleviate misunderstandings that can quickly grow and spread with increased use of mobile phone calls, text messages, emails and social media.

A revised view of mutinies

Mutinies grab public attention owing to the dramatic way they challenge the hierarchical structures that are the basis of any military organisation. Yet the value of examining mutinies extends beyond the moment of confrontation between junior ranks and their superiors. Mutinies provide a unique glimpse into a group whose voice is normally and intentionally stifled through a system of strict hierarchy. They serve to provide a rare insight into the way junior ranks view their conditions. Additionally, mutineers reveal what they expect from their military leaders as well as from the political leadership, whom they often approach directly during mutinies.

While there was an increasing amount of scholarly work on African militaries in the 1960s and 1970s, the perspective adopted was usually that of the officer corps.[2] The 'process of diffusion of force away from the state and official armies ... on the African continent in the 1980s and 1990s' coincided with a decline in academic work on militaries. Academic focus shifted from African militaries to rebel groups and non-state combatants. Within the structures of these groups, the junior ranks have been acknowledged and in many cases researched (for example, studies on child soldiers or junior ex-combatants). However, the interest in these junior members did not lead to a similar academic focus on the junior ranks of state militaries, and enlisted soldiers continue to 'remain invisible'.[3] This is a significant oversight consid-

AN ALTERED VIEW OF MUTINIES

ering that the junior ranks of the military are the 'physical production of force'.[4] They are the individuals that the international community is largely entrusting with peacekeeping missions, and the junior ranks are the primary defence against an external attack. Therefore, it is important to understand common concerns within this sector, as internal tensions and low morale can also hinder their effectiveness. In more extreme cases, their dissatisfaction has threatened state and regional stability.

This book has suggested that mutinies serve as a way for junior ranks to communicate with their superiors. By mutinying, soldiers draw attention to problems that have gone unaddressed through the normal chain of command. Chapter 3 demonstrated that mutineers usually use bold tactics that the government would find hard to ignore, such as kidnapping political leaders and taking over strategic locations. Mutineers often attempt a balancing act by trying to push the government far enough to force their demands but not to the point where the government will counter-attack with force or issue severe punishments. In an attempt to force the government into a dialogue about their complaints, they threaten violence while often refraining from the use of violence. Yet this is a fine line to walk, especially in mass mutinies, which involve a variety of participants and individualised goals. As mutinies regularly take place in urban centres, civilians unrelated to the cause of the mutiny are typically the victims when mutinies turn violent.

Since mutineers want to grab attention, the act itself is not particularly secretive, especially at the execution phase. However, even in the planning phase mutineers often send direct warnings to military or political leadership in the hope that any problems will be resolved before they commit a mutiny. Examples of this kind of tactic include Nigerian soldiers contacting international media outlets to warn of a revolt and Sierra Leonean soldiers sending letters to the Ministry of Defence (and copies to foreign embassies) with similar threats. The pattern can also be seen beyond the West and Central African region. Soldiers in Tanganyika, for instance, had approached State House twice before the 1964 mutinies in an attempt to seek an audience with the president over their grievances.[5] Similarly, 'anonymous letters of grievance had been emanating from the army for some weeks' before the 1964 mutiny, but 'they were considered no cause for alarm'.[6]

These early warnings demonstrate that mutinies are not always immediate reactions. This counters the claims made in some of the classic studies on mutinies, such as the work by Geoffrey Parker as well as more recent work by Joel Hamby, both of whom portray mutinies as reactions to immediate hardships and place heavy emphasis on environmental conditions.[7] Instead, this book has shown that in many cases mutinies in West and Central Africa were not spontaneous but were logical and planned actions. Mutinying soldiers take risks in conducting the revolt, which is universally illegal under military codes, but there is also a degree of caution involved. Soldiers mutiny when they believe there is a reasonable chance of success, and therefore it is often not a reckless or impulsive action but rather a strategic one.

Grievances over pay or living conditions are the most common complaints voiced by mutineers. However, too often the military or political leadership focuses only on these material complaints. Academics have also been guilty of simplifying mutinies to demands for material redress. Even some of the most-detailed academic work on African militaries, such as *Barrel of a Gun* by Ruth First, downplays mutinies by describing them as 'pay mutinies' or 'pay revolts' and providing little analysis of the events.[8] The term 'pay mutiny' does not require much explanation, as the cause and solution are both implied. This represents a common belief, especially in early independence years, that revolts by the rank and file are generally straightforward and do not require much investigation.

This book has argued for a move away from 'pay revolts' and 'pay mutinies' by showing that the material grievances are usually linked to perceptions of injustice and signal deeper discontent in the military. Junior ranks regularly blame their officers when they are unpaid, at times directly accusing them of stealing parts of their pay. Similarly, grievances over living conditions are regularly accompanied by claims of economic mismanagement by their superiors. The tensions between the ranks, which regularly form around accusations of corruption and favouritism, are difficult and time-intensive to resolve.

Chapters 2 and 3 argued that the divisions between the ranks, which are often revealed in mutinies, correspond to the manner in which militaries have developed in the region. A history of military involvement in politics throughout West and Central Africa has resulted in close ties between senior military leaders and politicians. The relationship often includes significant financial opportunities for senior officers, leading the military to be seen as a powerful, if not prestigious, organisation in most African states. However, the junior ranks rarely share in the benefits and regularly live in poor conditions. The rank-and-file soldiers are in an unusual position in that they are part of a powerful organisation, but they often fail to gain as many tangible benefits as the senior ranks from their membership. This becomes particularly problematic when there are limited opportunities for career advancement. Perceptions of injustice in a system they feel advantages the senior ranks often fuels mutinies.

Mutineers often express the idea that their leaders have broken the implicit contract in which the hierarchy will take care of soldiers' welfare and pay in return for discipline and obedience. Mutineers then justify their disobedience with the observation that officers have also neglected their part of the deal. This trend appears particularly prevalent in deployment-related mutinies owing to soldiers' heightened sense of entitlement alongside the increased dangers of the mission, as explained in Chapter 5.

Although a mutiny is a revolt against superiors, mutineers' actions should not be seen as an attack against the military structure. Mutineers regularly show respect for the concept of military hierarchy while still objecting to individuals or particular behaviour within their chain of command. This affirmation of hierarchy was especially evident in the case study of members of the Tiger unit in Sierra Leone, both in their obedience to their immediate officers and in the creation of the junta leadership based on rank. Nestor Luanda observed a similar trend in the 1964 Tanganyika mutinies, in which the mutineers sought to 'recreate (rather than destroy) hierarchy—even to the point of promoting themselves—while at the same time attempting to negotiate with "legitimate authority" over the heads of their officers'.[9] Similar to the Tanganyika mutinies, soldiers in mutinies in West and Central Africa may use bold tactics, but their requests are generally not particularly radical. Mutineers often request promotion, for example, but usually only by one rank, suggesting that they value the hierarchy.

Mutineers do not ask for a system in which all ranks are equal but rather identify specific concerns within their terms of service. By doing so, they can be seen as 'appeals to authority, rather than rejections of it'.[10] This provides an opportunity for the government or military leadership to address these issues and also provides the possibility for a stronger hierarchy to emerge from a mutiny. However, often the material issues alone are addressed, allowing the divisions and suspicions among the ranks to grow. In cases like Burkina Faso, mutinies have become a pattern in which the same complaints are recycled and each subsequent mutiny has increased in violence.

While dynamics between the ranks are an important aspect of mutinies, this book has also placed emphasis on the relationship between junior ranks and civilians. Although the junior ranks are at times in direct opposition to civilians (for example, when tasked with putting down mass protests), they are often also in close daily contact with them. As a result of military housing shortages, junior ranks often live in towns (instead of bases) and spend their free time in the same places as their civilian peers. The ways in which the rank and file seem to straddle both the military and civilian sectors is apparent in mutinies. Mutineers often borrow tactics that are common in civilian demonstrations. For example, mutineers regularly gather in public spaces or near political offices and make public statements through spokesmen, like civilian organisations. However, their military membership is also regularly used to intimidate and warn of their ability to unleash violence.

Chapter 4 demonstrated that it is not just civilian protest tactics that mutineers use; mutineers also borrowed themes from popular political movements, particularly in the 1990s. Just as civilians demonstrated a growing awareness of corruption and began calling for political accountability, soldiers also voiced similar concerns in a military environment. In public statements, mutineers often referred to elections, international organisations and issues of rule of law, all topics that had gained attention in the civilian realm. This overlap in the occurrence and themes of mutinies and mass civilian demonstrations extends beyond the 1990s. The case study of Burkina Faso in 2011 showed how unrest in both the civilian and military sectors was sparked by similar grievances about the justice system.

The book's findings suggest that two changes need to be made in the way mutinies are viewed. I have suggested that they should be seen as signs of deeper problems within the military and a means of communicating these issues. However, this would not be a popular shift for many in the military. While I use the rather neutral term 'communication' to describe the desire for junior ranks to present their grievances to superiors, one soldier used the word 'expose' to describe the goal of a mutiny. This single word highlights the divisions between the ranks that are often revealed in a mutiny and demonstrates the feelings of injustice that lie below the material demands of mutineers. Few in a military hierarchy would be keen to allow mutineers an open forum in which to elaborate on these perceived injustices, most of which they blame on their officers. It is therefore in the best interest of some to continue to treat mutinies as indiscipline or pay disputes in which the solution is punishment or payment (or a combination of both).

Although mutinies can be seen as a timeless tactic, there are regions that have been successful at reducing their occurrence. For example, Lawrence James notes that 'mutiny has become an unfashionable crime' in a modern Western context.[11] He argues that this is because 'its causes have been removed' and hierarchies have often learned from their mistakes.[12] However, mutiny has not lost its appeal as a tactic within West and Central African militaries, and there is no indication that mutinies will become passé in the near term. A significant reduction in mutinies in the region is not an unreasonable goal, but reducing the number of mutinies would entail more than simply addressing the tangible demands. It would also require tackling the root problems, which often include ingrained aspects of the military structure. Doing so would not be an easy task, as many of the class issues and favouritism that contribute to mutinies have developed through a history of close relations between the military and political elite. However, without a change to the way that mutinies are viewed and dealt with, they will likely remain an 'unfailingly timely topic' in the region and hierarchies will ultimately be left anticipating the next revolt.[13]

NOTES

1. THE POPULAR ALLURE AND ACADEMIC NEGLECT OF MUTINIES

1. Jane Hathaway, 'Introduction', in Jane Hathaway (ed.), *Rebellion, Repression, Reinvention: Mutiny in Comparative Perspective*, Westport, CT: Praeger, 2001, p. xi.
2. The use of the word 'soldier' throughout this book reflects the fact that militaries in West Africa overwhelming consist of armies, although some states have smaller navies and air forces. Additionally, the vast majority of mutineers in the region have been soldiers. Service personnel from navies or air forces will be denoted as such. Specialised services such as the gendarmerie will also be denoted.
3. Mark Weitz, 'Desertion as Mutiny: Upcountry Georgians in the Army of Tennessee', in Hathaway, *Rebellion, Repression, Reinvention*, p. 3.
4. Festus B. Aboagye, *The Ghana Army: A Concise Contemporary Guide to Its Centennial Regimental History, 1897–1999*, Accra: Sedco Publishing, 1999, pp. 95–6; David Killingray, 'The Mutiny of the West African Regiment in the Gold Coast, 1901', *International Journal of African Historical Studies*, 16, 3 (1983), p. 443.
5. Timothy H. Parsons, *The 1964 Army Mutinies and the Making of Modern East Africa*, Westport, CT: Praeger, 2003, p. 13.
6. Ibid.
7. Ibid.
8. Jama Mohamed, 'The 1937 Somaliland Camel Corps Mutiny: A Contrapuntal Reading', *International Journal of African Historical Studies*, 33, 3 (2000), p. 100.
9. Ibid., p. 95.
10. John Iliffe, *Honour in African History*, Cambridge: Cambridge University Press, 2005, p. 241.
11. Catherine Hoskyns, *The Congo since Independence: January 1960–December 1961*, London: Oxford University Press, 1965.
12. Parsons, *1964 Army Mutinies*, p. 2.

13. Gebru Tareke, *The Ethiopian Revolution: War in the Horn of Africa*, New Haven: Yale University Press, 2009, pp. 34–44; Robin Luckham, 'Radical Soldiers, New Model Armies and the Nation-State in Ethiopia and Eritrea', in Kees Koonings and Dirk Kruijt (eds), *Political Armies: The Military and National Building in the Age of Democracy*, London: Zed Books, 2002, pp. 238–66.
14. These sentences were commuted in 2015.
15. Eboe Hutchful and Abdoulaye Bathily, 'Introduction', in Eboe Hutchful and Abdoulaye Bathily (eds), *The Military and Militarism in Africa*, Dakar: CODESRIA, 1998, p. vi; Robin Luckham, 'The Military, Militarisation and Democratisation in Africa: A Survey of Literature and Issues', in Hutchful and Bathily (eds.), *Military and Militarism in Africa*, pp. 22–3.
16. Richard Watt, *Dare Call It Treason*, New York: Simon & Schuster, 1963, pp. 155–6, cited in Elihu Rose, 'The Anatomy of Mutiny', *Armed Forces and Society*, 8, 4 (Summer 1982), p. 561.
17. Rose, 'Anatomy of Mutiny', p. 568; latter quote from Julie Rawe et al., 'Mutiny on the Convoy?', *Time Magazine*, 25 October 2004, http://www.time.com/time/magazine/article/0,9171,995475,00.html (accessed 10 September 2013).
18. Ibid., p. 562.
19. This system is used in nearly all militaries; however, the terminology can vary by country (and even vary within different branches in the same country). The terms 'ranks', 'other ranks' and 'rank and file' all refer to enlisted soldiers, while 'officers' refers to commissioned officers, which make up the officer corps. For those unfamiliar with military hierarchies, confusion may come about with the term 'non-commissioned officers' (NCOs). These are the top levels of the enlisted ranks, but they are not part of the officer corps and are always subordinate to commissioned officers.
20. Rose, 'Anatomy of Mutiny', pp. 562–3.
21. Geoffrey Parker, 'Mutiny and Discontent in the Spanish Army of Flanders 1527–1607', *Past & Present*, 58 (February 1973), p. 45.
22. Nestor Luanda, 'The Tanganyika Rifles and the Mutiny of January 1964', in Hutchful and Bathily (eds.), *Military and Militarism in Africa*, p. 203.
23. Geoffrey Parker, 'Foreword', in Hathaway, *Rebellion, Repression, Reinvention*, p. viii.
24. Christopher Ankersen, 'Beyond Mutiny? Instrumental and Expressive Understandings of Contemporary "Collective Indiscipline"', in Craig Leslie Mantle (ed.), *The Unwilling and the Reluctant: Theoretical Perspectives on Disobedience in the Military Kingdom*, Ontario: Canadian Defence Academy Press, 2006, p. 121.
25. Ibid., p. 123.
26. Hutchful and Bathily, *Military and Militarism in Africa*, p. vi.
27. Luckham, 'Military, Militarisation and Democratisation in Africa', pp. 22–3.
28. Ankersen, 'Beyond Mutiny?', p. 124.
29. Rose, 'Anatomy of Mutiny', p. 563.

30. Hathaway, 'Introduction', p. xv.
31. Rose, 'Anatomy of Mutiny', p. 566.
32. Ibid.
33. Parker, 'Mutiny and Discontent in the Spanish Army', p. 47.
34. Ali A. Mazrui and Donald Rothchild, 'The Soldier and the State in East Africa: Some Theoretical Conclusions on the Army Mutinies of 1964', *Western Political Quarterly*, 20, 1 (March 1967), p. 82.
35. Rose, 'Anatomy of Mutiny', p. 572.
36. Howard G. Coombs, 'Dimensions of Military Leadership: The Kinmel Park Mutiny of 4–5 March 1919', in Craig Leslie Mantle (ed.), *The Apathetic and the Defiant: Case Studies of Canadian Mutiny and Disobedience, 1812 to 1919*, Kingston, Ontario: Canadian Defence Academy, 2007, p. 407.
37. Christopher Bell, 'Mutiny and the Royal Canadian Navy', in Mantle, *Unwilling and the Reluctant*, p. 97.
38. Parsons, *1964 Army Mutinies*, p. 8.
39. Lawrence James, *Mutiny in the British and Commonwealth Forces, 1797–1956*, London: Buchan & Enright, 1987, p. 12.
40. Parker, 'Foreword', p. viii.
41. Joel Hamby, 'The Mutiny Wagon Wheel: A Leadership Model for Mutiny in Combat', *Armed Forces & Society*, 28, 4 (2002), p. 596; Hathaway, 'Introduction', p. xii; Cornelis J. Lammers, 'Strikes and Mutinies: A Comparative Study of Organizational Conflicts between Rulers and the Ruled', *Administrative Science Quarterly*, 14, 4 (December 1969), p. 570. Christopher Bell and Bruce Allen Elleman, *Naval Mutinies of the Twentieth Century: An International Perspective*, London: Frank Cass, 2003.
42. Jimmy D. Kandeh, 'Civil–Military Relations', in Adekeye Adebajo and Ismail Rashid (eds), *West Africa's Security Challenges: Building Peace in a Troubled Region*, Boulder, CO: Lynne Rienner, 2004, p. 150.
43. Paul Nugent, *Africa since Independence*, 2nd edn, New York: Palgrave Macmillan, 2012, pp. 261–3.
44. Samuel Decalo, *Coups and Army Rule in Africa: Studies in Military Style*, New Haven: Yale University Press, 1976, pp. 14–15.
45. Pierre Englebert and Kevin C. Dunn, *Inside African Politics*, Boulder, CO: Lynne Rienner, 2013, p. 154.
46. Christopher Tuck, '"Every Car and Moving Object Gone": The ECOMOG Intervention in Liberia', *African Studies Quarterly*, 4, 1 (2000); Dionne Searcey, '"They Told Us They Were Here to Help Us": Then Came Slaughter', *New York Times*, 28 February 2017.
47. Parker, 'Mutiny and Discontent in the Spanish Army', p. 46.

2. OUT OF THE SHADOWS OF COUPS

1. Christopher Bell and Bruce Allen Elleman (eds), *Naval Mutinies of the Twentieth Century: An International Perspective*, London: Frank Cass, 2003, p. 1.
2. Dean C. Black, 'Murder by Spitfire? Probing for Mutiny and Indiscipline in Canada's Second World War Air Force', in Howard G. Coombs (ed.), *The Insubordinate and the Noncompliant: Case Studies of Canadian Mutiny and Disobedience, 1920 to Present*, Ontario: Canadian Defence Academy Press, 2007, p. 146.
3. Elihu Rose, 'Anatomy of Mutiny', p. 561.
4. James, *Mutiny in the British and Commonwealth Forces*, p. 10; Lammers, 'Strikes and Mutinies', p. 560.
5. United Kingdom Armed Forces Act 2006; similar wording is present in the acts that preceded the 2006 act.
6. This book focuses specifically on militaries, not police forces.
7. Naunihal Singh, *Seizing Power: The Strategic Logic of Military Coups*, Baltimore, MD: Johns Hopkins University Press, 2014, p. 10.
8. Jimmy Kandeh, *Coups from Below: Armed Subalterns and State Power in West Africa*, New York: Palgrave Macmillan, 2004, p. 42.
9. Jonathan M. Powell and Clayton L. Thyne, 'Global Instances of Coups from 1950 to 2010: A New Dataset', *Journal of Peace Research*, 48, 2 (2011), p. 255.
10. Ruth First, *The Barrel of a Gun: Political Power in Africa and the Coup d'État*, London: Penguin, 1970, p. 205; Luckham, 'Military, Militarisation and Democratisation in Africa', pp. 23–4.
11. Patrick J. McGowan, 'African Military Coups d'état, 1956–2001: Frequency, Trends and Distribution', *Journal of Modern African Studies*, 41, 3 (2003), p. 343.
12. Powell and Thyne, *Global Instances of Coups*, p. 250.
13. Edward Luttwak, *Coup d'état: A Practical Handbook*, London: Penguin, 1968, p. 24.
14. Kandeh, *Coups from Below*, p. 43.
15. First, *Barrel of a Gun*, p. 19.
16. Decalo, *Coups and Army Rule in Africa*, pp. 20–1.
17. Singh, *Seizing Power*, pp. 112–13.
18. 'Nigerian Soldiers Given Death Penalties for Mutiny', BBC, 17 December 2014.
19. Similar observations have been made in Kandeh, *Coups from Below*, p. 40; Luckham, 'Military, Militarisation and Democratisation in Africa', p. 17; and Parsons, *1964 Army Mutinies*, p. 5.
20. Parsons, *1964 Army Mutinies*, p. 5.
21. Luckham, 'Radical Soldiers, New Model Armies and the Nation-State', p. 243.
22. Luckham, 'Military, Militarisation and Democratisation in Africa', p. 23; Boubacar N'Diaye, 'Guinea', in Alan Bryden, Boubacar N'Diaye and 'Funmi Olonisakin

(eds), *Challenges of Security Sector Governance in West Africa*, Geneva: Geneva Centre for Democratic Control of Armed Forces, 2008, p. 143.
23. Countries covered in the study include: Benin, Burkina Faso, Cameroon, Cape Verde, Central African Republic, Chad, Democratic Republic of Congo, Equatorial Guinea, Gabon, The Gambia, Ghana, Guinea, Guinea-Bissau, Liberia, Mali, Niger, Nigeria, Republic of Congo, São Tomé and Príncipe, Senegal, Sierra Leone and Togo.
24. McGowan, 'African Military Coups d'État', p. 356; Pat McGowan and Thomas H. Johnson, 'African Military Coups d'état and Underdevelopment: A Quantitative Historical Analysis', *Journal of Modern African Studies*, 22, 4 (December 1984), p. 649.
25. Rose, 'Anatomy of Mutiny', p. 572; Hamby, 'Mutiny Wagon Wheel', p. 593.
26. The Central African Republic 1996–7 and Burkina Faso 2011 mutinies lasted several months. For these cases, the events were broken into phases, based on when negotiations or concessions occurred.
27. See datasets by Patrick McGowan and Powell and Thyne.
28. The cases of overlap are: Togo, January 1963 (listed as successful coup); Republic of Congo, June 1966 (listed as unsuccessful coup attempt); Guinea, February 1996 (listed as unsuccessful coup attempt); Côte d'Ivoire, December 1999 (listed as successful coup); and Côte d'Ivoire, September 2002 (listed as unsuccessful coup attempt). The coup dataset by Powell and Thyne can be found at http://www.uky.edu/~clthyn2/coup_data/home.htm

3. THE TYPICAL MUTINY: PATTERNS IN PARTICIPANTS, TACTICS AND OUTCOMES

1. As quoted in Rose, 'Anatomy of Mutiny', p. 565.
2. Ibid.
3. Robin Luckham, 'The Military, Militarization and Democratization in Africa: A Survey of Literature and Issues', *African Studies Review*, 37, 2 (September 1994), pp. 13–75; Michael F. Lofchie, 'The Uganda Coup: Class Action by the Military', *Journal of Modern African Studies*, 10, 1 (May 1972), pp. 19–35; Kandeh, *Coups from Below*.
4. A.H.M. Kirk-Greene, '*Stay by your radios*': *Documentation for a Study of Military Government in Tropical Africa*, Cambridge: African Studies Centre, 1981, pp. 12–13.
5. Mathurin Houngnikpo, *Guarding the Guardians: Civil–Military Relations and Democratic Governance in Africa*, Burlington, VT: Ashgate, 2010, p. 20.
6. Samuel Decalo, 'Modalities of Civil–Military Stability in Africa', *Journal of Modern African Studies*, 27, 4 (December 1989), p. 573.
7. Ibid., pp. 573–4.
8. Ibid., p. 567.

9. Herbert M. Howe, *Ambiguous Order: Military Forces in African States*, Boulder, CO: Lynne Rienner, 2001, p. 41; for example, his research provides numerous examples of senior officers in Nigeria receiving commissions as high as 20 per cent from sales of equipment with price tags in the tens and hundreds of millions (USD). I heard numerous examples of similar patterns during field research.
10. Kandeh, *Coups from Below*, p. 208.
11. 'Guinea Mutiny Reveals Rift between Top Brass and Ordinary Soldiers', AFP, 5 June 2008.
12. *Africa Research Bulletin*, February 1997, p. 12578.
13. *Africa Research Bulletin*, May 2008, pp. 17526–7; *West Africa*, 12 August 1991, p. 1336.
14. Samsudeen Sarr, *Coup d'état by the Gambian National Army*, Philadelphia, PA: Xlibris, 2007.
15. *West Africa*, 5 May 1996, p. 667.
16. Ibid.
17. 'Guinea Mutiny Reveals Rift'.
18. Howe, *Ambiguous Order*, pp. 44–5; Bernd Horn, 'A Law unto Themselves? Elitism as a Catalyst for Disobedience', in Mantle, *Unwilling and the Reluctant*, pp. 127–38.
19. Quote from spokesperson of Guinea mutiny in 2008; 'Guinea Mutiny Reveals Rift'.
20. Author interview with Sierra Leonean enlisted soldier, April 2012.
21. Author interview with Sierra Leonean enlisted soldier, May 2011.
22. 'Burkina Faso President Leaves Capital amid Mutiny', AFP, 15 April 2011.
23. 'Guinea Meets Soldiers' Demands to End 2-Day Mutiny', Reuters, 27 May 2008.
24. Emile Ouédraogo, 'Advancing Military Professionalism in Africa', African Center for Strategic Studies, Research Paper no. 6, 2014.
25. Kent Hughes Butts and Steven Metz, 'Armies and Democracy in the New Africa: Lessons from Nigeria and South Africa', Strategic Studies Institute, US Army War College, 1996.
26. Author interview with Burkinabé enlisted soldier, March 2012.
27. Kandeh, *Coups from Below*, p. 7.
28. Author interviews in Burkina Faso, 2012. More details will be provided in Chapter 8.
29. Author interview with Burkinabé enlisted soldier, March 2012.
30. The name 'Bangura' is a pseudonym.
31. Author interview with Sierra Leonean enlisted soldier, April 2012; regulations in the 1990s required all citizens to assist in cleaning the city one day a month.
32. Rose, 'Anatomy of Mutiny', p. 572.
33. Hamby, 'Mutiny Wagon Wheel', p. 595.
34. Ibid., p. 576.

NOTES

35. Examples include Luttwak, *Coup d'état*; and Harvey G. Kebschull, 'Operation "Just Missed": Lessons from Failed Coup Attempts', *Armed Forces and Society*, 20, 4 (1994), pp. 565–79; Singh, *Seizing Power*.
36. *West Africa*, 2 July 1966, p. 757.
37. *West Africa*, 27 May 1996, p. 812.
38. 'Mutiny: 27 Soldiers Get Life Sentence', *This Day*, 28 April 2009.
39. *West Africa*, 28 May 1990, pp. 877–8.
40. *West Africa*, 30 July 1966, p. 869; *West Africa*, 7 October 1991, pp. 1674–5; *Africa Research Bulletin*, February 1992, p. 10471.
41. *Africa Research Bulletin*, February 1997, p. 12578.
42. *Africa Research Bulletin*, May 1993, p. 11012.
43. *West Africa*, 5 May 1996, p. 667.
44. Ibid.
45. Kadir Badsha Mukhtar and Misbahu Bashir, 'Nigeria: Darfur Operations; Nigerian Soldiers Threaten Mutiny; Ask to be Airlifted Home', *Daily Trust*, 26 June 2012.
46. iReport-NG.com is one of the many sites that posted the report.
47. Samuel Huntington, *The Soldier and the State: The Theory and Politics of Civil–Military Relations*, Cambridge, MA: Harvard University Press, 1957, p. 13.
48. Rose, 'Anatomy of Mutiny', p. 568; Hathaway, 'Introduction', p. xvi.
49. Andreas Mehler, 'The Production of Insecurity by African Security Forces: Insights from Liberia and the Central African Republic', GIGA Working Papers, no. 114, 2009.
50. Edgar O'Ballance, *The Congo–Zaire Experience, 1960–98*, London: Macmillan, 2000, pp. 101–3; *West Africa*, 7 October 1991, pp. 1674–5.
51. *West Africa*, 30 September 2002, p. 25; *Africa Research Bulletin*, February 1998, p. 13014.
52. Hathaway, 'Introduction', p. xv.
53. *West Africa*, 4 May 1997, p. 665; *Africa Research Bulletin*, March 1997, p. 12664.
54. Rose, 'Anatomy of Mutiny', p. 569.
55. Author interview with editorial chief for Ouaga FM, March 2012.
56. Author interviews in Burkina Faso, March 2012.
57. Author interview with former enlisted soldier, currently working in defence industry, March 2012.
58. *Africa Research Bulletin*, May 1993, p. 11012; *West Africa*, 31 May 1993, p. 922; *Africa Confidential*, 13 August 1996, p. 6.
59. *West Africa*, 20 April 1963, p. 444.
60. *Africa Research Bulletin*, December 1999, pp. 13783–6.
61. Tom Kamara, 'Côte d'Ivoire: Implications of the December 1999 Coup d'État', 1 April 2000, Writnet Paper, January 2000, available at: http://www.unhcr.org/refworld/docid/3ae6a6c74.html (accessed 4 December 2012).
62. *Africa Research Bulletin*, December 1999, pp. 13783–6.
63. *West Africa*, 16 June 1996; *West Africa*, 23 June 1996.

64. Hamby, 'Mutiny Wagon Wheel', p. 592; Rose, 'Anatomy of Mutiny', p. 572.
65. *Africa Research Bulletin*, 1–31 March 2007; *Africa Research Bulletin*, 1 February 2008.
66. *Africa Research Bulletin*, 1–31 March 2007, p. 17015.
67. Hamby, 'Mutiny Wagon Wheel', p. 592; Rose, 'Anatomy of Mutiny', p. 571.
68. *West Africa*, 18 March 1961, p. 298.
69. Lila Chouli, 'People's Revolt in Burkina Faso', in Firoze Manji and Sokari Ekine (eds), *Africa Awakening: The Emerging Revolutions*, Oxford: Pambazuka Press, 2012, p. 143.
70. At the time of writing, the sentences were still being appealed.
71. James, *Mutiny in the British and Commonwealth Forces*, pp. 13–15, as summarised in Coombs, *Insubordinate and the Noncompliant*, p. 16.

4. PUBLIC DISCOURSE, PROTESTS AND REVOLTS

1. Several examples of volumes dedicated to the topic include Larry Diamond and Marc Plattner (eds), *Democratization in Africa: Progress and Retreat*, 2nd edn, Baltimore: Johns Hopkins University Press, 2010; Abdul Raufu Mustapha and Lindsay Whitfield (eds), *Turning Points in African Democracy*, Woodbridge: James Currey, 2009; E. Gyimah-Boadi (ed.), *Democratic Reform in Africa: The Quality of Progress*, Boulder, CO: Lynne Rienner, 2004.
2. Richard Joseph, 'Challenges of a "Frontier" Region', in Diamond and Plattner (eds.), *Democratization in Africa*, p. 4.
3. Eboe Hutchful, 'Military Issues in the Transition to Democracy', in Hutchful and Bathily (eds.), *Military and Militarism in Africa*, p. 608.
4. Ibid.
5. 'Rediscovery of a popular voice', borrowed from Nugent, *Africa since Independence*, p. 377.
6. Samuel Decalo, 'The Morphology of Military Rule in Africa', in John Markakis and Michael Waller (eds), *Military Marxist Regimes in Africa*, London: Frank Cass, 1986, pp. 122–44.
7. Nugent, *Africa since Independence*, p. 246.
8. Adebayo Olukoshi, 'State, Conflict, and Democracy in Africa: The Complex Process of Renewal', in Richard Joseph (ed.), *State Conflict and Democracy in Africa*, Boulder, CO: Lynne Rienner, 1999, p. 454.
9. Nugent, *Africa since Independence*, pp. 330–1.
10. Christopher Clapham, *Africa and the International System: The Politics of State Survival*, Cambridge: University of Cambridge Press, 1996, p. 170.
11. Ibid., p. 172.
12. Wuyi Omitoogun, 'Introduction', in Wuyi Omitoogun and Eboe Hutchful (eds), *Budgeting for the Military Sector in Africa: The Processes and Mechanism of Control*, Oxford: Oxford University Press, 2006, p. 1.

13. Nicolas Van De Walle, *African Economies and the Politics of Permanent Crisis, 1979–1999*, Cambridge: Cambridge University Press, 2001, pp. 64–112.
14. Omitoogun, 'Introduction', pp. 1–2.
15. Nadir A.L. Mohammed, 'Trends, Determinants and the Economic Effects of Military Expenditures in Sub-Saharan Africa', in Hutchful and Bathily (eds.), *Military and Militarism in Africa*, pp. 93–4; Mohammed draws his conclusions from an analysis of thirteen African countries.
16. Dataset can be accessed at http://www.sipri.org
17. All figures are set to USD 2014 exchange rate within the SIPRI dataset. See dataset titled 'Military Expenditures by Region in Constant US Dollars, 1988–2015'.
18. Geoff Harris, 'The Case for Demilitarisation in sub-Saharan Africa', in Geoff Harris (ed.), *Achieving Security in Sub-Saharan Africa*, Pretoria: Institute for Security Studies, 2004, p. 3.
19. Ibid., p. 4.
20. Jeffrey Herbst, 'African Militaries and Rebellion: The Political Economy of Threat and Combat Research', *Journal of Peace Research*, 41 (2004), p. 359.
21. Michael Bratton and Nicolas Van de Walle, *Democratic Experiments in Africa: Regime Transitions in Comparative Perspective*, Cambridge: Cambridge University Press, 1997, p. 244.
22. Chris Allen, 'Understanding African Politics', *Review of African Political Economy*, 22, 65 (September 1995), p. 312.
23. Michael Bratton, 'International versus Domestic Pressures for Democratisation in Africa', in William Hale and Eberhard Kienle (eds), *After the Cold War: Security and Democracy in Africa and Asia*, London: Tauris Academic Studies, 1997, p. 160.
24. William G. Thom, 'An Assessment of Prospects for Ending Domestic Military Conflict in Sub-Saharan Africa', *CSIS Africa Notes*, 177 (1995), p. 3.
25. Howe, *Ambiguous Order*, p. 80.
26. Robin Luckham, 'Taming the Monster: Democratisation and Demilitarisation', in Hutchful and Bathily (eds.), *Military and Militarism in Africa*, p. 589.
27. Bratton, 'International versus Domestic Pressures', p. 179.
28. Elizabeth Schmidt, *Foreign Intervention in Africa: From the Cold War to the War on Terror*, New York: Cambridge University Press, 2013, p. 180.
29. Ibid., p. 180.
30. Bratton, 'International versus Domestic Pressures', p. 165.
31. *West Africa*, 28 May–3 June 1990, p. 877.
32. John Wiseman, 'Introduction', in John Wiseman (ed.), *Democracy and Political Change in Sub-Saharan Africa*, New York: Routledge, 1995, p. 3.
33. Bratton, 'International versus Domestic Pressures', p. 184; Allen, 'Understanding African Politics', p. 313.
34. Wiseman, 'Introduction', p. 5.

35. Bratton and Van de Walle, *Democratic Experiments in Africa*, p. 3.
36. Wiseman, 'Introduction', p. 5.
37. Abdul Raufu Mustapha and Lindsay Whitfield, 'African Democratisation: The Journey So Far', in Mustapha and Whitfield (eds.), *Turning Points in African Democracy*, p. 1; Michael Bratton and Robert Mattes, 'Support for Democracy in Africa: Intrinsic or Instrumental?', Afrobarometer Paper, no. 1, 2000, p. 2.
38. Chris Allen, Carolyn Baylies and Morris Szeftel, 'Editorial: Surviving Democracy?', *Review of African Political Economy*, 54 (July 1992), p. 8.
39. Abdul Raufu Mustapha and Lindsay Whitfield, 'The Politics of African States in the Era of Democratisation', in Mustapha and Whitfield, *Turning Points in African Democracy*, p. 225.
40. Wiseman, 'Introduction', p. 5.
41. Robert A. Dahl, *A Preface to Democratic Theory: Expanded Edition*, Chicago: University of Chicago Press, 2006, p. 3.
42. Bratton and Mattes, 'Support for Democracy in Africa', p. 3.
43. Jennifer Widner, 'The 1990 Elections in Côte d'Ivoire', *Issue: A Journal of Opinion*, 20, 1 (Winter 1991), pp. 31–41.
44. Ibid.
45. Ibid., p. 32.
46. Richard Crook, 'Côte d'Ivoire: Multi-party Democracy and Political Change; Surviving the Crisis', in Wiseman, *Democracy and Political Change in Sub-Saharan Africa*, p. 16.
47. Ibid.; *West Africa*, 18–24 June 1990, p. 1022.
48. *West Africa*, 28 May 1990, pp. 877–8; *Africa Research Bulletin*, June 1990, p. 9693.
49. *West Africa*, 28 May 1990, pp. 877–8; *West Africa*, 25 June 1990, p. 1090; *Africa Research Bulletin*, June 1990, p. 9693.
50. *West Africa*, 28 May–3 June 1990, p. 877.
51. John Wiseman and Elizabeth Vidler, 'The July 1994 Coup d'état in the Gambia: The End of an Era', *Round Table*, 333, 1 (January 1995), p. 57.
52. *West Africa*, 29 April–5 May 1996, p. 667.
53. Ibid.
54. *West Africa*, January 1997, p. 89.
55. Numerous examples can be found in A.H.M. Kirk-Greene, 'Stay by your radios'.
56. *West Africa*, 29 April–5 May 1996, p. 667.
57. *Africa Research Bulletin*, March 1998, p. 13052.
58. 'Soldiers End Burkina Faso Mutiny', AP, 16 July 1999.
59. *West Africa*, 1 August 1993, p. 1313.
60. *West Africa*, December 1996, p. 1909.
61. Ibid.
62. *West Africa*, 5 May 1996, p. 667.
63. *West Africa*, November 1996, p. 1705.

64. *West Africa*, February 1997.
65. Hutchful, 'Military Issues in the Transition to Democracy', p. 608.
66. Bratton and Van de Walle, *Democratic Experiments in Africa*, p. 244.
67. Hutchful, 'Military Issues in the Transition to Democracy', p. 609.
68. Ibid.
69. Ibid.
70. Rose, 'Anatomy of Mutiny', p. 568.
71. Wiseman, *Democracy and Political Change in Sub-Saharan Africa*, p. 5; Nugent, *Africa since Independence*, p. 382.
72. Nugent, *Africa since Independence*, pp. 389–92.
73. Ibid., p. 389.
74. Eboe Hutchful, 'Institutional Decomposition and Junior Ranks' Political Action in Ghana', in Hutchful and Bathily, *Military and Militarism in Africa*, p. 249.
75. Ibid.
76. This figure involves mutinies from 1972 onwards because the Freedom in the World index started in this year. The Freedom House index was selected over other similar indexes such as the Ibrahim Index owing to the long history of its reports, which allowed for greater analysis over time. More information about the Freedom in the World index can be found on the organisation's website: https://www.freedomhouse.org
77. 'Gambia Executions: Senegal Angry after Nationals Killed', BBC, 29 August 2012.
78. Author interview with Sierra Leonean enlisted soldier, May 2012.
79. Olukoshi, 'State, Conflict, and Democracy in Africa', p. 454.
80. Goran Hyden and Michael Leslie, 'Communications and Democratization in Africa', in Goran Hyden, Michael Leslie and Folu F. Ogundimu (eds), *Media and Democracy in Africa*, New Brunswick, NJ: Transaction, 2002, p. 4.
81. Ibid., p. 11.
82. Ibid., p. 12.
83. Ibid.; Goran Hyden and Charles Okigbo, 'The Media and the Two Waves of Democracy', in Hyden, Leslie and Ogundimu (eds.), *Media and Democracy in Africa*, p. 48.
84. Hyden and Leslie, 'Communications and Democratization', p. 5.
85. *Africa Research Bulletin*, July 2002, pp. 14972–5.
86. Ibid.
87. Committee to Protect Journalists, 'CJP Concerned about Climate for Independent Journalism', 4 September 2002; IRIN, 'Niger: Second Journalist Arrested over Mutiny Reports', 28 August 2002.
88. *Africa Research Bulletin*, September 2002, p. 14999.
89. *Africa Research Bulletin*, May 2003, p. 15317.
90. 'Amnesty International Report 2004: Niger', available at http://www.refworld.org/docid/40b5a1fd8.html

91. *The Point*, 10 February 1992.
92. *Foroyaa*, 15 February 1992.
93. *The Gambia Weekly*, 21 February 1992.
94. Dahl, *Preface to Democratic Theory*, p. 3.
95. Hutchful, 'Military Issues in the Transition to Democracy', p. 608.

5. THE PRICE OF HARDSHIP: DEPLOYMENTS AND PEACEKEEPING

1. Paul D. Williams, 'Peacekeeping in Africa after the Cold War: Trends and Challenges', in James Hentz (ed.), *Routledge Handbook on African Security*, New York: Routledge, 2014, p. 66.
2. United Nations, 'Current Contributions to UN Peacekeeping', August 2016, available at http://www.un.org/en/peacekeeping/contributors/2016/aug16_2.pdf (accessed 3 January 2017).
3. Chiyuki Aoi, Cedric de Coning and Ramesh Thakur (eds), *Unintended Consequences of Peacekeeping Operations*, New York: United Nations University Press, 2007.
4. Paul D. Williams, *War & Conflict in Africa*, Cambridge: Polity, 2011, p. 202.
5. These cases and the missions the soldiers were involved in include: Ghana (1961, ONUC), The Gambia (1991, 1992 ECOMOG Liberia), Guinea (1996 ECOMOG Liberia), Burkina Faso (1999 MINURCA/ECOMOG Liberia), Côte d'Ivoire (1999 MINURCA), Benin (2000 ECOMOG Liberia/Guinea Bissau), Nigeria (2000 ECOMOG Liberia/Sierra Leone), Guinea Bissau (2004 ECOMOG/ECOMIL Liberia), Nigeria (2008 UNMIL), Chad (2013, 2014 MINUSMA).
6. Quote from Ankersen, 'Beyond Mutiny?', p. 121; topic also discussed in Rachel Lea Heide, 'After the Emergency: Demobilization Strikes, Political Statements, and the Moral Economy in Canada's Air Forces, 1919–1946', in Coombs, *Insubordinate and the Noncompliant*, pp. 178–9.
7. 'United Nations Operations: Principles and Guidelines', 2008, pp. 17–20.
8. Ibid.
9. James D. Fearon and David Laitin, 'Neotrusteeship and the Problem of Weak States', *International Security*, 28, 4 (Spring 2004), p. 25; William J. Durch et al., *The Brahimi Report and the Future of United Nations Peace Operations*, Washington, DC: Henry L. Stimson Center, 2003, p. 71.
10. James D. Fearon, 'International Institutions and Collective Authorization of the Use of Force', in A. Alexandroff (ed.), *Can the World Be Governed? Possibilities for Effective Multilateralism*, Waterloo, Ontario: W. Laurier University Press, 2008, p. 20.
11. 'Funmi Olonisakin, 'Lessons Learned from an Assessment of Peacekeeping and Peace Support Operations in West Africa', Kofi Annan International Peacekeeping Training Centre, Accra: 2008, p. 17.
12. Ibid.

13. Author interview with Sierra Leonean enlisted soldier, May 2011; in 1992, the conversion rate for leones to US dollars averaged 482 to 1, according to the US Department of Treasury, Reporting Rates of Exchange. Therefore, 10,000 leones a month would be roughly $20.
14. Author interview with Gambian former enlisted soldier, October 2012.
15. Author interview with Sierra Leonean enlisted soldier, May 2011; Sierra Leone has increased the peacekeeping pay since the time of this interview.
16. Iliffe, *Honour in African History*, p. 4.
17. Ibid.
18. Author interview with Sierra Leonean officer, May 2011.
19. 'Boko Haram Crisis: Nigerian Soldiers Mutiny over Weapons', BBC, 19 August 2014.
20. Herbert Howe, 'Lessons of Liberia: ECOMOG and Regional Peacekeeping', *International Security*, 21, 3 (Winter 1996–7), pp. 151–2; Eboe Hutchful, 'The ECOMOG Experience with Peacekeeping in Africa', in *Whither Peacekeeping in Africa?*, Monograph no. 36, Institute for Security Studies, Pretoria: April 1999.
21. The Anglophone countries contributing troops included Liberia, Sierra Leone, The Gambia, Nigeria and Ghana. The only Francophone country to contribute troops at the initial stage was Guinea.
22. Howe, 'Lessons of Liberia', p. 167.
23. Ibid.
24. After Action Reports are commonly used following military operations. They allow for the unit and/or its leadership to analyse the operation and make recommendations to improve performance in future missions. Olonisakin, 'Lessons Learned', p. 29
25. 'Funmi Olonisakin, *Reinventing Peacekeeping in Africa: Conceptual and Legal Issues in ECOMOG Operations*, The Hague: Kluwer Law International, 2000, pp. 163, 172–5.
26. Hutchful, 'ECOMOG Experience with Peacekeeping in Africa'.
27. Tuck, '"Every Car or Moving Object Gone"'.
28. Adekeye Adebajo, *Liberia's Civil War: Nigeria, ECOMOG and Regional Security in West Africa*, Boulder, CO: Lynne Rienner, 2002, p. 251.
29. 'Chadian Troops Abandon North Mali Posts in Protest', Reuters, 18 September 2013; Kemo Cham, 'Sierra Leone AU Troops "Want out of Somalia"', *Africa Review*, 11 May 2014.
30. Author interviews in Sierra Leone, 2016.
31. Abdulkadir Badsha and Misbahu Bashir, 'Nigeria: Darfur Operations; Nigerian Soldiers Threaten Mutiny; Ask to Be Airlifted Home', *Daily Trust*, 26 June 2012.
32. Ibid.
33. Amy B. Adler, Brett T. Litz and Paul T. Bartone, 'The Nature of Peacekeeping Stressors', in Thomas W. Britt and Amy B. Adler (eds), *The Psychology of the Peacekeeper*, Westport, CT: Praeger, 2003, pp. 152–3.

34. Olonisakin, *Reinventing Peacekeeping in Africa*, pp. 178–86.
35. Author interview with Gambian former enlisted soldier, October 2012.
36. Author interview with Gambian former officer, August 2012.
37. Author interview with Gambian former officer, September 2012; author interview with Gambian enlisted soldier, May 2012.
38. Author interview with Gambian former officer, August 2012.
39. Author interview, Gambian academic, June 2012.
40. Hutchful, 'ECOMOG Experience with Peacekeeping in Africa'.
41. Howe, *Ambiguous Order*, p. 138.
42. Olonisakin, *Reinventing Peacekeeping in Africa*, p. 170.
43. Tuck, '"Every Car and Moving Object Gone"'.
44. Howe, 'Lessons of Liberia', pp. 157, 169; W. Ofuatey-Kodjoe, 'The Impact of Peacekeeping on Target States: Lessons from the Liberian Experience', in Ricardo Rene Laremont (ed.), *The Causes of War and the Consequences of Peacekeeping in Africa*, Portsmouth, NH: Heinemann, 2002, p. 136.
45. While the original ECOMOG mission to Liberia ended in 1999, a second mission was established in 2003 called ECOMIL. However, it was soon transitioned into a UN mission titled UNMIL.
46. Mark Malan, 'Transition with Minimal Assistance: Lessons from Guinea-Bissau?', Kofi Annan International Peacekeeping Training Centre, Accra, paper no. 5, March 2005, pp. 14–15.
47. Katharina P. Coleman, 'The Political Economy of UN Peacekeeping: Incentivizing Effective Participation', New York: International Peace Institute, May 2014, p. 26.
48. Kwesi Aning, 'Unintended Consequences of Peace Operations for Troop-Contributing Countries from West Africa: The Case of Ghana', in Chiyuki Aoil, Cedric de Coning and Ramesh Thakur (eds), *Unintended Consequences of Peacekeeping Operations*, Tokyo: United Nations University Press, 2007, p. 140.
49. Emma Birikorang, 'Ghana's Regional Security Policy: Costs, Benefits, and Consistency', Kofi Annan International Peacekeeping Training Centre, Accra, KAIPTC paper no. 20, September 2007, p. 10.
50. It is Ghanaian policy that all troops must test negative for HIV before being able to deploy on a peacekeeping mission.
51. Aning, 'Unintended Consequences of Peace Operations', p. 140.
52. Author interviews in Sierra Leone, 2016.
53. Emma Birikorang, 'Ghana's Regional Security Policy: Costs, Benefits, and Consistency', Kofi Annan International Peacekeeping Training Centre, Accra, paper no. 20, September 2007, p. 8.
54. Ibid., p. 6.
55. Aning, 'Unintended Consequences of Peace Operations', pp. 135–7.
56. United Nations, 'Financing Peacekeeping', available at http://www.un.org/en/peacekeeping/operations/financing.shtml

NOTES

57. Coleman, 'Political Economy of UN Peacekeeping', p. 10.
58. Author interview with Sierra Leonean enlisted soldier, April 2012. In 2013, the government of Sierra Leone publicly stated that it increased its payments to peacekeepers. However, in interviews during 2011 and 2012, Sierra Leonean soldiers made $450 per month. The change is explained in a Ministry of Defence document titled 'The Purpose of Deducting USD 200 from Allowances of Troops in Foreign Peacekeeping Mission in Somalia'.
59. Author interview with Sierra Leonean enlisted soldier, May 2011; the calculations were estimates made by the soldier.
60. Author interview with Sierra Leonean enlisted soldier, May 2011.
61. The AMISOM mission is led by the AU but similar patterns regarding differences exist in what the troop-contributing countries are reimbursed compared with what soldiers are paid.
62. The document can be found at: http://www.mod.gov.sl/docs/Purpose_of_USD_200_Deductions_fm_RSLAF_PK_Troops.pdf
63. Musdapha Ilo, 'Army Short Changes Nigerian Peacekeepers', International Centre for Investigative Reporting, 19 October 2013.
64. In Nigerian parlance, *oga* can be understood as leader, boss or senior.
65. Author interview with Sierra Leonean enlisted soldier, May 2011.
66. Kemo Cham, 'Pay Scandal Rocks Sierra Leone's Troops in Somalia', *Africa Review*, 17 October 2013.
67. Aning, 'Unintended Consequences of Peace Operations', p. 144.
68. Ibid., pp. 144–8.
69. Author interview with Burkinabé former officer, currently working in the security sector, March 2012.
70. Similar argument to corruption delegitimising organisations and impeding the peacebuilding efforts, as explained by Philippe Le Billon, 'Corrupting Peace? Peacebuilding and Post-conflict Corruption', *International Peacekeeping*, 15, 3 (2008), pp. 344–61.
71. John Michael Lee, *African Armies and Civil Order*, London: Chatto and Windus, 1969, pp. 92–3; William Gutteridge, *Military Regimes in Africa*, London: Methuen, 1975, pp. 28–9; First, *Barrel of a Gun*, pp. 22–3.
72. For more on this topic, see Gregory Mann, *Native Sons: West African Veterans and France in the Twentieth Century*, Durham, NC: Duke University Press, 2006. The Tirailleurs Sénégalais was a corps of colonial troops in the French military, primarily recruited from West Africa.
73. Olonisakin, *Reinventing Peacekeeping in Africa*, p. 179.
74. Ibid., pp. 179–80.
75. Author interview with Gambian officer, May 2012.
76. Olonisakin, *Reinventing Peacekeeping in Africa*, p. 180.
77. Operation Liberty was launched by ECOMOG in late 1990 to push the rebel group, NPFL, out of Monrovia. Ibid.

78. Ibid., p. 181.
79. Sarr, *Coup d'état*, p. 120.
80. Hutchful, 'ECOMOG Experience with Peacekeeping in Africa'.
81. Olonisakin, *Reinventing Peacekeeping in Africa*, p. 194. The initial ECOMOG pay rate was $5 per day, although troops often did not receive the full pay for a variety of reasons.
82. Coleman, 'Political Economy of UN Peacekeeping', p. 28.
83. Ibid.
84. Author interviews in Sierra Leone, 2016
85. Guy L. Siebold, 'The Essence of Military Group Cohesion', *Armed Forces & Society*, 33, 2 (2007), p. 288.
86. Anthony King, *The Combat Soldier: Infantry Tactics and Cohesion in the Twentieth and Twenty-First Centuries*, Oxford: Oxford University Press, 2013, p. 18.
87. Ibid., p. 31.
88. Siebold, 'Essence of Military Group Cohesion', p. 293.
89. King, *Combat Soldier*, p. 32.
90. Olonisakin, *Reinventing Peacekeeping in Africa*, p. 205.
91. Hutchful, 'ECOMOG Experience with Peacekeeping in Africa'.
92. Elizabeth Dickinson, 'For Tiny Burundi, Big Returns in Sending Peacekeepers to Somalia', *Christian Science Monitor*, 22 December 2011.
93. Cedric de Coning, 'The Evolution of Peace Operations in Africa: Trajectories and Trends,' *Journal of International Peacekeeping*, 14 (2010), p. 26.

6. A COUP HIDDEN IN A MUTINY: CASE STUDY OF SIERRA LEONE

1. There was a coup in 1967, followed several days later by an internal counter-coup. Details on this event can be found in Humphrey J. Fisher, 'Elections and Coups in Sierra Leone, 1967', *Journal of Modern African Studies*, 7, 4 (December 1969), pp. 611–36. A second coup was conducted in 1968. Additionally, Patrick McGowan's dataset shows three coup attempts and two coup plots between 1961 and 1992.
2. Thomas S. Cox, *Civil–Military Relations in Sierra Leone: A Case Study of African Soldiers in Politics*, Cambridge, MA: Harvard University Press, 1976, pp. 220–3.
3. Ibid., p. 223.
4. John Cartwright, *Political Leadership in Sierra Leone*, London: Croom Helm, 1978, pp. 80–1.
5. Cox, *Civil–Military Relations in Sierra Leone*, p. 90.
6. Kandeh, *Coups from Below*, p. 146.
7. E.D.A. Turay and A. Abraham, *The Sierra Leone Army*, London: Macmillan, 1987, p. 137.
8. Ibid.
9. Ibid., p. 147.

10. David Fasholé Luke, 'Continuity in Sierra Leone: From Stevens to Momoh', *Third Word Quarterly*, 10, 1 (January 1988), p. 71.
11. Later renamed the Special Security Division (SSD).
12. Lansana Gberie, *A Dirty War in West Africa*, London: Hurst, 2005, p. 29.
13. David Keen, *Conflict and Collusion in Sierra Leone*, New York: Palgrave, 2005, p. 17.
14. Turay and Abraham, *Sierra Leone Army*, p. 161.
15. Luke, 'Continuity in Sierra Leone', pp. 75–6.
16. William Reno, *Corruption and State Politics in Sierra Leone*, New York: Cambridge University Press, 1995, p. 153.
17. John L. Hirsch, *Sierra Leone: Diamonds and Struggle for Democracy*, Boulder, CO: Lynne Rienner, 2001, p. 30.
18. A. Zack-Williams and Stephen Riley, 'Sierra Leone: The Coup and Its Consequences', *Review of African Political Economy*, 56 (1993), p. 92.
19. Keen, *Conflict and Collusion*, p. 26.
20. Earl Conteh-Morgan and Mac Dixon-Fyle, *Sierra Leone at the End of the Twentieth Century*, New York: Lang, 1999, pp. 125–126.
21. Hirsch, *Sierra Leone*, p. 30.
22. Jimmy D. Kandeh, 'In Search of Legitimacy: The 1996 Election', in Ibrahim Abdullah (ed.), *Between Democracy and Terror: The Sierra Leone Civil War*, Dakar: CODESRIA, 2004, p. 125.
23. Ismail Rashid, 'Student Radicals, Lumpen Youth and Origins of Revolutionary Groups in Sierra Leone 1977–1996', in Abdullah, *Between Democracy and Terror*, p. 84.
24. Gberie, *Dirty War in West Africa*, pp. 37–8.
25. Transcripts of the speeches can be found in *West Africa*, 11 May 1992.
26. Keen, *Conflict and Collusion*, p. 37.
27. Stephen Ellis, *The Mask of Anarchy*, 2nd edn, London: Hurst, 2007, pp. 92–3; David Harris, *Sierra Leone: A Political History*, London: Hurst, 2013, p. 86.
28. Paul Richards, *Fighting for the Rain Forest: War, Youth & Resources in Sierra Leone*, Oxford: James Currey, 1996, p. 23.
29. Gberie, *Dirty War in West Africa*, p. 70.
30. Keen, *Conflict and Collusion*, p. 83.
31. Based on author interviews with soldiers in Sierra Leone, 2011 and 2012.
32. Keen, *Conflict and Collusion*, p. 87.
33. Author interview with Sierra Leonean enlisted soldier, April 2012.
34. Author interview with Sierra Leonean officer (enlisted rank in 1992), May 2011.
35. Ibid.
36. Author interview with Sierra Leonean enlisted soldier, May 2011.
37. Author interview with Sierra Leonean enlisted soldier, April 2012.
38. Author interview with Sierra Leonean officer (enlisted rank in 1992), May 2011.

39. Author interview with Sierra Leonean enlisted soldier, April 2012.
40. Author interview with Sierra Leonean enlisted soldier, May 2011.
41. Author casual conversation with soldier, April 2012.
42. *West Africa*, 3 April 1995, pp. 498–9.
43. Brigadier (retired) Kellie H. Conteh, testimony before TRC hearing held in Freetown, June 2003, quoted in Mohamed Sesay, 'Military Reform and Post-conflict Peace Building in Sierra Leone', MPhil, Fourah Bay College, 2009.
44. *New African*, June 1992, p. 18.
45. Author interview with Sierra Leonean enlisted soldier, May 2011.
46. Author interview with Sierra Leonean enlisted soldier, April 2012.
47. *West Africa*, 15 June 1992, p. 1002.
48. *New African*, June 1992, p. 18.
49. Author interview with Sierra Leonean enlisted soldier, May 2011.
50. Author interview with Valentine Strasser, May 2011.
51. *West Africa*, 15 June 1992, p. 1002.
52. Author interview with Valentine Strasser, May 2011.
53. *West Africa*, 11 May 1992, p. 788; Zack-Williams and Riley, 'Sierra Leone', p. 94.
54. Several of these publications include Arthur Abraham, 'State Complicity as a Factor in Perpetuating the Sierra Leone Civil War', in Abdullah, *Between Democracy and Terror*, p. 105; Hirsch, *Sierra Leone*, p. 32; Gberie, *Dirty War in West Africa*, p. 68; Richards, 'Fighting for the Rain Forest', p. 9.
55. Hirsch, *Sierra Leone*, p. 32.
56. These accounts include *Daily Mail*, 4 May 1992; *Rural Post*, June 1992; and *Progress*, 9 May 1992.
57. This narrative was told by several different interviewees.
58. Author interview with Valentine Strasser, May 2011.
59. Author interview with Sierra Leonean enlisted soldier, May 2011.
60. Author interview with Sierra Leonean enlisted soldier, April 2012.
61. Author interview with Sierra Leonean enlisted soldier, May 2011; this story was verified by numerous sources, although there were variations in the name of the major.
62. Author interview with Sierra Leonean officer, May 2011.
63. First, *Barrel of a Gun*, p. 19; Kandeh, *Coups from Below*, p. 43.
64. Based on author interviews and casual conversations, Sierra Leone, 2011 and 2012.
65. Based on author interviews, Sierra Leone, 2011 and 2012.
66. Author interview with Sierra Leonean officer, May 2011.
67. Author interview with Sierra Leonean enlisted soldier, May 2011.
68. Ibid.
69. Ibid.
70. Ibid.
71. Keen, *Conflict and Collusion*, p. 94.

72. Musa was a figure that the rank and file rallied around until his death in battle in 1998. He appeared in the post-coup newspaper reporting more often than Strasser and was nicknamed the 'Action Man' in the press owing to the many initiatives he led under the National Provisional Ruling Council (NPRC).
73. Robin Luckham, *The Nigerian Military: A Sociological Analysis of Authority and Revolt, 1960–1967*, Cambridge: Cambridge University Press, 1971, p. 83.
74. Author interview with Sierra Leonean officer, May 2011.
75. Several such accounts include *West Africa*, 29 June 1992, Robert Edgerton, *African Armies: From Honor to Infamy*, Boulder, CO: Westview, 2002; p. 164; Zack-Williams and Riley, 'Sierra Leone', p. 92.
76. The roughly one-year time frame for the coup plan is consistent with descriptions given by Strasser to the media immediately after the coup, as quoted in *West Africa*, 11 June 1992.
77. First, *Barrel of a Gun*, p. 22.
78. *West Africa*, 11 May 1992.
79. Rashid, 'Student Radicals', p. 85.
80. Joseph A. Opala, '"Ecstatic Renovation!" Street Art Celebrating Sierra Leone's 1992 Revolution', *African Affairs*, 93, 371 (April 1994), pp. 195–218.
81. Keen, *Conflict and Collusion*, p. 108.
82. Author interview with Sierra Leonean officer, May 2011.
83. Author interview with Sierra Leonean officer (enlisted soldier in 1992), May 2011.
84. Strasser was one of the only interviewees who had a long list of achievements by the NPRC.
85. Author interview with Sierra Leonean enlisted soldier, May 2011.
86. Ibid.
87. Ibid.
88. Gberie, *Dirty War in West Africa*, p. 91.
89. Ibid., pp. 91–3.
90. Kandeh, 'In Search of Legitimacy', p. 129.
91. Abraham, 'State Complicity', p. 119.
92. Harris, *Sierra Leone*, p. 98; Gberie, *Dirty War in West Africa*, pp. 84–5.
93. Harris, *Sierra Leone*, p. 106.
94. Gberie, *Dirty War in West Africa*, p. 101.
95. Kandeh, *Coups from Below*, pp. 169–74; Lansana Gberie, 'The 25 May Coup d'état in Sierra Leone: A Lumpen Revolt?', in Abdullah, *Between Democracy and Terror*, p. 147.
96. Krijn Peters, *War and the Crisis of Youth in Sierra Leone*, Cambridge: Cambridge University Press, 2011, pp. 75–6.
97. Author interview with Sierra Leonean officer, May 2011.
98. Peters, *War and the Crisis of Youth*, pp. 76–7.
99. Identification of the sources of interviewees who provided details on a potential

future mutiny will be kept confidential owing to the sensitivity of the topic. Information about future mutinies was provided to me in 2011 and 2012.

100. The largest contribution to this effort was the UK International Military Training and Advisory Team (IMATT), which provided training and assistance to the Sierra Leone Armed Forces for nearly twelve years (2002–13).
101. West Side boys was a notorious gang/rebel group.
102. Author interview with Sierra Leonean officer, May 2011.
103. Research for this chapter involved visits to ten military bases throughout Sierra Leone.
104. Author interview with Sierra Leonean officer, April 2012.
105. American Embassy Freetown, 'Sierra Leone Army "Dream Team" Airs Grievances', 4 February 2009.
106. Peter Albrecht and Cathy Haenlein, 'Sierra Leone's Post-conflict Peacekeepers', *RUSI Journal*, 160, 1 (2015), p. 30.
107. 'Pay Scandal Rocks Sierra Leone AMISOM Mission', *Daily Nation*, 17 October 2013.
108. Umaru Fofana, 'Bring on the Alleged Mutineers', *Politico*, 28 January 2014.
109. Mohamed Massaquoi, 'After Almost 14 Weeks Incommunicado', *Concord Times* (Freetown), 6 December 2013.
110. Kemo Cham, 'Sierra Leone Mutiny Trial Hit by Cash Crunch', *Africa Review*, 11 February 2014; Press Release by Centre for Accountability and Rule of Law (CARL), 7 April 2014.
111. 'Sierra Leone Court Acquits 13 Soldiers Accused of Mutiny', Reuters, 6 August 2015.
112. For example, he explained that it is up to each country what it will pay its peacekeepers and Sierra Leone has decided on $828 per month per soldier, with the balance of the UN pay going towards 'operational costs'. He emphasised that it is not the responsibility of the Sierra Leone government or the Ministry of Defence to provide food for the peacekeepers and commented that he knew nothing about the allegations of bribery.

7. MUTINIES WITH UNINTENDED CONSEQUENCES: CASE STUDY OF THE GAMBIA

1. McGowan, 'African Military Coups d'État', pp. 363–4.
2. Arnold Hughes, 'The Attempted Gambian Coup d'état of 30 July 1981', in Arnold Hughes (ed.), *The Gambia: Studies in Society and Politics*, Birmingham University African Studies Series 3, Birmingham: University of Birmingham, pp. 96–7.
3. John Wiseman, 'Revolt in the Gambia: A Pointless Tragedy', *Round Table: The Commonwealth Journal of International Affairs*, 71, 284 (1981), p. 374; there was one incident in October 1980 in which the deputy commander of the field force,

Eku Mahoney, was killed by a junior member of the unit. Investigations were conducted to determine if the perpetrator, Mustapha Danso, was linked to radical political groups but no link was ever determined. Furthermore, there was no indication that the murder had anything to do with complaints within the field force, it was rather was assessed to be an individual act of aggression. For more information on this topic, see *The Voice of the People: The Story of the PPP, 1959–1989*, Banjul: Baroueli Publications, 1992, p. 98; Dawda K. Jawara, *Kairaba*, Haywards Heath: Alhaji Sir Dawda Kairaba Jawara, 2009, pp. 315–17.

4. Zaya Yeebo, *State of Fear in Paradise: The Military Coup in the Gambia and its Implications for Democracy*, London: Africa Research and Information Bureau, 1995, p. 46; Abdoulaye Saine, *The Paradox of Third-Wave Democratization in Africa*, Plymouth, UK: Lexington Books, 2009, p. 26.
5. Arnold Hughes and David Perfect, *A Political History of The Gambia: 1816–1994*, Rochester, NY: University of Rochester Press, 2006, p. 212; Kandeh, *Coups from Below*, p. 180.
6. Hughes, 'Attempted Gambian Coup d'État', p. 99.
7. Ibid.
8. Ibid., p. 103; Jawara, *Kairaba*, 311–12.
9. Hughes and Perfect, *Political History of The Gambia*, pp. 211–14; Hughes, 'Attempted Gambian Coup d'État', p. 99.
10. Nicodemus Fru Awasom, 'The Senegambia in Historical and Contemporary Perspective', in Siga Fatima Jagne (ed.), *Nation-States and the Challenges of Regional Integration in West Africa: The Case of the Gambia*, Paris: Editions Karthala, 2010, p. 52.
11. Hughes and Perfect, *Political History of The Gambia*, p. 215; Jawara, *Kairaba*, p. 311; the estimates of the number of Senegalese troops sent in the response to the coup attempt vary widely. Jawara, in his autobiography, states that 300 airborne troops were initially dropped with more arriving later. Hughes gives an estimate as high as 3,000 in total; Britain's Special Air Service (SAS) was also utilised specifically to deal with the hostage situation.
12. McGowan and Johnson, 'African Military Coups d'État', p. 635; Harvey G. Kebschull, 'Operation "Just Missed": Lessons from Failed Coup Attempts', *Armed Forces and Society*, 20, 4 (1994), p. 570.
13. Jawara, *Kairaba*, p. 341.
14. *Gambia Times*, 14 February 1990.
15. Hughes and Perfect, *Political History of the Gambia*, p. cit. p. 220.
16. Sarr, *Coup d'État*, p. 120.
17. Binneh Minteh, *Rethinking the Military and Democratization*, Saarbrucken, Germany: Lambert Publishing, 2010, p. 7.
18. It took time for The Gambia to recruit and train its army and therefore The Gambia did not begin contributing troops to the joint unit until 1985, even though the Confederal Army was established years earlier.

19. Ebrima Chongan, *The Price of Duty*, Lulu: n.p., 2010, p. 26.
20. Yeebo, *State of Fear*, p. 47.
21. Author interview with Gambian former enlisted soldier, October 2012.
22. Author confidential interview, 2012.
23. John Wiseman and Elizabeth Vidler, 'The July 1994 Coup d'état in The Gambia: The End of an Era?', *Round Table*, 333, 1 (January 1995), p. 55.
24. Ibid.
25. Hughes and Perfect, *Political History of The Gambia*, p. 265.
26. Awasom, 'Senegambia in Historical and Contemporary Perspective', p. 55.
27. Ibid.; Wiseman and Vidler, 'July 1994 Coup d'état in The Gambia', p. 55.
28. Jawara, *Kairaba*, p. 354.
29. Wiseman and Vidler, 'July 1994 Coup d'état in The Gambia', p. 55.
30. Hughes and Perfect, *Political History of The Gambia*, p. 265.
31. Author interview with Gambian former enlisted soldier, October 2012.
32. *Gambia Weekly*, 10 August 1990; the exact number of Gambian troops involved in the first ECOMOG mission varies depending on the source, although all state that over 100 troops were deployed. *Gambia Weekly* (government-sponsored newspaper) and Jawara's autobiography quote 105 troops, whereas other media sources and academic writing puts the number at 150.
33. *Foroyaa* published numerous and regular criticism of the mission from 1989 into the early 1990s; author interview with Gambian former officer, September 2012.
34. Author interview with Gambian former enlisted soldier, October 2012.
35. Sarr, *Coup d'État*, pp. 126–7.
36. Author interview with Gambian former officer, September 2012.
37. Olonisakin, *Reinventing Peacekeeping in Africa*, p. 166.
38. Sarr, *Coup d'État*, p. 40.
39. Olonisakin, *Reinventing Peacekeeping in Africa*, p. 47.
40. Ibid.
41. Author interview with Gambian former officer, September 2012.
42. Author interview with Gambian former enlisted soldier, October 2012.
43. Author interview with Gambian officer and Gambian enlisted soldier, May 2012.
44. *Foroyaa*, 15 May 1991.
45. Author interview with Gambian former enlisted soldier, October 2012.
46. *Foroyaa*, 15 May 1991.
47. Sarr, *Coup d'État*, pp. 127–8; *Foroyaa*, 30 June 1991.
48. *Foroyaa*, 30 June 1991.
49. Author interview with Gambian officer, May 2012; Sarr, *Coup d'État*, pp. 127–8.
50. *West Africa*, 10 February 1992; author interview with Gambian former officer, September 2012.
51. *West Africa*, 10–16 October 1994.

52. Author interview with Gambian former officer, August 2012.
53. *West Africa*, 10–16 October 1994.
54. Author interview with Dr Abdoulaye Saine, June, 2012.
55. Author interview with Gambian former enlisted soldier, October 2012.
56. Author interview with Gambian former officer, September 2012.
57. *West Africa*, 10–16 October 1994.
58. Author interview with Gambian former enlisted soldier, October 2012.
59. *The Nation*, 20 July 1991.
60. *West Africa*, 8–14 July 1991.
61. Comment by Lt Col. Rtd Jim Shaw on blog titled 'Mutiny in Gambia, Former Army Lieutenant Kejau Touray Breaks His Silence', 28 August 2007, http://www.bloggernews.net/19753
62. Author interview with Gambian former enlisted soldier, September 2012.
63. *Foroyaa*, 15 July 1991.
64. Ibid.
65. *The Point*, 23 March 1992.
66. *Foroyaa*, 15 February 1992
67. Sarr, *Coup d'État*, p. 129.
68. *The Point*, 10 February 1992.
69. *Foroyaa*, 15 February 1992.
70. *West Africa*, 10 February 1992.
71. *The Point*, 10 February 1992.
72. Ibid.
73. Interview with Gambian officer, May 2012.
74. Author interview with Gambian former enlisted soldier, September, 2012.
75. Author interview with Gambian former officer, August 2012.
76. *Foroyaa*, 15 March 1992; *The Point*, 27 April 1992.
77. *The Point*, 27 July 1992.
78. *The Point*, 20 July 1992.
79. Author interview with Gambian former enlisted soldier, October 2012.
80. Author interview with Gambian former officer, September 2012.
81. Ibid.
82. Sarr, *Coup d'État*, pp. 32, 55.
83. Author interview with Gambian former enlisted soldier, October 2012.
84. Sarr, *Coup d'État*, p. 33.
85. Ibid., p. 50.
86. Author interview with Gambian former officer, September 2012; Sarr, *Coup d'État*, p. 19.
87. Author interview with Gambian former officer, August 2012.
88. Author confidential interview, May 2012.
89. Abdoulaye Saine and Ebrima Ceesay, 'Post-coup Politics and Authoritarianism in

The Gambia: 1994–2012', in Abdoulaye Saine, Ebrima Ceesay and Ebrima Sall (eds), *State and Society in The Gambia since Independence: 1965–2012*, Trenton, NJ: Africa World Press, 2013, p. 156.
90. Author interview with Gambian former officer, September 2012.
91. Sarr, *Coup d'État*, p. 47; Chongan, *Price of Duty*, p. 31.
92. *Gambia Weekly*, 28 February 1992.
93. When the gendarmerie was converted into the TSG, many gendarmes requested transfer to the army. One such individual was Lieutenant Yahya Jammeh.
94. Chongan, *Price of Duty*, p. 32.
95. Sarr, *Coup d'État*, p. 47; author interview with Gambian former officer, September 2012.
96. Author interview with Gambian former officer, August 2012; Chongan, *Price of Duty*, p. 32; author interview with Gambian former enlisted soldier, October 2012.
97. A sample of such articles includes *Daily Observer*, 30 May 1994; *Daily Observer*, 21 June 1994; *The Point*, 17 February 1994.
98. *Daily Observer*, 1–3 July 1994; *Daily Observer*, 14 July 1994.
99. *Foroyaa*, 15 March 1993; *Foroyaa*, 28 April 1993; *Foroyaa*, 15 May 1993; *Foroyaa*, 30 May 1994.
100. *Daily Observer*, 7 April 1994; *Foroyaa*, 15 July 1994.
101. Wiseman and Vidler, 'July 1994 Coup d'état in The Gambia', p. 58; Kandeh, *Coups from Below*, p. 183.
102. Author confidential interview, May 2012.
103. For tactical level details of the coup, see Sarr, *Coup d'État*, and Chongan, *Price of Duty*.
104. *Daily Observer*, 22 June 1994.
105. *The Point*, 21 July 1994.
106. Ebrima Chongan is of the former opinion, while Samsudeen Sarr is of the latter.
107. Jawara had arrived home from England the day before, and Gambian officers, including Yayha Jammeh, came to the airport armed to meet him. They were disarmed and sent away by the NATAG. In an interview just two days after the coup, Jammeh complains that he was publicly humiliated at the airport for 'no apparent reason' and that this event 'was the last straw' (*Daily Observer*, 25 July 1994). It remains unclear why the Gambian soldiers were armed but rumours began to spread that they had been planning to stage a coup at the airport.
108. Jawara, *Kairaba*, p. 380.
109. Wiseman and Vidler, 'July 1994 Coup d'état in The Gambia', p. 53.
110. A text of the radio announcement can be found in *Foroyaa*, 24 July 1994.
111. Transcript of the interview published in ibid.
112. Sarr, *Coup d'État*, p. 131.

113. Hughes and Perfect, *Political History of The Gambia*, p. 281.
114. Sarr, *Coup d'État*, p. 89.
115. Author interview with Gambian former enlisted soldier, October 2012.
116. Sarr, *Coup d'État*, p. 19; there have been numerous deaths of military personnel at the hands of the AFRC in the later years of the regime's rule. For more details on this topic, see Chapter 6 in Saine, *Paradox of Third-Wave Democratization*.
117. Examples include *Africa South of the Sahara*, 1995 edn and *West Africa*, 1–7 August 1994.
118. There seems to be particular misperceptions about Jammeh's involvement in ECOMOG. Civilian interviewees and academic writers such as Adekeye Adebajo claimed that Jammeh 'himself served with ECOMOG in Liberia'. However, this appears to be only a rumour. Military sources that I interviewed say he never served in Liberia (or elsewhere abroad) and his biography on the official Gambian State House webpage does not list any deployments.
119. Sarr, *Coup d'État*, p. 41.
120. Ibid., p. 91.
121. Ibid., p. 129.
122. Transcript of the press conference can be found in *Foroyaa*, 29 July 1994.
123. Chongan, *Price of Duty*, p. 8.
124. Author interview with Gambian enlisted soldier, May 2012.
125. Author interview with Gambian civil servant, May 2012.
126. Sarr, *Coup d'État*, p. 196; 'Another Army Promotion at the State Guards', *Freedom Newspaper*, 17 October 2011.
127. For example, many of the individuals who have held the position of chief of defence staff (CDS) have been Jola, including Baboucarr Jatta (1999–2004), Lang Tombong Tamba (2005–9) and Ousman Badjie (2012–17).
128. Matthew K. Jallow, 'Yahya Jammeh's Tribalism and the Tyranny of the Jola Minority', *Freedom Newspaper*, 31 July 2011.
129. David Perfect, *Historical Dictionary of The Gambia*, 5th edn, Lanham, MD: Rowman & Littlefield, 2016, p. 247.
130. Abdoulaye Saine, 'The Gambia's 2006 Presidential Election: Change or Continuity?', *African Studies Review*, 51, 1 (April 2008), p. 75.
131. Saine, *Paradox of Third-Wave Democratization*, pp. 84, 121.
132. 'Government Clears Air on "Terrorist" Attack', *The Standard* (The Gambia), 8 January 2015.
133. 'Jammeh Says Tuesday Episode a "Terror Attack" Not Attempted Coup', *Daily Observer*, 2 January 2015; 'Court Martial Underway in the Gambia', *The Point*, 16 February 2015.
134. 'Families Targeted and Persecuted after Failed Coup d'état in The Gambia', *Article 19*, 2 February 2015.

8. AN ESCALATING CYCLE OF MUTINIES: CASE STUDY OF BURKINA FASO

1. '"Just What Were They Thinking When They Shot at People": Crackdown on Anti-government Protests in Burkina Faso', Amnesty International, 2015, p. 9.
2. Marie-Soleil Frère and Pierre Englebert, 'Burkina Faso: The Fall of Blaise Compaoré', *African Affairs*, 114, 455 (2015), p. 4.
3. Author interview with editorial chief for private radio station in Burkina Faso, March 2012.
4. McGowan, 'African Military Coups d'État', p. 367; supplemented with Jonathan Powell and Clayton Thyne's dataset, available at http://www.uky.edu/~clthyn2/coup_data/home.htm
5. Michael Wilkins, 'The Death of Thomas Sankara and the Rectification of the People's Revolution in Burkina Faso', *African Affairs*, 88, 352 (July 1989), p. 381.
6. *Africa Research Bulletin*, May 1983, p. 6849; *Africa Research Bulletin*, June 1983; p. 6684; *Africa Confidential*, 8 June 1983, pp. 7–8; *West Africa*, 27 June 1983, pp. 1490–1.
7. Victoria Brittain, 'Introduction to Sankara and Burkina Faso', *Review of African Political Economy*, 32 (April 1985), p. 45.
8. Pierre Englebert, *Burkina Faso: Unsteady Statehood in West Africa*, Boulder, CO: Westview, 1996, p. 55.
9. Brittain, 'Introduction to Sankara and Burkina Faso', p. 45.
10. Ibid., p. 42.
11. Ibid.
12. Englebert, *Burkina Faso*, pp. 152–5.
13. Ibid., p. 43.
14. Wilkins, 'Death of Thomas Sankara', p. 383.
15. *West Africa*, 20 August 1983.
16. Thomas Sankara, 'Political Orientation Speech', presented by Sankara on behalf of the NCR, 2 October 1983, from *Thomas Sankara: Speeches from the Burkina Faso Revolution 1983–87*, New York: Pathfinder Press, 2002, p. 47.
17. Ernest Harsch, *Thomas Sankara: An African Revolutionary*, Athens, OH: Ohio University Press, 2014, p. 66.
18. In 2015, after Compaoré resigned as president, an international arrest warrant was issued for his alleged to the murder of Sankara. As of 2017, Compaoré remains in Côte d'Ivoire with no indication that the warrant will be acted on.
19. Institute for Democracy and Electoral Assistance, http://www.idea.int/vt/countryview.cfm?CountryCode=BF
20. Col. H.L. Nombre, 'Civil–Military Relations and National Security in Burkina Faso: An Assessment', July 2008, p. 29.
21. 'Burkina Faso Soldiers End Protest', BBC, 15 July 1999.
22. 'Soldiers End Mutiny in Burkina Faso', AP, 15 July 1999.

23. Ibid.
24. Nombre, 'Civil–Military Relations', p. 29.
25. Ernest Harsch, 'Trop, c'est trop! Civil Insurgence in Burkina Faso 1989–1999', *Review of African Political Economy*, 26, 81 (September 1999), p. 401.
26. Nombre, 'Civil–Military Relations', p. 34; similar account provided in 'Fragile Democracy Being Tested', IRIN, 27 December 2006.
27. Nombre, 'Civil–Military Relations', p. 35.
28. American Embassy in Ouagadougou, 'Burkina Faso: Military Retirees Surprise Government with Aggressive Demands for Improved Benefits, Movement of Camps Outside of Main Cities', 28 April 2008.
29. Large country-wide demonstrations occurred in 1998 when government officials were suspected of killing the journalist Norbert Zongo.
30. Justin Zongo is not a direct relative of Norbert Zongo, but some speculate that the matching surname brought back memories of Norbert Zongo's suspected murder, further fuelling the anger of protestors.
31. Author interview with Chrysogone Zougmore, president of MBDHP, March 2012.
32. Author interview with Bazie Bassolina, secretary general of CGT-B, April 2012; CGT-B is the abbreviation for Confédération Générale du Travail du Burkina, a confederation of twelve national trade unions.
33. Author interview with Bazie Bassolina, secretary general of CGT-B, April 2012.
34. Author interview with Hamidou Idogo, editor in chief of *Journal du Jeudi*, March 2012.
35. 'Burkina Faso Cotton Growers Protest Low Prices', Reuters, 28 April 2011; 'Mort d'un élève à Koudougou: Violence et répression excessives', *Bendré*, 28 February 2011; 'Burkina Faso Teachers' Strike: Union Agrees Deal', BBC, 25 May 2011.
36. Author interview with editorial chief of private radio station, March 2012.
37. Some examples of this type of rhetoric in the local media include *L'indépendant*, no. 9, 1 March 2011; *Le Reporter*, no. 66, 15–31 March 2011; and *L'observateur Paalga*, no. 7840, 16 March 2011.
38. Author interview with former Burkinabé officer, currently working in the security sector, March 2012.
39. Ibid.
40. Author interview with Burkinabé former enlisted soldier, currently working in security sector, March 2012.
41. Author interview with Burkinabé former officer, currently working in security sector, March 2012.
42. American Embassy Ouagadougou, 'Burkina Faso: Military Court Hands Out Sentences', October 2009.
43. Ibid.
44. Ibid.

45. Author interview with Burkinabé former officer, March 2012.
46. Author interview with Burkinabé officer, March 2012.
47. Chouli, 'People's Revolt in Burkina Faso', p. 138.
48. 'Burkina Troops Free Rapist Comrade', AFP, 28 March 2011.
49. Ibid.
50. S. Yonaba, 'Mutineries de Militaires au Burkina Faso: L'Etat de droit mis à rude épreuve', *Liberté*, no. 33, September 2011, p. 10.
51. 'Burkinabé Soldiers Fire Rocket at Court', AFP, 29 March 2011.
52. Chouli, 'People's Revolt in Burkina Faso', p. 138.
53. 'Compaore to Meet Troops amid Protests', AFP, 31 March 2011.
54. Chouli, 'People's Revolt in Burkina Faso', p. 138.
55. Ibid., p. 139.
56. 'Gunfire Spread in Burkina Faso Capital', AFP, 15 April 2011.
57. 'Compaore Leaves Capital amid Army Mutiny', AFP, 15 April 2011; 'Troops Loot Burkina Faso for 2nd Night', AP, 16 April 2011.
58. 'Compaore Leave Capital amid Army Mutiny'.
59. 'Burkina Faso Gets New PM, Mutiny Spreads', AFP, 19 April 2011.
60. Ibid.
61. Chouli, 'People's Revolt in Burkina Faso', p. 139; 'Burkina Army Revolt Spreads', AFP, 17 April 2011.
62. 'Burkina Faso Troops and Cops Riot, Loot', AFP, 18 April 2011.
63. Chouli, 'People's Revolt in Burkina Faso', p. 140.
64. Mathieu Hilgers and Augustin Loada, 'Tensions et protestations dans un régime semi-autoritaire: Croissance des révoltes populaires et maintien du pouvoir au Burkina Faso', *Politique Africaine*, 131 (2013), pp. 187–208.
65. Ibid.
66. 'Burkina Faso Lifts Curfew after Unrest', SAPA, 17 May 2011.
67. Chouli, 'People's Revolt in Burkina Faso', p. 143.
68. Author interview with former Burkinabé officer, currently working in the security sector, March 2012; the gendarmeries who took part in the raid against the mutineers were specifically from the Security and Intervention Unit.
69. Chouli, 'People's Revolt in Burkina Faso', p. 143; author interview with Burkinabé former enlisted soldier, currently working in security sector, March 2012.
70. Author interviews, 2012.
71. Chouli, 'People's Revolt in Burkina Faso', p. 143.
72. Author interview with Burkinabé former enlisted soldier, March 2012.
73. 'Burkina Faso: With or Without Compaoré, Times of Uncertainty', International Crisis Group, Africa Report no. 205, 22 July 2013, p. 33.
74. Ibid., p. 34.
75. Ibid.
76. Author interview with Burkinabé professor, March 2012.

77. Author interview with Burkinabé enlisted soldier, March 2012.
78. Interview with foreign military officer working alongside Burkinabé military, March 2012, and confirmed in various other conversations.
79. Author interview with Burkinabé enlisted soldier, March 2012.
80. Author interview with Burkinabé former officer, currently working in security sector, March 2012.
81. Author interview with Burkinabé former enlisted soldier, March 2012.
82. Author interview with Burkinabé enlisted soldier, March 2012.
83. Ibid.
84. 'Burkina Faso: With or Without Compaoré, Times of Uncertainty', p. 32.
85. Ibid.; the International Crisis Group's figures also roughly match estimates in *The Military Balance*, 116, 1 (2016), p. 432, which estimate the army at 6,400 and the air force at 600.
86. Data on current and past UN troop contributions can be found at: http://www.un.org/en/peacekeeping/resources/statistics/contributors_archive.shtml
87. Author interview with Burkinabé former enlisted soldier, currently working in security sector, March 2012.
88. Author interview with Burkinabé enlisted soldier, March 2012.
89. Author interview with Burkinabé former officer, currently working in the security sector, March 2012.
90. Author interview with Burkinabé enlisted soldier, March 2012.
91. Author interview with Burkinabé former enlisted soldier, currently working in the security sector, March 2012. Ouaga 2000 is the wealthiest area of Ouagadougou; it houses the Presidential Palace as well as numerous Western embassies and expensive hotels.
92. Author interview with Burkinabé enlisted soldier, March 2012.
93. Author interview with Burkinabé former enlisted soldier, March 2012.
94. 'Burkina Faso: With or Without Compaoré, Times of Uncertainty', p. 32.
95. Nombre, 'Civil–Military Relations', p. 41.
96. Author interview with Burkinabé former enlisted soldier, currently working in the security sector, March 2012.
97. 'Burkina Faso: With or Without Compaoré, Times of Uncertainty', p. 33.
98. A sample of such predictions includes 'Burkina Faso: Next Regime to Fall?', United Press International, 15 April 2011; 'A Coup in the Making in Burkina Faso?', Stratfor, 16 April 2011; Alex Thurston, 'Burkina Faso's Compaore Facing Perfect Storm?', *World Politics Review*, 3 May 2011.
99. Author interview with Burkinabé enlisted soldier, March 2012; author interview with Burkinabé enlisted soldier, March 2012.
100. Author interview with Burkinabé enlisted soldier, March 2012.
101. Sources explained that there may have been a few individual gendarmes who revolted but no whole units.

102. American Embassy in Ouagadougou, 'Burkina Faso: Military Retirees Surprise Government with Aggressive Demands for Improved Benefits, Movement of Camps Outside of Main Cities', 28 April 2008.
103. Niagalé Bagayoko, 'Security Systems in Francophone and Anglophone Africa', *IDS Bulletin*, 43, 4 (July 2012), p. 69.
104. Author interview with Burkinabé former enlisted soldier, March 2012; confirmed in author interview with Burkinabé military officer, March 2012.
105. Author interview with Burkinabé former officer, currently working in the security sector, March 2012.
106. Author interview with Burkinabé former enlisted soldier, March 2012
107. A good example of this trend can be found in Klaas van Walraven's description of the formation of the Nigerien gendarmerie. Klaas van Walraven, *The Yearning for Relief: A History of the Sawaba Movement in Niger*, Leiden: Brill, 2013, pp. 581–2.
108. Bagayoko, 'Security Systems', p. 70.
109. Ibid.
110. Simon Gongo, 'Burkina Faso President Named Defense Minister in New Cabinet', Bloomberg, 22 April 2011.
111. Student focus group at university of Ouagadougou conducted by author, April 2012.
112. Author interview with Burkinabé former enlisted soldier, currently working in the security sector, March 2012.
113. Author interview with Burkinabé officer, March 2012.
114. Author interview with Burkinabé former enlisted soldier, currently working in the security sector, March 2012; 'Burkina Faso: With or Without Compaoré, Times of Uncertainty', p. 33.
115. Author interview with Burkinabé former enlisted soldier, March 2012.
116. Author interview with Burkinabé enlisted soldier, March 2012.
117. 'Forces armées nationales (FAN) du Burkina Faso: La discipline faisant la force principale', 11 November 2013, http://www.lefaso.net/spip.php?article56669&rubrique0
118. Ibid.
119. Student debate, University of Ouagadougou, March 2012.
120. Author interview with Moussa Diallo, secretary general of social issues for CGT-B, March 2012; interview with Burkinabé professor, March 2012.
121. Author interview with Burkinabé former officer, currently working in security sector, March 2012.
122. Author interview with Burinabé professor, March 2012.
123. Author interview with Burinabé professor, March 2012.
124. '"Le foulard noir," un film adapté de la mutinerie au Burkina a reçu l'onction du président', 14 February 2012, http://burkina24.com/news/2012/02/14/"le-

foulard-noir"'-un-filmadapte-de-la-mutinerie-au-burkina-a-recu-l'onction-du-president/
125. See the official government website at http://www.gouvernement.gov.bf/spip. php?article920
126. 'Projection en avant-première du "Foulard noir", le dernier film de Boubacar Diallo', 14 February 2012, http://www.gouvernement.gov.bf/spip.php?article920
127. Ibid.
128. Ibid.
129. 'See our sons sink'.
130. Dimitri Kaboré, 'Les militaires radiés en 2011 demandent leur réintégration', 26 April 2015, http://www.fasozine.com/situation-nationale-les-militaires-radies-de-2011-demandent-leur-reintegration-dans-larmee/#disqus_thread
131. 'Burkina Faso Presidential Guard Should Be Disbanded, Panel Says', Reuters, 14 September 2015.
132. 'Commission de reconciliation natrionale et des reformes: plus de 5000 dossiers de crimes enregistrés', Ouga.com, 15 September 2015.
133. For a detailed account of the events leading up to the disbanding of the RSP, see blog entries from Daniel Eizenga from 16 September to 2 October 2015 on sahelblog.wordpress.com

9. AN ALTERED VIEW OF MUTINIES

1. Author interviews with Burkinabé soldiers, 2012.
2. For example, classic texts from this period, such as *Barrel of a Gun* (1970) by Ruth First, *The Nigerian Military: A Sociological Analysis of Authority and Revolt* (1971) by Robin Luckham, and *Military Regimes in Africa* (1975) by W.F. Gutteridge, all place heavy emphasis on the officer corps, with limited analysis of the actions of the rank and file.
3. Hutchful and Bathily, 'Introduction', p. vi.
4. Hutchful, 'Institutional Decomposition' and Junior Ranks', p. 248.
5. Luanda, 'Tanganyika Rifles', p. 203.
6. First, *Barrel of a Gun*, p. 206.
7. Parker, 'Foreword', p. viii; Hamby, 'Mutiny Wagon Wheel'.
8. First, *Barrel of a Gun*, p. 436.
9. Luanda, 'Tanganyika Rifles', p. 203.
10. Iliffe, *Honour in African History*, p. 245.
11. James, *Mutiny in the British and Commonwealth Forces*, p. 3.
12. Ibid.
13. Hathaway, *Rebellion, Repression, Reinvention*, p. xi.

BIBLIOGRAPHY

Abdullah, Ibrahim, *Between Democracy and Terror: The Sierra Leone Civil War*, Dakar: CODESRIA, 2004.

Aboagye, Festus B., *ECOMOG: A Sub-regional Experience in Conflict Resolution Management and Peacekeeping in Liberia*, Accra: Sedco Publishing, 1999.

—— *The Ghana Army: A Concise Contemporary Guide to its Centennial Regimental History, 1897–1999*, Accra: Sedco Publishing, 1999.

Abraham, Arthur, 'State Complicity as a Factor in Perpetuating the Sierra Leone Civil War', in Ibrahim Abdullah (ed.), *Between Democracy and Terror: The Sierra Leone Civil War*, pp. 104–22, Dakar: CODESRIA, 2004.

Adebajo, Adekeye, *Liberia's Civil War: Nigeria, ECOMOG, and Regional Security in West Africa*, Boulder, CO: Lynne Rienner, 2002.

Adler, Amy B., Brett T. Litz and Paul T. Bartone, 'The Nature of Peacekeeping Stressors', in Thomas W. Britt and Amy B. Adler (eds), *The Psychology of the Peacekeeper*, pp. 149–68, Westport, CT: Praeger, 2003.

Afrifa, A.A., *The Ghana Coup: 24th February 1966*, London: Frank Cass, 1966.

Agyeman-Duah, Baffour, 'Military Coups, Regime Change, and Interstate Conflicts in West Africa', *Armed Forces and Society*, 16, 4 (1990), pp. 547–70.

Albrecht, Peter and Cathy Haenlein, 'Sierra Leone's Post-conflict Peacekeepers', *RUSI Journal*, 160, 1 (2015), pp. 26–36.

Alexander, H.T., *African Tightrope: My Two Years as Nkrumah's Chief of Staff*, London: Pall Mall Press, 1965.

Allen, Chris, 'Understanding African Politics', *Review of African Political Economy*, 22, 65 (September 1995), pp. 301–20.

Allen, Chris, Carolyn Baylies and Morris Szeftel, 'Editorial: Surviving Democracy?', *Review of African Political Economy*, 54 (July 1992), pp. 3–10.

Aning, Kwesi, 'Unintended Consequences of Peace Operations for Troop-Contributing Countries from West Africa: The Case of Ghana', in Chiyuki Aoil, Cedric de Coning and Ramesh Thakur (eds), *Unintended Consequences of*

BIBLIOGRAPHY

Peacekeeping Operations, pp. 133–55, Tokyo: United Nations University Press, 2007.

Ankersen, Christopher, 'Beyond Mutiny? Instrumental and Expressive Understandings of Contemporary "Collective Indiscipline"', in Craig Leslie Mantle (ed.), *The Unwilling and the Reluctant: Theoretical Perspectives on Disobedience in the Military*, pp. 113–26, Kingston, Ontario: Canadian Defence Academy Press, 2006.

Aoi, Chiyuki, Cedric de Coning and Ramesh Thakur (eds), *Unintended Consequences of Peacekeeping Operations*, New York: United Nations University Press, 2007.

Arlinghaus, Bruce E. and Pauline H. Baker (eds), *African Armies: Evolution and Capabilities*, Boulder: Westview, 1986.

Awasom, Nicodemus Fru, 'The Senegambia in Historical and Contemporary Perspective', in Siga Fatima Jagne (ed.), *Nation-States and the Challenges of Regional Integration in West Africa: The Case of the Gambia*, pp. 41–62, Paris: Editions Karthala, 2010.

Bagayoko, Niagalé, 'Security Systems in Francophone and Anglophone Africa', *IDS Bulletin*, 43, 4 (July 2012).

Ball, Nicole, 'J. Kayode Fayemi, 'Funmi Olonisakin, Rocklyn Williams and Martin Rupiya, 'Governance in the Security Sector', in Nicolas Van De Walle, Nicole Ball and Vijaya Ramachandran (eds), *Beyond Structural Adjustment*, pp. 263–304, New York: Palgrave Macmillan, 2003.

Bell, Christopher, 'Mutiny and the Royal Canadian Navy', in Craig Leslie Mantle (ed.), *The Unwilling and the Reluctant: Theoretical Perspectives on Disobedience in the Military*, pp. 87–112, Kingston: Ontario Canadian Defence Academy Press, 2006.

Bell, Christopher and Bruce Allen Elleman (eds), *Naval Mutinies of the Twentieth Century: An International Perspective*, London: Frank Cass, 2003.

Bienen, Henry, *Armies and Parties in Africa*, New York: Holmes and Meier Publishing, 1978.

—— 'Military Rule and Political Process: Nigerian Examples', *Comparative Politics*, 10, 2 (1978), pp. 205–25.

Birikorang, Emma, 'Ghana's Regional Security Policy: Costs, Benefits, and Consistency', KAIPTC Paper, no. 20, September 2007.

Black, Dean C., 'Murder by Spitfire? Probing for Mutiny and Indiscipline in Canada's Second World War Air Force', in Howard G. Coombs (ed.), *The Insubordinate and the Noncompliant: Case Studies of Canadian Mutiny and Disobedience, 1920 to Present*, pp. 143–72, Kingston: Ontario Canadian Defence Academy Press, 2007.

Bratton, Michael, 'Deciphering Africa's Divergent Transitions', *Political Science Quarterly*, 112, 1 (1997), pp. 67–93.

—— 'International versus Domestic Pressures for Democratisation in Africa', in William Hale and Eberhard Kienle (eds), *After the Cold War: Security and Democracy in Africa and Asia*, pp. 156–93, London: Tauris Academic Studies, 1997.

BIBLIOGRAPHY

Bratton, Michael and Robert Mattes, 'Support for Democracy in Africa: Intrinsic or Instrumental?', *Afrobarometer Paper*, 1 (2000).

Bratton, Michael and Nicolas Van de Walle, *Democratic Experiments in Africa: Regime Transitions in Comparative Perspective*, Cambridge: Cambridge University Press, 1997.

Britt, Thomas W. and Amy B. Adler (eds), *The Psychology of the Peacekeeper: Lessons from the Field*, Westport, CT: Praeger, 2003.

Bryden, Alan, Boubacar N'Diaye and 'Funmi Olonisakin (eds), *Challenges of Security Sector Governance in West Africa*, Geneva: Geneva Centre for Democratic Control of Armed Forces, 2008.

Butts, Kent Hughes and Steven Metz, 'Armies and Democracy in the New Africa: Lessons from Nigeria and South Africa', Strategic Studies Institute, 1996.

Callahan, Raymond, 'The Indian Army, Total War and the Dog that Didn't Bark in the Night', in Jane Hathaway (ed.), *Rebellion, Repression, Reinvention: Mutiny in Comparative Perspective*, pp. 119–30, Westport, CT: Praeger, 2001.

Cartwright, John, *Political Leadership in Sierra Leone*, London: Croom Helm, 1978.

Chabal, Patrick, *Power in Africa: An Essay in Political Interpretation*, London: Macmillan, 1992.

Chabal, Patrick and Jean-Pascal Daloz, *Africa Works: Disorder as Political Instrument*, Bloomington, IN: Indiana University Press, 1999.

Chongan, Ebrima, *The Price of Duty*, Lulu: n.p. 2010.

Chouli, Lila, 'People's Revolt in Burkina Faso', in Firoze Manji and Sokari Ekine (eds), *Africa Awakening: The Emerging Revolutions*, pp. 131–46, Oxford: Pambazuka Press, 2012.

Clapham, Christopher, *Africa and the International System: The Politics of State Survival*, Cambridge: University of Cambridge Press, 1996.

Coleman, Katharina P., 'The Political Economy of UN Peacekeeping: Incentivizing Effective Participation', New York: International Peace Institute, May 2014.

Collier, Paul and Anke Hoeffler, 'Coup Traps: Why Does Africa Have So Many Coups d'états?', Centre for the Study of African Economies, University of Oxford, 2005.

Coning, Cedric de. 'The Evolution of Peace Operations in Africa: Trajectories and Trends', *Journal of International Peacekeeping*, 14 (2010), pp. 6–26.

Conteh-Morgan, Earl and Mac Dixon-Fyle, *Sierra Leone at the End of the Twentieth Century*, New York: Peter Lang, 1999.

Coombs, Howard G., 'Dimensions of Military Leadership: The Kinmel Park Mutiny of 4–5 March 1919', in Craig Leslie Mantle (ed.), *The Apathetic and the Defiant: Case Studies of Canadian Mutiny and Disobedience, 1812 to 1919*, pp. 405–38, Ontario: Canadian Defence Academy, 2007.

—— (ed.), *The Insubordinate and the Noncompliant: Case Studies of Canadian Mutiny and Disobedience, 1920 to Present*, Kingston: Ontario Canadian Defence Academy Press, 2007.

BIBLIOGRAPHY

Cox, Thomas S., *Civil–Military Relations in Sierra Leone: A Case Study of African Soldiers in Politics*, Cambridge, MA: Harvard University Press, 1976.

Crook, Richard, 'Côte d'Ivoire: Multi-party Democracy and Political Change; Surviving the Crisis', in John Wiseman (ed.), *Democracy and Political Change in Sub-Saharan Africa*, pp. 11–44, London: Routledge, 1995.

Dahl, Robert A., *A Preface to Democratic Theory: Expanded Edition*, Chicago: University of Chicago Press, 2006.

Decalo, Samuel, *Africa: The Lost Decades*, Gainesville, FL: Florida Academic Press, 2012.

—— *Coups and Army Rule in Africa: Studies in Military Style*, New Haven: Yale University Press, 1976.

—— 'Modalities of Civil–Military Stability in Africa', *Journal of Modern African Studies*, 27, 4 (1989), pp. 547–78.

—— 'Morphology of Military Rule in Africa', in John Markakis and Michael Waller (eds), *Military Marxist Regimes in Africa*, pp. 122–44, London: Frank Cass, 1986.

—— *Psychoses of Power: African Personal Dictatorships*, 2nd edn, Gainesville, FL: Florida Academic Press, 1989.

Devlin, Larry, *Chief of Station, Congo: Fighting the Cold War in a Hot Zone*, New York: PublicAffairs, 2007.

Diamond, Larry and Marc Plattner (eds), *Democratization in Africa: Progress and Retreat*, 2nd edn, Baltimore: Johns Hopkins University Press, 2010.

Edgerton, Robert, *African Armies: From Honor to Infamy*, Boulder, CO: Westview, 2002.

Ellis, Stephen, *The Mask of Anarchy*, 2nd edn, London: Hurst, 2007.

Embaló, Birgit, 'Civil–Military Relations and Political Order in Guinea-Bissau', *Journal of Modern African Studies*, 50, 2 (June 2012), pp. 253–81.

Englebert, Pierre, *Burkina Faso: Unsteady Statehood in West Africa*, Boulder, CO: Westview, 1996.

—— *State Legitimacy and Development in Africa*, London: Lynne Rienner, 2000.

Englerbert, Pierre and Kevin C. Dunn, *Inside African Politics*, Boulder, CO: Lynne Rienner, 2013.

Fearon, James D., 'International Institutions and Collective Authorization of the Use of Force', in A. Alexandroff (ed.), *Can the World Be Governed? Possibilities for Effective Multilateralism*, pp. 160–95, Waterloo, Ontario: W. Laurier University Press, 2008.

Fearon, James D. and David Laitin, 'Neotrusteeship and the Problem of Weak States', *International Security*, 28, 4 (Spring 2004), pp. 5–43.

Feaver, Peter D., 'The Civil–Military Problematique: Huntington, Janowitz, and the Question of Civilian Control', *Armed Forces and Society*, 23, 2 (1996), pp. 149–78.

Finer, S.E., *The Man on Horseback: The Role of the Military in Politics*, London: Pall Mall Press, 1962.

BIBLIOGRAPHY

First, Ruth, *The Barrel of a Gun: Political Power in Africa and the Coup d'État*, London: Penguin, 1970.

Fisher, Humphrey J., 'Elections and Coups in Sierra Leone, 1967', *Journal of Modern African Studies*, 7, 4 (December 1969), pp. 611–36.

Frère, Marie-Soleil and Pierre Englebert, 'Burkina Faso: The Fall of Blaise Compaoré', *African Affairs*, 114, 455 (2015), pp. 295–307.

Gberie, Lansana, 'The 25 May Coup d'état in Sierra Leone: A Lumpen Revolt?', in Ibrahim Abdullah (ed.), *Between Democracy and Terror: The Sierra Leone Civil War*, pp. 144–63, Dakar: CODESRIA, 2004.

——— *A Dirty War in West Africa*, London: Hurst, 2005.

——— 'Liberia's War and Peace Process: A Historical Overview', in Festus Aboagye and Alhaji M.S. Bah (ed.), *Tortuous Road to Peace: The Dynamics of Regional, UN and International Humanitarian Interventions in Liberia*, pp. 51–71, Pretoria: Institute for Security Studies, 2005.

Gershoni, Yekutiel, 'The Changing Pattern of Military Takeovers in Sub-Saharan Africa', *Armed Forces and Society*, 23, 2 (1996), pp. 235–48.

Goldsworthy, David, 'On Structural Explanation of African Military Interventions', *Journal of Modern African Studies*, 24, 1 (1986), pp. 179–85.

Guttenridge, W.F., *Military Regimes in Africa*, London: Methuen, 1975.

Hamby, Joel E., 'Mutiny Wagon Wheel: A Leadership Model for Mutiny in Combat', *Armed Forces and Society*, 28, 4 (2002), pp. 575–600.

Harris, David, *Sierra Leone: A Political History*, London: Hurst, 2013.

Harris, Geoff, 'The Case for Demilitarisation in sub-Saharan Africa', in Geoff Harris (ed.), *Achieving Security in Sub-Saharan Africa*, Pretoria: Institute for Security Studies, 2004.

Harsch, Ernest, *Thomas Sankara: An African Revolutionary*, Athens, OH: Ohio University Press, 2014.

——— 'Trop, c'est trop! Civil Insurgence in Burkina Faso 1989–1999', *Review of African Political Economy*, 26, 81 (September 1999), pp. 395–406.

Hathaway, Jane (ed.), *Rebellion, Repression, Reinvention: Mutiny in Comparative Perspective*, Westport, CT: Praeger, 2001.

Heide, Rachel Lea, 'After the Emergency: Demobilization Strikes, Political Statements, and the Moral Economy in Canada's Air Forces, 1919–1946', in Howard G. Coombs (ed.), *The Insubordinate and the Noncompliant: Case Studies of Canadian Mutiny and Disobedience, 1920 to Present*, pp. 178–9, Ontario: Canadian Defense Academy Press, 2007), 178–179.

Herbst, Jeffrey, 'African Militaries and Rebellion: The Political Economy of Threat and Combat Research', *Journal of Peace Research*, 41 (2004), pp. 357–69.

Hilgers, Mathieu and Augustin Loada, 'Tensions et protestations dans un régime semi-autoritaire: Croissance des révoltes populaires et maintien du pouvoir au Burkina Faso', *Politique Africaine*, 131 (2013), pp. 187–208.

BIBLIOGRAPHY

Hirsch, John L., *Sierra Leone: Diamonds and the Struggle for Democracy*, Boulder, CO: Lynne Rienner, 2001.

Horn, Bernd, 'A Law unto Themselves? Elitism as a Catalyst for Disobedience', in Craig Leslie Mantle (ed.), *The Unwilling and the Reluctant: Theoretical Perspectives on Disobedience in the Military*, pp. 127–38, Kingston: Ontario Canadian Defence Academy Press, 2006.

Hoskyns, Catherine, *The Congo since Independence: January 1960–December 1961*, London: Oxford University Press, 1965.

Houngnikpo, Mathurin, *Guarding the Guardians: Civil–Military Relations and Democratic Governance in Africa*, Burlington, VT: Ashgate, 2010.

Howe, Herbert M., *Ambiguous Order: Military Forces in African States*, Boulder, CO: Lynne Rienner, 2001.

—— 'Lessons of Liberia: ECOMOG and Regional Peacekeeping', *International Security*, 21, 3 (Winter 1996–7), pp. 145–76.

Hughes, Arnold, 'The Attempted Gambian Coup d'état of 30 July 1981', in Arnold Hughes (ed.), *The Gambia: Studies in Society and Politics*, Birmingham University African Studies Series 3, Birmingham: Birmingham University, 1991.

Hughes, Arnold and David Perfect, *A Political History of The Gambia: 1816–1994*, Rochester, NY: University of Rochester Press, 2006.

Huntington, Samuel, 'Democracy's Third Wave', *Journal of Democracy*, 2, 2 (Spring 1991), pp. 12–34.

—— *The Soldier and the State: The Theory and Politics of Civil–Military Relations*, Cambridge, MA: Harvard University Press, 1957.

Hutchful, Eboe, 'Institutional Decomposition and Junior Ranks' Political Action in Ghana', in Eboe Hutchful and Abdoulaye Bathily (eds), *The Military and Militarism in Africa*, pp. 211–56, Dakar: CODESRIA, 1998.

—— 'The ECOMOG Experience with Peacekeeping in Africa', in *Whither Peacekeeping in Africa?*, Monograph no. 36, Institute for Security Studies, April 1999.

—— 'Military Issues in the Transition to Democracy', in Eboe Hutchful and Abdoulaye Bathily (eds), *The Military and Militarism in Africa*, pp. 599–617, Dakar: CODESRIA, 1998.

Hutchful, Eboe and Abdoulaye Bathily (eds), *The Military and Militarism in Africa*, Dakar: CODESRIA, 1998.

Hydén, Göran and Michael Leslie, 'Communication and Democratization in Africa', in Göran Hydén, Michael Leslie and Folu F. Ogundimu (eds), *Media and Democracy in Africa*, pp. 1–28, Newark, NJ: Transaction Publishers, 2002.

Hydén, Göran and Charles Okigbo, 'The Media and the Two Waves of Democracy', in Göran Hydén, Michael Leslie and Folu F. Ogundimu (eds), *Media and Democracy in Africa*, pp. 29–54, Newark, NJ: Transaction Publishers, 2002.

Iliffe, John, *Honour in African History*, Cambridge: Cambridge University Press, 2005.

BIBLIOGRAPHY

International Crisis Group, 'Burkina Faso: With or Without Compaoré, Times of Uncertainty', *Africa Report* no. 205, 22 July 2013.

Jackman, Robert W., 'Politicians in Uniform: Military Governments and Social Change in the Third World', *American Political Science Review*, 70, 4 (1976), pp. 1078–97.

——— 'The Predictability of Coups d'état: A Model with African Data', *American Political Science Review*, 72, 4 (1978), pp. 1262–75.

James, Lawrence, *Mutiny in the British and Commonwealth Forces, 1797–1956*, London: Buchan & Enright, 1987.

Janowitz, Morris, *Sociology and the Military Establishment, 3rd Edition*, Beverly Hills, CA: Palgrave, 1974.

Janowitz, Morris and James Burke, *On Social Organization and Social Control*, Chicago: University of Chicago Press, 1991.

Jawara, Dawda K., *Kairaba*, Haywards Heath: Alhaji Sir Dawda Kairaba Jawara, 2009.

Jenkins, J. Craig and Augustine J. Kposowa, 'Political Origins of African Military Coups: Ethnic Competition, Military Centrality, and Struggle over the Postcolonial State', *International Studies Quarterly*, 36, 3 (1992), pp. 271–91.

Joseph, Richard, 'Challenges of a "Frontier" Region', in Larry Diamond and Marc F. Plattner (eds), *Democratization in Africa: Progress and Retreat*, 2nd edn, pp. 3–17, Baltimore: Johns Hopkins University Press, 2010.

Kandeh, Jimmy, *Coups from Below: Armed Subalterns and State Power in West Africa*, New York: Palgrave Macmillan, 2004.

——— 'Civil–Military Relations', in Adekeye Adebajo and Ismail Rashid (eds), *West Africa's Security Challenges: Building Peace in a Troubled Region*, pp. 45–68, Boulder, CO: Lynne Rienner, 2004.

——— 'In Search of Legitimacy: The 1996 Election', in Ibrahim Abdullah (ed.), *Between Democracy and Terror: The Sierra Leone Civil War*, pp. 123–43, Dakar: CODESRIA, 2004.

Kebschull, Harvey G., 'Operation "Just Missed": Lessons from Failed Coup Attempts', *Armed Forces and Society*, 20, 4 (1994), pp. 565–79.

Keen, David, *Conflict and Collusion in Sierra Leone*, New York: Palgrave, 2005.

Khobe, Mitikishe Maxwell, 'The Evolution and Conduct of the ECOMOG Operations in West Africa', in International Security Studies Monograph no. 44, February 2000.

Kieh, George Klay and Pita Ogaba Agbese (eds), *The Military and Politics in Africa: From Engagement to Democratic and Constitutional Control*, Burlington, VT: Ashgate, 2004.

Killingray, David, 'The Mutiny of the West African Regiment in the Gold Coast, 1901', *International Journal of African Historical Studies*, 16, 3 (1983), pp. 441–54.

King, Anthony, *The Combat Soldier: Infantry Tactics and Cohesion in the Twentieth and Twenty-First Centuries*, Oxford: Oxford University Press, 2013.

BIBLIOGRAPHY

Kirk-Greene, A.H.M. '"*Stay by your radios*": Documentation for a Study of Military Government in Tropical Africa*, Cambridge: African Studies Centre, 1981.

Lammers, Cornelius, 'Review of *Mutiny in Comparative Perspective*', *International Review of Social History*, 48 (2003), pp. 473–82.

―――― 'Strikes and Mutinies: A Comparative Study of Organizational Conflicts between Rulers and Ruled', *Administrative Science Quarterly*, 14, 4 (1969), pp. 558–72.

Le Billon, Philippe, 'Corrupting Peace? Peacebuilding and Post-conflict Corruption', *International Peacekeeping*, 15, 3 (2008), pp. 344–61.

Lee, J.M., *African Armies and Civil Order*, London: Chatto and Windus, 1969.

Lofchie, Michael F., 'The Uganda Coup: Class Action by the Military', *Journal of Modern African Studies*, 10, 1 (May 1972), pp. 19–35.

Lonsdale, John, 'Political Accountability in African History', in Patrick Chabal (ed.), *Political Domination in Africa: Reflections on the Limits of Power*, Cambridge: Cambridge University Press, 1986.

Luanda, Nestor, 'The Tanganyika Rifles and the Mutiny of January 1964', in Eboe Hutchful and Abdoulaye Bathily (eds), *The Military and Militarism in Africa*, pp. 175–210, Dakar: CODESRIA, 1998.

Luckham, A.R. 'A Comparative Typology of Civil–Military Relations', *Government and Opposition*, 6, 1 (1971), pp. 5–35.

Luckham, Robin, 'Radical Soldiers, New Model Armies and the Nation-State in Ethiopia and Eritrea', in Kees Koonings and Dirk Kruijt (eds), *Political Armies: The Military and National Building in the Age of Democracy*, pp. 238–66, London: Zed Books, 2002.

―――― 'The Military, Militarism and Democratisation in Africa: A Survey of Literature and Issues', in Eboe Hutchful and Abdoulaye Bathily (eds), *The Military and Militarism in Africa*, pp. 1–46, Dakar: CODESRIA, 1998.

―――― 'The Military, Militarization and Democratization in Africa: A Survey of Literature and Issues', *African Studies Review*, 37, 2 (September 1994), pp. 13–75.

―――― *The Nigerian Military: A Sociological Analysis of Authority and Revolt, 1960–67*, Cambridge: Cambridge University Press, 1971.

―――― 'Taming the Monster: Democratisation and Demilitarisation', in Eboe Hutchful and Abdoulaye Bathily (ed.), *The Military and Militarism in Africa*, pp. 589–98, Dakar: CODESRIA, 1998.

Luke, David Fasholé, 'Continuity in Sierra Leone: From Stevens to Momoh', *Third Word Quarterly*, 10, 1 (1988), pp. 67–78.

Luttwak, Edward, *Coup d'état: A Practical Handbook*, London: Penguin, 1968.

Malan, Mark, 'Transition with Minimal Assistance: Lessons from Guinea-Bissau?', KAIPTC Paper no. 5, March 2005.

Mann, Gregory, *Native Sons: West African Veterans and France in the Twentieth Century*, Durham, NC: Duke University Press, 2006.

BIBLIOGRAPHY

Mantle, Craig Leslie, 'The "Moral Economy" as a Theoretical Model to Explain Acts of Protest in the Canadian Expeditionary Force, 1914–1919', Report for Canadian Forces Leadership Institute, March 2004.

Martin, Michel Louis, 'Soldiers and Governments in Postpraetorian Africa: Cases in the Francophone Area', in Giuseppe Caforio (ed.), *Handbook of the Sociology of the Military*, New York: Springer, 2006.

Mazrui, Ali and Donald Rothchild, 'The Soldiers and the State in East Africa: Some Theoretical Conclusions on the Army Mutinies of 1964', *Western Political Quarterly*, 20, 1 (1967), pp. 82–96.

McGowan, Patrick J., 'African Military Coups d'état, 1956–2001: Frequency, Trends and Distribution', *Journal of Modern African Studies*, 41, 3 (2003), pp. 339–70.

——— 'Coups and Conflict in West Africa, 1955–2004: Part II, Empirical Finding', *Armed Forces and Society*, 32 (2006), pp. 234–53.

McGowan, Patrick J. and Thomas H. Johnson, 'African Military Coups d'état and Underdevelopment: A Quantitative Historical Analysis', *Journal of Modern African Studies*, 22, 4 (1984), pp. 633–66.

Mehler, Andreas, 'The Production of Insecurity by African Security Forces: Insights from Liberia and the Central African Republic', GIGA working papers, no. 114, 2009.

Minteh, Binneh, *Rethinking the Military and Democratization*, Saarbrucken, Germany: Lambert Publishing, 2010.

Mohamed, Jama, 'The 1937 Somaliland Camel Corps Mutiny: A Contrapuntal Reading', *International Journal of African Historical Studies*, 33, 3 (2000), pp. 615–34.

Mohammed, Nadir A.L., 'Tank Tractor Trade-off in Sudan: The Socio-economic Impact of Military Expenditure', in Eboe Hutchful and Abdoulaye Bathily (eds), *The Military and Militarism in Africa*, pp. 129–74, Dakar: CODESRIA, 1998.

——— 'Trends, Determinants and the Economic Effects of Military Expenditure in Sub-Saharan Africa', in Eboe Hutchful and Abdoulaye Bathily (eds), *The Military and Militarism in Africa*, pp. 47–104, Dakar: CODESRIA, 1998.

Mustapha, Marda and Joseph J. Bangura (eds), *Sierra Leone beyond the Lome Peace Accords*, New York: Palgrave Macmillan, 2010.

Mustapha, Abdul Raufu and Lindsay Whitfield, 'African Democratisation: The Journey So Far', in Abdul Raufu Mustapha and Lindsay Whitfield (eds), *Turning Points in African Democracy*, Woodbridge: James Currey, 2009.

——— 'The Politics of African States in the Era of Democratisation', in Abdul Raufu Mustapha and Lindsay Whitfield (eds), *Turning Points in African Democracy*, Woodbridge: James Currey, 2009.

N'Diaye, Boubacar, 'Guinea', in Alan Bryden, Boubacar N'Diaye and 'Funmi Olonisakin (eds), *Challenges of Security Sector Governance in West Africa*, pp. 133–50, Geneva: Geneva Centre for Democratic Control of Armed Forces, 2008.

BIBLIOGRAPHY

Nombre, Colonel H.L., 'Civil–Military Relations and National Security in Burkina Faso: An Assessment', July 2008.

Nordlinger, Eric, 'Soldiers in Mufti: The Impact of Military Rule upon Economic and Social Change in the Non-Western States', *American Political Science Review*, 64 (1970), pp. 1131–48.

Nugent, Paul, *Africa since Independence*, 2nd edn, New York: Palgrave Macmillan, 2012.

O'Ballance, Edgar, *The Congo-Zaire Experience, 1960–98*, London: Macmillan, 2000.

Okran, A.K., A Myth Is Broken: An Account of the Ghana Coup d'état of 24th February, 1966, Harlow: Longman, Green & Co., 1968.

Ofuatey-Kodjoe, W., 'The Impact of Peacekeeping on Target States: Lessons from the Liberian Experience', in Ricardo Rene Laremont (ed.), *The Causes of War and the Consequences of Peacekeeping in Africa*, Portsmouth, NH: Heinemann, 2002.

Olonisakin, 'Funmi, 'African Peacekeeping and the Impact on African Military Personnel', in Thomas W. Britt and Amy B. Adler (eds), *The Psychology of the Peacekeeper*, pp. 299–310, Westport, CT: Praeger, 2003.

——— 'Lessons Learned from an Assessment of Peacekeeping and Peace Support Operations in West Africa', Kofi Annan International Peacekeeping Training Centre, 2008.

——— *Peacekeeping in Sierra Leone: The Story of UNAMSIL*, Boulder, CO: Lynne Rienner, 2008.

——— *Reinventing Peacekeeping in Africa: Conceptual and Legal Issues in ECOMOG Operations*, The Hague: Kluwer Law International, 2000.

Olukoshi, Adebayo, 'State, Conflict, and Democracy in Africa: The Complex Process of Renewal', in Richard Joseph (ed.), *State Conflict and Democracy in Africa*, pp. 451–66, Boulder, CO: Lynne Rienner, 1999.

Omitoogun, Wuyi, 'Introduction', in Wuyi Omitoogun and Eboe Hutchful (eds), *Budgeting for the Military Sector in Africa: The Processes and Mechanism of Control*, Oxford: Oxford University Press, 2006.

Onwumechili, Chuka, *African Democratization and Military Coups*, Westport, CT: Praeger, 1998.

Opala, Joseph A., '"Ecstatic Renovation!" Street Art Celebrating Sierra Leone's 1992 Revolution', *African Affairs*, 93, 371 (April 1994), pp. 195–218.

Ouédraogo, Emile, 'Advancing Military Professionalism in Africa', African Center for Strategic Studies, Research Paper no. 6, 2014.

Parsons, Timothy H., *The 1964 Army Mutinies and the Making of Modern East Africa*, Westport, CT: Praeger, 2003.

Parker, Geoffrey, 'Foreword', in Jane Hathaway (ed.), *Rebellion, Repression, Reinvention: Mutiny in Comparative Perspective*, pp. vii–ix, Westport, CT: Praeger, 2001.

——— 'Mutiny and Discontent in the Spanish Army of Flanders 1572–1607', *Past & Present*, 58 (February 1973), pp. 38–52.

BIBLIOGRAPHY

People's Progressive Party, *The Voice of the People: The Story of the PPP, 1959–1989*, Banjul: Baroueli Publications, 1992.

Peters, Krijn, *War and the Crisis of Youth in Sierra Leone*, New York: Cambridge University Press, 2011.

Perfect, David, *Historical Dictionary of The Gambia*, 5th edn, Lanham, MD: Rowman & Littlefield, 2016.

Pitts, Michelle, 'Sub-regional Solutions for African Conflict: The ECOMOG Experiment', *Journal of Conflict Studies*, 19, 1 (Spring 1999).

Powell, Jonathan M. and Clayton L. Thyne, 'Global Instances of Coups from 1950 to 2010: A New Dataset', *Journal of Peace Research*, 48, 2 (2011), pp. 249–59.

Prairie, Michel (ed.), *Thomas Sankara: Speeches from the Burkina Faso Revolution 1983–87*, New York: Pathfinder Press, 2002.

Rashid, Ismail, 'Student Radicals, Lumpen Youth and Origins of Revolutionary Groups in Sierra Leone 1977–1996', in Ibrahim Abdullah (ed.), *Between Democracy and Terror: The Sierra Leone Civil War*, pp. 66–89, Dakar: CODESRIA, 2004.

Reno, William, *Corruption and State Politics in Sierra Leone*, New York: Cambridge University Press, 1995.

Richards, Paul, *Fighting for the Rain Forest: War, Youth & Resources in Sierra Leone*, Portsmouth: James Currey, 1996.

Rose, Elihu, 'The Anatomy of Mutiny', *Armed Forces and Society*, 8, 4 (1982), pp. 561–74.

Rubinstein, Robert A., *Peacekeeping under Fire: Culture and Intervention*, Boulder, CO: Paradigm Publishers, 2008.

Saine, Abdoulaye, 'The Coup d'état in The Gambia, 1994: The End of the First Republic', *Armed Forces and Society*, 23, 1 (1996), pp. 97–111.

—— *The Paradox of Third-Wave Democratization in Africa*, Plymouth, UK: Lexington Books, 2009.

Saine, Abdoulaye and Ebrima Ceesay, 'Post-coup Politics and Authoritarianism in The Gambia: 1994–2012', in Abdoulaye Saine, Ebrima Ceesay and Ebrima Sall (eds), *State and Society in The Gambia since Independence: 1965–2012*, pp. 151–84, Trenton, NJ: Africa World Press, 2013.

Sarr, Samsudeen, *Coup d'état by the Gambia National Army*, Philadelphia, PA: Xlibris, 2007.

Schmidt, Elizabeth, *Foreign Intervention in Africa: From the Cold War to the War on Terror*, New York: Cambridge University Press, 2013.

Sesay, Mohamed, 'Military Reform and Post-conflict Peace Building in Sierra Leone', MPhil Thesis, Fourah Bay College, 2009.

Siebold, Guy L., 'The Essence of Military Group Cohesion', *Armed Forces & Society*, 33, 2 (January 2007), pp. 286–95.

Singh, Naunihal, *Seizing Power: The Strategic Logic of Military Coups*, Baltimore, MD: Johns Hopkins University Press, 2014

Souaré, Issaka K., 'The African Union as a Norm Entrepreneur on Military Coups

BIBLIOGRAPHY

d'état in Africa (1952–2012): An Empirical Assessment', *Journal Of Modern African Studies*, 52, 1 (March 2014), pp. 60–94.

Souley, Abdoulaye Niandou, 'Mutineries militaires en période démocratiation', in Kimba Idrissa (ed.), *Armée et Politique au Niger*, Dakar, Senegal: CODESRIA, 2008.

Tareke, Gebru, *The Ethiopian Revolution: War in the Horn of Africa*, New Haven: Yale University Press, 2009.

Thom, William G., 'An Assessment of Prospects for Ending Domestic Military Conflict in Sub-Saharan Africa', *CSIS Africa Notes*, 177 (1995).

Tuck, Christopher, '"Every Car or Moving Object Gone": The ECOMOG Intervention in Liberia', *Africa Studies Quarterly*, 4, 1 (2000).

Turay, E.D.A. and A. Abraham, *The Sierra Leone Army: A Century of History*, London: Macmillan, 1987.

Van De Walle, Nicolas, *African Economies and the Politics of Permanent Crisis, 1979–1999*, Cambridge: Cambridge University Press, 2001.

Van Walraven, Klaas, 'Sawaba's Rebellion in Niger (1963–1964): Narrative and Meaning', in Jon Abbink, Mirjam de Bruijn and Klaas van Walraven (eds), *Rethinking Resistance: Revolt and Violence in African History*, Leiden: Brill, 2003.

—— *The Yearning for Relief: A History of the Sawaba Movement in Niger*, Leiden: Brill, 2013.

Weitz, Mark, 'Desertion as Mutiny: Upcountry Georgians in the Army of Tennessee', in Jane Hathaway (ed.), *Rebellion, Repression, Reinvention: Mutiny in Comparative Perspective*, pp. 3–24, Westport, CT: Praeger, 2001.

Welch, Claude E., 'African Military and Political Development: Reflections on a Score of Years, and Several Score of Studies', *Journal of Opinion*, 13 (1984), pp. 41–4.

—— 'Military Disengagement from Politics: Lessons from West Africa', *Armed Forces & Society*, 9, 4 (Summer 1983), pp. 541–54.

Wells, Alan, 'The Coup d'état in Theory and Practice: Independent Black Africa in the 1960s', *American Journal of Sociology*, 79, 4 (1974), pp. 871–87.

Widner, Jennifer, 'The 1990 Elections in Côte d'Ivoire', *Issue: A Journal of Opinion*, 20, 1 (Winter, 1991), pp. 31–41.

Wilkins, Michael, 'The Death of Thomas Sankara and the Rectification of the People's Revolution in Burkina Faso', *African Affairs*, 88, 352 (July 1989), pp. 375–88.

Williams, Paul, *War & Conflict in Africa*, Cambridge Polity, 2011.

Wiseman, John, 'Introduction', in John Wiseman (ed.), *Democracy and Political Change in Sub-Saharan Africa*, pp. 1–10, New York: Routledge, 1995.

—— 'Revolt in the Gambia: A Pointless Tragedy', *Round Table: The Commonwealth Journal of International Affairs*, 71, 284 (1981), pp. 373–80.

Wiseman, John and Elizabeth Vidler, 'The July 1994 Coup d'état in the Gambia: The End of an Era', *Round Table*, 333, 1 (January 1995), pp. 53–65.

Yeebo, Zaya, *State of Fear in Paradise: The Military Coup in the Gambia and its*

BIBLIOGRAPHY

Implications for Democracy, London: Africa Research and Information Bureau, 1995.

Yin, Robert K., *Case Study Research: Design and Methods*, 2nd Ed, Thousand Oaks, CA: Sage, 1994.

Young, Crawford, 'The Third Wave of Democratization in Africa: Ambiguities and Contradictions', in Richard Joseph (ed.), *State, Conflict, and Democracy in Africa*, pp. 15–38, Boulder, CO: Lynne Rienner, 1999.

Zack-Williams, A. and Stephen Riley, 'Sierra Leone: The Coup and its Consequences', *Review of African Political Economy*, 56 (1993), pp. 91–8.

Zimmermann, Ekkart, 'Toward a Causal Model of Military Coups d'État', *Armed Forces and Society*, 5, 3 (1979), pp. 387–413.

Zolberg, Aristide R., 'The Structure of Political Conflict in the New States of Tropical Africa', *American Political Science Review*, 62, 1 (1968), pp. 70–87.

INDEX

Abacha, Sani, 97
Abidjan, 42, 51, 65
accountability, 6, 63, 64, 68, 78, 182
aircrafts, 61, 84
airports, 42, 43, 46, 65, 129, 208
air force, 36, 42, 65, 158, 166, 167, 185
African Commission of Human and People's Right, 77
African Union, 80, 98
African Union Mission in Somalia (AMISOM), 80, 86, 95, 102, 120, 121, 122
All People's Congress (APC), 104, 105, 111
ammunition, 41, 84, 85, 108, 113, 114, 127, 168
Amnesty International, 68, 77
Angola, 60
Aning, Kwesi, 89, 91
Ankersen, Christopher, 5, 6
Armed Forces Provisional Ruling Council (AFPRC), 141, 142
Armed Forces Revolutionary Council (AFRC), 118
armoury, 41, 46, 49, 127, 134
arms trafficking, 79
Australia, 96

Bangura, Thaimu, 105
Banjul, The Gambia, 21, 127, 131, 132, 134, 135, 139, 140, 141, 142, 143
Bakau, The Gambia, 139
Barrow, Adama, 146, 147
Bassolé, Djibril, 166
Bédié, Henri, 51
Belgian Congo, 2
Benin, 26, 60, 80
Bio, Maada, 117
Bobo Dioulasso, Burkina Faso, 155, 159, 161
Boko Haram, 2, 11, 13, 80, 85
boots, 35, 36, 84, 85, 108, 162
Boukary, Dabo, 155
Brahimi Report, 81
Bratton, Michael, 71
bribes, 80, 121
Brikama, The Gambia, 139
Burkina Faso, 2, 7, 11, 13, 20, 21, 22, 23, 26, 27, 38, 39, 43, 48, 49, 50, 52, 53, 54, 60, 69, 74, 76, 78, 80, 92, 115, 149–174, 178, 181, 182
Burundi, 80

Camp de Thiaroye, 2
Camp Lamizana, 158

INDEX

Canada, 90
Cape Verde, 126
casualties, 10, 47, 81, 83, 85, 93, 94, 108, 114, 115, 155, 160, 176
Central African Republic, 26, 27, 35, 41, 44, 45, 47, 48, 50, 52, 53, 60, 61, 67, 68, 69, 70, 153
Chad, 26, 27, 61, 80, 86
Cham, Ndure, 144
checkpoints, 22, 43, 72, 73, 80, 112
Civil Defence Force (CDF), 118
civil liberties, 58, 68, 74, 75, 76, 77, 78, 126, 143, 146
class, 3, 5, 22, 30–33, 39, 104, 151, 183
Cobra unit (Sierra Leone), 105, 107, 109, 110
cohesion, 23, 47, 55, 95–97, 107, 117, 123, 124, 146
Cold War, 12, 58, 61, 62, 63, 79, 81
Compaoré, Blaise, 2, 69, 149, 151, 152, 153, 154, 156, 158, 159, 160, 161, 164, 166, 167, 171, 172
Conseil National de la Révolution (CNR), 151, 152
Confederal Army, 128, 129, 130, 138
conflict minerals, 79
conscription, 9
contagion, of mutinies 50, 51
Conteh, Kellie, 108
corruption, 7, 25, 39, 50, 51, 53, 64, 65, 75, 78, 86, 90, 91, 92, 98, 177, 180, 182
 in The Gambia, 66, 125, 129, 130, 132, 133, 135, 136, 137, 139, 141, 145, 146
 in Sierra Leone, 104, 109, 119, 120, 124
 in Burkina Faso, 153, 154, 159, 162, 164, 168, 173
Côte d'Ivoire, 18, 26, 27, 42, 47, 50, 51, 52, 60, 61, 62, 64, 65, 66, 67, 80, 81, 126

coup d'état, 2, 11, 12, 13, 15–19, 22, 23, 24, 25, 27, 28, 31, 43, 47, 49, 50, 51, 58, 67, 175, 176
 in Sierra Leone, 101, 102, 108, 111, 113, 114, 115, 118, 123, 124
 in The Gambia, 125, 126, 127, 128, 138, 139, 140, 141, 142, 143, 144, 145
 in Burkina Faso, 150, 151, 152, 164, 165
court marital, 54, 77, 85, 111, 122, 134, 135, 136, 145
Cuba, 103
curfew, 141, 158

Dada, Abubakar, 134, 136
Dahl, Robert, 64
Dakar, Senegal, 2, 141
Darfur, 45, 82, 86, 91, 120, 121, 163
Daru, Sierra Leone, 109, 111
death penalty, 2, 20, 54, 85
Decalo, Samuel, 11, 31, 32
Dedougou, Burkina Faso, 159, 160
democracy, 2, 6, 11, 54, 57, 58, 63, 64, 67, 68, 69, 70, 71, 72, 73, 74, 75, 78, 117, 119, 125, 126, 141, 150, 169, 182
Democratic Republic of Congo, 26, 42, 47, 48, 50, 60, 61, 76, 138
Denton Bridge, 135, 140, 142
Diallo, Boubacar, 171
Diendéré, Gilbert, 172
Diouf, Abdou, 127
Dori, Burkina Faso, 159

East African mutinies of 1964, 2, 5, 7, 50, 138, 179
Ebola, 86
Economic Community of West African States (ECOWAS), 61, 80, 85, 87, 88, 93, 130, 133, 147, 154

INDEX

Economic Community of West African States Monitoring Group (ECOMOG), 66, 83, 85, 86, 87, 88, 93, 94, 95, 97, 114, 118, 130, 131, 132, 133, 134, 135, 136, 142, 146
ECOWAS Mission to Liberia (ECOMIL), 88
elections, 57, 64, 66, 117, 125, 126, 149, 153, 182
Equatorial Guinea, 74
equipment, 5, 31, 34, 61, 62, 81, 84, 85, 86, 90, 93, 94, 97, 98, 103, 106, 108, 132, 138, 152, 176
Ethiopia, 2, 18, 20, 60
Ethnicity, 3, 11, 33, 46, 107, 144
Executive Outcomes, 117

Fada N'Gourma, Burkina Faso, 157, 158
favouritism, 35, 53, 120, 129, 136, 144, 146, 162, 163, 164, 168, 172, 173, 177, 180, 183
Field Force (The Gambia), 126, 127, 128
First, Ruth, 17, 180
First World War, 96
food, grievances about, 5, 34, 40, 80, 84, 85, 93, 94, 108, 121, 137, 141, 161, 162, 164, 167, 168
Fourah Bay College, 113
France, 16, 45, 62, 65, 67, 90, 96, 128, 166
Freedom House, 73, 74, 114, 143
Freetown, Sierra Leone, 38, 101, 103, 105, 106, 107, 109, 110, 111, 112, 113, 114, 116, 117, 118, 123, 124, 141
fuel, 104, 137

Gambia, 7, 13, 20, 21, 22, 23, 26, 35, 47, 50, 61, 66, 67, 69, 74, 77, 78, 80, 82, 87, 92, 93, 94, 125–147, 165, 173
Gambia Revolutionary Socialist Party (GRSP), 126
gendarmerie, 36, 41, 128, 135, 138, 142, 150, 159, 160, 162, 164–166, 167, 172, 185
Generals, 34, 37, 51, 104, 134, 172
Ghana, 26, 54, 73, 80, 89, 90, 91, 94, 115, 130, 151
Gold Coast Artillery Corps, 1
'good governance', 63, 64, 70
Guéï, Robert, 51
Guinea, 20, 22, 26, 27, 34, 35, 36, 38, 47, 48, 53, 56, 60, 61, 68, 80, 83, 89, 94, 103
Guinea Bissau, 26, 60, 80, 83
Gurkha Security Guards, 117

HIV, 89
honour, 2, 6, 83, 84, 114, 156
hostages, 41, 42, 43, 46, 48, 49, 55, 127, 172
Houphouët-Boigny, Félix, 62, 65
housing, 5, 30, 32, 34, 35, 37, 40, 50, 53, 55, 72, 80, 119, 124, 132, 137, 151, 153, 154, 158, 161, 162, 181, 182
Howe, Herbert, 32, 61
human rights, 22, 63, 64, 66, 68, 70, 71, 122, 126, 143, 146, 155
Hutchful, Eboe, 57, 71
Hydara, Sadibou, 141

Iliffe, John, 2, 83, 84
immunity, 68, 156, 172
impunity, 32, 39, 66, 137, 155, 156, 157, 168
intelligence, 20, 21, 24, 85, 140, 142, 144
Internal Security Unit (ISU), Sierra Leone, 103, 114

233

INDEX

International Monetary Fund (IMF), 70
internet, 45, 46, 76, 94, 177

jail, 54, 75, 77, 103, 122, 142, 144, 154, 156
Jammeh, Yahya, 21, 74, 126, 131, 141, 142, 143, 144, 145, 146, 147, 151
Jawara, Dawda, 66, 126, 127, 129, 131, 132, 133, 134, 137, 139, 140, 141, 143
Johnson, Thomas, 24
Jola, 144

Kabbah, Ahmed, 117
Kafando, Michel, 149, 172
Kailahun, Sierra Leone, 109
Kamajors, 117, 118, 119
Kandeh, Jimmy, 17, 30, 39
Kaur Declaration, 127
Kaya, Burkina Faso, 158, 159
Kenema, Sierra Leone, 109, 110
Kenya, 2, 50, 95, 138
King, Anthony, 96
Kofi Annan International Peacekeeping Training Centre (KAIPTC), 89, 90
Koroma, Ernest, 121
Koupela, Burkina Faso, 159

land, access to, 32
Le Foulard Noir (film), 170
Liberia, 11, 26, 50, 61, 66, 75, 81, 82, 83, 85, 87, 88, 93, 97, 105, 114, 130, 131, 142, 146
Lofchie, Michael, 30
logistics, 81, 84, 85, 86, 97, 108, 109, 112, 116, 142, 176
looting, 36, 48, 49, 87, 88, 127, 156, 157, 158
Lougué, Kouamé, 153
Luanda, Nestor, 5

Luckham, Robin, 11, 17, 20, 30, 115

maintenance of equipment, 61
Makeni, Sierra Leone, 121
Mali, 2, 22, 27, 71, 74, 81, 83, 86, 89, 153, 163, 167
Mareneh, Daba, 144
Mauritania, 129
Mazrui, Ali, 7
McGowan, Patrick, 24
medals, military, 77, 83
media, use by mutineers, 8, 24, 25, 35, 44–46, 55, 69, 75–78, 91, 131–132, 158, 177, 179
Medical care/medicine, 38, 84, 91, 108, 111, 120
Mile Two prison (The Gambia), 127, 144
mobile phones, 112, 164, 178
Momoh, Joseph, 83, 101, 104, 105, 109, 114, 115, 116, 125
Monrovia, Liberia, 130
Morocco, 128
Movement for Justice in Africa (MOJA), 126
Musa, Solomon 'Saj', 106, 114

National Assembly
 of Central African Republic, 41
 of Burkina Faso, 149
National Patriotic Front of Liberia (NPFL), 105
National Provisional Ruling Council (NPRC), Sierra Leone, 115, 116, 117, 118, 141
navies, 8, 9, 10, 36, 139, 140, 141, 185
negotiation, 33, 34, 43, 46, 48, 49, 51, 70, 109, 145, 154, 158, 160
nepotism, 39, 92, 101, 105, 107, 123, 129, 133, 146, 162
Niamey, Niger, 77

INDEX

Niger, 26, 27, 41, 42, 50, 53, 54, 60, 61, 69, 70, 76, 77, 78

Nigeria, 20, 26, 27, 38, 41, 42, 45, 46, 54, 76, 81, 86, 91, 179
  and Boko Haram, 2, 11, 80, 85
  and ECOMOG 93, 94, 97, 130, 132, 133
  and NATAG, 125, 134, 136, 137, 138, 140, 141, 146

Nigerian Army Training Assistance Group (NATAG), 125, 134, 136, 137, 138, 140, 141, 146

Njie, Ndow, 66, 132, 133, 134

Nugent, Paul, 72

Nyuma, Tom, 104, 110

Olonisakin, 'Funmi, 94, 97

Ouagadougou, Burkina Faso, 48, 150, 154, 155, 156, 157, 158, 159, 160, 170, 172

Ouédraogo, Jean-Baptiste, 151

Ousmane, Mahamane, 69

Pademba Road Prison, Sierra Leone, 113, 118

Pan African Union (PANAFU), 104

Pakistan, 128

paratroopers, 62, 160

parade, military, 77

Patassé, Ange-Félix, 67, 69, 70

peacekeeping, 3, 9, 38, 50, 61, 62, 66, 79–99, 102, 173, 176, 177, 179
  and Sierra Leone, 120–123, 124, 125
  and The Gambia, 130–133, 144
  and Burkina Faso, 153, 163

People's Progressive Party (PPP), 77, 126, 139

Pô, Burkina Faso 150, 151, 158, 159

police, 33, 128, 135, 138, 140, 142, 151, 153, 154, 155, 157, 158, 160, 165, 166, 167, 172, 188

political conditionality, 63

presidential guards, 36, 50
  in The Gambia, 129, 140
  in Burkina Faso, 149, 158, 161, 168, 172

Presidential Palace (Burkina Faso), 149

presidential term limits, 149

prisoners, 42, 118, 127, 154

procurement, 38

promotions, 11, 31, 33, 35, 46, 50, 53, 55, 83, 89, 102, 120, 136, 144, 163, 173

protests, 4, 24, 27, 33, 104, 139, 181, 182
  in 1990s, 6, 57–73
  in Burkina Faso, 22, 149, 150, 154–160, 170, 172, 173, 174
  in The Gambia, 139

radio, 44, 45, 65, 67, 72, 73, 76, 112, 113, 114, 115, 122, 124, 127, 141, 150

rape, 48, 49, 157, 158, 169, 170, 171

Rawlings, Jerry, 115, 151

Régiment de Défense Opérationnelle du Territoire, Central African Republic, 50

Régiment de Sécurité Présidentiel (RSP), 158, 160, 161, 172, 173

Report of the Panel on United Nations Peace Operations, 81

Republic of Congo, 26, 27, 35, 41, 42, 48, 50, 60, 61

Revolutionary United Front (RUF), 101, 102, 104, 105, 108, 115, 117, 118, 119

rice, 34, 35, 36, 53, 104, 111, 168

roadblocks, 151

Rose, Elihu, 4, 6, 7, 16, 29, 40, 48, 52, 54, 72

Rothchild, Donald, 7

INDEX

Royal Niger Constabulary, 1
Royal West African Frontier Force (RWAFF), 126

Sabally, Sana, 141, 142
Sankara, Thomas, 115, 150, 151, 152, 155
Sankoh, Foday, 104
Sanneh, Lamin, 145
Sanyang, Kukoi Samba, 126
Sao Tomé and Principe, 27
Second World War, 1, 8, 93
self-contained mutinies, 47, 48
Sembène, Ousmane, 2
Senegal, 2, 21, 64, 127, 128, 129, 138, 141
Senegambia Confederation, 127, 128, 129, 130
Sergeants Revolt (Sierra Leone), 103
Serrekunda, The Gambia, 135
Sierra Leone, 11, 13, 20, 21, 22, 23, 24, 26, 36, 37, 38, 39, 40, 51, 60, 61, 74, 75, 76, 81, 82, 83, 84, 86, 89, 90, 93, 101–124, 125, 141, 146, 165, 173, 177, 179, 181
Sierra Leone Frontier Force, 1
Singhateh, Edward, 141, 142
social contracts, 7, 17, 80, 81, 83, 98, 181
social media, 45, 46, 95, 122, 177, 178
Somali Camel Corps, 2
Somalia, 76, 91, 121
South Africa, 60
Soviet Union, 61
Special Security Division (SSD), Sierra Leone, 114
State House, 41, 44, 179
   in The Gambia, 69, 132, 139, 140, 141, 143, 144, 146
   in Sierra Leone, 109, 113, 114, 123
State of Emergency, 76
Stevens, Siaka, 103, 104

Strasser, Valentine, 105, 106, 108, 110, 114, 115, 116, 117, 141, 151
Stockholm International Peace Research Institute (SIPRI), 59, 60
Structural Adjustment Programmes (SAPs), 59, 63
students, 21, 22, 33, 65, 69, 72, 104, 139, 151, 158, 159, 160, 168
subsidies, 65, 104
success rates, of mutinies, 52–54
Sudan, 82

Tactical Support Group (TSG), 138, 140
tactics, 41–44, 46, 52
Tandja, Mamadou, 76
Tanganyika, 5, 179
tanks, 61
Tanzania, 2, 50, 138
taxes, 65, 139, 159
taxi drivers, 65, 126, 139
Taylor, Charles, 105
Tenkodogo, Burkina Faso, 158, 159
Tiger unit (Sierra Leone), 101–118, 123, 124, 146, 181
Tirailleurs Sénégalais, 93
Togo, 26, 27
trade unions, 22, 33, 69, 155, 159, 172
training, 10, 11, 12, 29, 31, 40, 41, 61, 62, 80, 85, 86, 89, 90, 93, 94, 96, 103, 106, 108, 116, 128, 160, 164, 166, 167
Truth and Reconciliation Commission (Sierra Leone), 108
Turkey, 128

Uganda, 2, 50, 138
uniforms, 11, 33, 34, 35, 36, 49, 72, 73, 80, 84, 85, 91, 93, 94, 98, 107, 112, 120, 152, 154, 162
United Kingdom, 2, 21, 90, 126, 128, 131, 132, 133

INDEX

United Nations, 79, 80, 81, 88, 89, 90, 94, 98, 117, 119, 163, 177
United Nations/African Union Mission in Darfur (UNAMID), 45, 91, 119, 163
United Nations Mission in the Central African Republic (MINURCA), 153
United Nations Mission to Liberia (UNMIL), 88
United Nations Multidimensional Integrated Stabilization Mission in Mali (MINUSMA), 86, 91, 163
United States, 21, 90, 96, 128, 139, 140, 141, 142
United States Africa Command (AFRICOM), 93

Van de Walle, Nicolas, 71
veterans, 7, 83, 84, 86, 97, 136
violence, 17, 19, 22, 24, 33, 46–49, 55, 56, 127, 155, 160, 168, 169, 170, 176, 179, 181, 182
violent mass mutinies, 23, 48, 150

weapons, 31, 32, 41, 43, 49, 55, 61, 65, 106, 112, 113, 114, 127, 134, 138, 156, 168, 169
  grievances about, 85, 108–109
West African Regiment, 1
West Side Boys, 119
World Bank, 70

Yamoussoukro, Côte d'Ivoire 65
youths, 21, 72, 73, 107, 116, 151, 160
Yundum barracks, 132, 134, 142

Zida, Yacouba Isaac, 149
Ziniaré, Burkina Faso, 158
Zongo, Justin, 154, 155, 157, 159
Zongo, Norbert, 153, 155, 171